THE CALAMITY PAPERS

THE
CALAMITY
PAPERS

WESTERN MYTHS
AND COLD CASES

Dale L. Walker

FORGE

A TOM DOHERTY ASSOCIATES BOOK
New York

A Forge Book
Published by Tom Doherty Associates, LLC
175 Fifth Avenue
New York, NY 10010

www.tor.com

Forge® is a registered trademark of Tom Doherty Associates, LLC.

ISBN 0-765-30831-2
EAN 978-0765-30831-3

First Edition: December 2004

Printed in the United States of America

0 9 8 7 6 5 4 3 2 1

To Three Great Ladies:

Eileen Walker Hall
(1916–2003),

Joy Ann Walker Elliott,

Alice McCord Walker

CONTENTS

Introduction   9

THE YAZOO PILGRIM   17

"OH, HOW HARD IT IS TO DIE"   35
    I. The Stand   37
    II. Theodosia   54

SAM HOUSTON'S DILEMMA   79

MEAGHER OF THE SWORD   99
    I. Ireland and Beyond   101
    II. Montana   112
    III. Fort Benton   126

UNDER THE WHITE SANDS   141
    I. Fountain and Fall   143
    II. Vanished   156
    III. Justice   166

WHO KILLED THE MAN WHO KILLED THE KID?   175

THE CALAMITY PAPERS   195
    I. Martha Canary   197
    II. The Album   221

THE JACK LONDON CASES   239
    I. Wolf House Burning   241
    II. Wolf Dying   259

Acknowledgments   275
Sources   277

INTRODUCTION

In police parlance, a "cold case" is an old crime that has languished unsolved, often for years, its details preserved in paperwork in file folders and boxes of evidence in a property room.

All the cases in *The Calamity Papers* are cold—one of them more than three hundred years cold—and even the most recent a chilly eighty-seven. But apart from their age and where the details are stored, these cold cases differ in several respects from the constabulary definition: Only one of the episodes in this book is about a real crime (although foul play is suspected in two others and seems obvious in a third); one of the cases has been "solved," by exposure of a hoax, another probably solved by exposure of historical sloppiness.

Besides being cold, everything in this book has in common that universal element of life: *curiosity*.

It is mostly a blessing, "the engine that drives the intellect," as historical writer Win Blevins puts it ("the stimulant underlying all advancement" in historian H.H. Bancroft's words), and all writers have tales of how their curiosity led them down a path that uncovered something overlooked by others less inquisitive, therefore something unique and wonderful. Such small triumphs make curiosity creative, give it a kind of righteousness, and result in adding something to the historical record rather than subtracting from it by the old dodge of rehashing what others have already written.

Naturally, the eternal hope is that the reader is pestered by the same craving to know and will share the writer's curiosity.

The Calamity Papers is a product not only of curiosity, but also of two principles that guide the historical writer. The first of these is the setting aside of preconceptions and prejudices, a matter aptly stated by Montana novelist Richard S. Wheeler: "Between curiosity and letting go everything that might block the quest for truth, historical researchers began to open new understandings." The second tenet is the fixed truth that in history nothing is "definitive," nothing is beyond a shadow of doubt.

For forty years, since publication of Vardis Fisher's *Murder or Suicide?*, I have been enthralled by that great enigma of American history, the awful, inexplicable death of Meriwether Lewis in the Tennessee wilderness in 1809. Over the years, I collected a home library of books and files on the case and eventually poured everything I had learned into a book of my own, *Legends and Lies* (Forge, 1997).

But the explorer's violent death—the murder or suicide question—continued to nag me long after that pouring out. The writing of *Legends and Lies* did not dampen my curiosity; there were too many aggravating questions, too much more to learn.

What, for example, to make of the startling prophecy Lewis was said to have made—"I am going to die, Theodosia. I cannot tell you how I know it, but I do"—that presaged his death and seemed to add significant weight to the theory that he died a suicide? Why have some historians ignored this, while others have used it? And who was Theodosia?

The Theodosia matter gave rise to a phenomenon well known to the habitually (some might say pathologically) curious: This is the realization that the time and resources spent in the process of finding out something often seem to outweigh the result. It took months, off and on, to trace the origin of the "I am going to die" letter, and in the midst of the search I kept asking myself, "Who *cares* about this?" while plodding on. In such moments, we see what Poe called the "Imp of the Perverse," that mental demon that impels us to proceed in some line of work or thought even when we know it is hurtful to do so. In any event, the Theodosia story herein turned out to be a mystery within a mystery and seemed to me to be worth the effort to get to the bottom of it.

I felt that way about the Killer of Pain, that forgotten Mississippi Indian who may have crossed the continent to the Pacific a century before Lewis and Clark; about the circumstances of Sam Houston's first wife fleeing from him after their wedding; about the story behind Calamity Jane's life and her relationship, if any, to Wild Bill Hickok, and all the other curiosities to be found in *The Calamity Papers*.

Two of the stories here are connected and spring from my own Southwestern backyard. At the little New Mexico settlement of Organ, atop San Augustín Pass, there is a historical marker at the place near where Pat Garrett was killed in 1908. Farther on, down from the pass on State Highway 70 and at the edge of the White Sands National Monument, is the site once called Chalk Hill, where Judge Albert Jennings Fountain and his son disappeared in 1896. I have stopped at these sites a dozen times over the years, always determining to learn more about both cases.

Similarly haunting is the burned-out shell of Jack London's Wolf House in the Valley of the Moon, an hour's drive north of San Francisco. People who visit those ruins and London's nearby grave invariably stop at the London State Park museum or the London Bookstore down the road in Glen Ellen and ask, "What happened to Wolf House?" and "Why did Jack die so young?"

Tom Meagher is another historical figure who elicits the "What happened?" and "Why did he die so young?" questioning. I had seen the monument commemorating Meagher and the Irish Brigade at the Antietam battlefield in Maryland, and the statue of him in front of the state capitol building in Helena, Montana, but beyond what their plaque inscriptions said, knew little else. Then I read Richard Wheeler's *Exile,* a superb, scrupulously researched novel about Meagher, and wanted to know more. In June 2003, I spent a day at the Montana Historical Society in Helena, reading and copying the society's voluminous Meagher files, and another day at Fort Benton, where the Irish hero died. New York literary agent Nat Sobel accompanied me on the trip to the old town on the Missouri River northeast of the capital, and en route I told him a bit about "Meagher of the Sword." Then, after we walked the Benton levee, we found a bench on the Walking Bridge that spans the fabled Big Muddy.

"Somewhere over there," I said, pointing toward the riverbank, "is where he went into the water."

Sobel looked, said, "All the way from Ireland and Tasmania to wind up dead out here. I can see why you got interested in him."

I wanted to know about the word and found this: it derives from the Latin *curiosus,* originally meaning "careful," but evolving, with Old French influence, into "inquisitive."

In his *Confessions,* Saint Augustine told the story of a curious soul who wondered what God did in the eons before creating heaven and earth. "He fashioned hell for the inquisitive," came the impatient reply.

In *Don Juan,* Lord Byron wrote, "I loathe that low vice curiosity," but the insatiably curious Albert Einstein had the last word:

> The important thing is not to stop questioning. Curiosity has its own reason for existing. One cannot help but be in awe when he contemplates the mysteries of eternity, of life, of the

marvelous structure of reality. It is enough if one tries merely to comprehend a little of this mystery every day. Never lose a holy curiosity.

—DALE L. WALKER
November 27, 2003

THE CALAMITY PAPERS

THE YAZOO PILGRIM

*Du Pratz said the
old man's actual name was
Moncacht-apé and that
it translated as
"Killer of Pain
and Fatigue."*

The annals of exploration tell us that the first man to cross the North American continent was Alexander Mackenzie (1764–1820), a Scotsman from Stornoway, on the Isle of Lewis in the Hebrides.

In his teens, Mackenzie emigrated to Canada and found work in Montreal as a clerk with the North West Company, an organization of fur traders established to compete with the lordly Hudson's Bay Company. In 1787, Mackenzie's superiors assigned him to the desolate trading post at Fort Capon in the wilds at the head of Lake Athabaska in today's far northeastern Alberta province. There, as the post factor, he traded for beaver and other prized furs among the Indians and listened to their tales of a mighty river that emptied into the Pacific Ocean—a river, Mackenzie dreamed, that could open the fur trade on an unprecedented scale.

In 1789, he took a small exploratory party north to the Great Slave Lake and found what seemed to be a broad and likely stream that flowed westerly from the lake. He and his men provisioned their canoes and followed the uncharted waterway, but it soon swung north, always north, with no westerly drift. They pushed on, and after a journey of 1,120 miles on the river, Mackenzie and his party found themselves paddling among the ice floes of the Beaufort Sea, the southern edge of the Arctic Ocean.

The next year he wintered at a North West Company fort on the Peace River and on May 9, 1793, set out again. With him now were another Scotsman, Alexander Mackay, six French Canadian voyageurs, and two Indians. Their canoes were loaded to the gunwales with a ton and a half of provisions and equipage, among the latter Mackenzie's sextant, a good telescope to find Jupiter's moons and compute longitude, and plenty of ink, pen nibs, and paper to keep a journal and draw maps.

After portaging across the Rockies, Mackenzie and his party struck out afoot for the coast and reached salt water at the northern end of the Strait of Georgia that separates Vancouver Island from the Canadian mainland.

There, using a mixture of grease and vermilion paint, the explorer wrote on a rock, ALEXANDER MACKENZIE, FROM CANADA, BY LAND, THE TWENTY-SECOND OF JULY, 1793.

He returned to Scotland later that year and was knighted for his great journey. His acclaimed book, *Voyages from Montreal, on the River St. Lawrence, Through the Continent of North America, to the Frozen and Pacific Ocean,* appeared in London in 1801, and among its enthusiastic readers were the American President Thomas Jefferson and his private secretary, Meriwether Lewis. Both studied the book at Monticello on the eve of Lewis's departure to launch another great westward exploration.

The first recorded crossing of the continental United States began on the rainy afternoon of May 14, 1804, at the mouth of the Missouri River, a few miles north of Saint Louis. The co-captains of this epochal enterprise were the Virginians Meriwether Lewis (age thirty, a captain of the First United States Infantry) and William Clark (thirty-four, a lieutenant of artillery and an experienced Indian fighter in Ohio Valley campaigns). At the outset, they commanded fourteen soldiers, nine Kentucky frontiersmen, and two French boatmen.

The Corps of Discovery, as Jefferson named it, had specific orders from the president:

> The object of your mission is to explore the Missouri river, & such principal streams of it, as, by its course, and communication with the waters of the Pacific ocean . . . may offer the

most direct & practicable water communication across this continent for the purpose of commerce.

The expedition was to undertake scientific work, as well: cartography (the captains had no maps of the terrain beyond the Rocky Mountains), the study and collection of flora and fauna and geologic formations, and observations of the native people the explorers encountered.

Among its scientific instruments, quite sophisticated for the era, the expedition took along a brass sextant; quadrants for measuring land feature altitudes; three Artificial Horizons that used water and glass as a reflecting surface to determine the altitude of the moon and stars; an English-made chronometer for longitudinal measurements; a device called a circumferentor to take the magnetic azimuth of the sun and polestar; pocket and surveying compasses; a two-pole chain for gauging distances up to thirty-three feet; and a log-line reel to measure rate and distance of boat travel.

On September 23, 1806, the Corps of Discovery returned to Saint Louis, completing its twenty-eight-month, eight-thousand-mile journey with stunning success (and with the loss of but a single man, whose death was unpreventable)—the most monumental exploration in American history. Lewis hurried a letter east to Jefferson:

> In obedience to your orders we have penitrated the Continent of North America to the Pacific Ocean, and sufficiently explored the interior of the country to affirm with confidence that we have discovered the most practical rout which dose exist across the continent.

Mackenzie, Lewis and Clark: the first to cross the continent north of Mexico? Or were they preceded, by over a century, by an American—a *native* American—Marco Polo, a figure almost, but not quite, lost to history?

The story of this original overlander is exasperatingly blurry because he traveled alone, wrote no journal, drew no maps, and had no instruments with which to measure the coordinates of his progress. Few historians have given his story much credence, but there is significant evidence that he not only reached the Oregon coast by pirogue, canoe, and on foot, but possibly the Atlantic coast, as well.

We would not know of him at all were it not for a French savant who believed his story and wrote it down.

The Frenchman had the euphonious name of Antoine Simon LePage du Pratz, and he was a Hollander by birth whose family must have emigrated to France when Antoine was a child. He was well educated, affluent, and is said to have served in a French dragoon regiment in the War of the Spanish Succession and as a military engineer. Little else is known of his history, and only because he wrote a valuable book is he remembered.

In the spring of 1718, at age twenty-three, du Pratz sailed from La Rochelle on the Bay of Biscay bound for New France. His ship reached Dauphin Island off the Louisiana coast that August, and he spent four months there before venturing to the mainland. His mission and duties in Louisiana are not known, not even if he came there in a military party sent as a garrison reinforcement, or as a civilian using his own funds.

His advent in New France did come at a propitious time: Only twenty years had passed since the Mississippi Valley had been claimed by the fur trader–explorer René-Robert Cavalier, Sieur de La Salle, and christened in the name of King Louis XIV. And 1718 was the year of the founding of New Orleans by Jean Baptiste Le Moyne, Sieur de Bienville, who named it after the Duc d'Orleans, regent of the child king Louis XV.

Du Pratz seems to have unlimited time on his hands and spent it traveling between the Gulf Coast of Louisiana and the eastern seaboard of the continent, venturing as far north as the coast of the British Carolinas, and pursuing studies of the "aboriginals" of the Mississippi Delta country.

Whether sent to New France as a soldier-scholar specifically to undertake this ethnological work, or as a wealthy civilian traveler with a scientific bent, du Pratz spent eight of his sixteen years in Louisiana living among the Natchez people "and their several nations" along the big river. In 1720, he bought from the Indians four hundred acres of land and a cabin located near a newly constructed French fort and the main Natchez Indian village. From this headquarters he began befriending the Natchez people, who he said "make good use of their reason, who think justly, who are prudent, faithful, generous, much more than certain civilized nations." He spent months learning their languages, customs, and rituals; talking with tribal elders; and learning also from a Natchez slave girl he acquired.

Du Pratz developed certain theories on the origin of America's natives—he was certain they were of oriental stock in the dim past—and in his studies among the natives encountered a persistent tradition that said they "came from between the north and the sun-setting." He asked to meet the wisest man of the tribe to talk about this and thus came to meet an old man of the Yazoo people, some forty leagues north of the Natchez village in which he was conducting his studies.

The elder was called L'Interprète by the French, who were at once mystified and awed by his grasp of many native languages far removed from his homeland. Du Pratz said the old man's actual name was Moncacht-apé and that it translated as "Killer of Pain and Fatigue."

At the time du Pratz spoke to him over the course of several days, Moncacht-apé's people, a small clan, were living on the lower course of the Yazoo River, a two-hundred-mile waterway in west-central Mississippi. It seems likely that the two men met before 1729, since after that year, the Yazoo and their Natchez brethren were scattered to the four winds, and after 1730 there were few Yazoos left to talk to.

Although there were French missions among the Natchez and neighboring tribes dating from 1699, the Yazoos, like the Chickasaws, were more influenced by British traders from the Carolinas and were no friends of the French. In 1729, the Yazoos had joined the Natchez in an attack on French settlements in their tribal lands, killing several hundred Frenchmen, including two Jesuit priests, and carrying off a great number of women and children. French troops pursued them and mounted a scorched-earth campaign in retribution, burning the Natchez villages and dispersing the Indians, capturing many and selling them into slavery in the West Indies. By 1843, the Natchez—and Yazoos—were said to be "culturally extinct."

Du Pratz makes no mention of reverting to his dragoon commission and joining in the Natchez War, but he was there, living among the Natchez tribes before the war and presumably continued his work afterward—although his Indian informants had dwindled to a handful.

Of all the elders he met in his ethnological studies, Moncacht-apé of the Yazoos proved the most fruitful. The old man had a long and astonishing story to tell of a journey across the continent.

The "ancient aboriginal," as du Pratz called him, told of having lost his wife and children in some unspecified circumstance that the interviewer did not pursue, after which he said, "I undertook my journey towards the sun-rising." He departed his village to travel first to the Chickasaw nation, probably in northern Mississippi, then moved on to the Wabash (Ohio) River to its source, which he said (or at least du Pratz interpreted), "is in the country of the Iroquois or Five Nations." Moncacht-apé told of being guided by Indian friends to the "Great Water" (the Atlantic Ocean), which "filled me with such joy and admiration that

I could not speak." The ebb and flow of the tides, he said, "filled me with great apprehension; but my companion quieted my fears . . . assuring me that the water observed certain bounds both in advancing and retiring."

After spending the winter with a people he called the Abenaquis, he viewed the "great fall of the river St. Laurence at Niagara," which he said "made my hair stand on end, and my heart almost leap out of its place."

Soon after witnessing this terrifying spectacle, he and a companion "took the shortest road to the Ohio," cut down a tree, and "formed it into a pettiaugre [pirogue—a dugout canoe] which served to conduct me down the Ohio and the Mississippi, after which, with much difficulty, I went up our small river; and at length arrived safe among my relations, who were rejoiced to see me in good health."

Moncacht-apé said, "This journey, instead of satisfying, only served to excite my curiosity." He told du Pratz that Yazoo tribal elders had for years talked of their forebears having come from much farther north than the Missouri River and, he said, "as I had longed to see, with my own eyes, the land from whence our first fathers came, I took my precautions for my journey westwards."

He packed some corn and other simple provisions and started out afoot up the eastern bank of the Mississippi to its confluence with the Ohio (at about present-day Cairo, Illinois), followed the Ohio and crossed it in "a raft of canes," and proceeded northward. He killed a buffalo "and took from it the fillets, the bunch [hump], and the tongue," and visited among a village of Illinois Indians he called the Tamaroas. At some point on the Illinois shore, he contrived to cross the Mississippi and proceeded north to the mouth of the Missouri, following its northern bank into "the nation of the Missouri tribe," where he "staid a long time to learn the language."

"In going along the Missouri," he said, "I passed through

meadows a whole day's journey in length, which were quite covered with buffaloes."

After wintering with the Missouri people, Moncacht-apé told of ascending the river in a pirogue, stopping frequently to visit Indian villages, learning languages and smatterings of information on regions beyond. He told of spending some time with "the Nation of the West, or the Canzas," and learned that if he proceeded on the river for one moon, he would reach certain high mountains "that were beset with dangers." There he would turn north and after several days would come to another river that flowed toward the west and into the Western Ocean.

The Yazoo said he ascended the Missouri for a month, "and although I had gone so far I did not turn to the right [north] as they [the Kanza tribe] had directed me, because for some days past I had seen many mountains which I dare not cross for fear of blistering my feet."

After ascending the river, he said he fell in with a hunting party of a tribe he called the Otters and accompanied thirty of these buffalo hunters, by canoe and overland march, for seventeen days. Then they arrived on the banks of "a river of beautiful clear water, called for this reason the Beautiful River." He said he feared bathing in the river and from his experience in Mississippi swamplands warned the others of the crocodiles that might inhabit it. He was informed that no such monsters infested these waters, and thus assured he was able to bathe with the rest of the tribe.

The Beautiful River, which du Pratz figured flowed at about latitude forty-five degrees north, took the Yazoo and his buffalo hunter companions to the Otter village where Moncacht-apé "was received with much kindness." After reaching the village, he accompanied an Otter delegation "who were going to carry a calumet [pipe] of peace to a nation beyond them." He and the Otters journeyed on the river in a dugout, landing now and then to reprovision, and after eighteen days reached the village. Moncacht-apé spent the winter with these unnamed people and learned their dialect. He was told that with this tongue "I should be able to understand all the nations which I would find, even to the Great Water which is to the west."

His hosts filled a canoe with pemmican, and he resumed his westward river journey, during the course of which, he said, "I met with several nations with whom I generally staid but one night." Among these was a village where the people wore their hair long and who regarded all "short hairs" as slaves.

The chief of this village accosted Moncacht-apé and asked "Who are you? Whence do you come? What seek you here with your short hair?" The Yazoo said he came from the land of the Otters though he was not one of them, seeking information, and that his heart was good, that he asked for no food, only information. "I have still far to go; my right arm and my bow are always equal to my necessities," he told the chief.

The chief and the chief's father, whose name du Pratz translated as "Big Roebuck" (probably "Big Elk" or "Great Elk" since a roebuck, a male roe deer, was an Old World animal unknown in America), took him into their tent and kept him there two days, telling him how to conduct himself among the other tribes he would encounter. When he was permitted to proceed, they gave him food and some meal "prepared from a small grain." He was advised that to be well received by all the nations thence to the Great Water he had but to say that Big Roebuck was his friend. The Yazoo testified that this proved true.

One day's journey from "the Great Water on the West" and about a league distant from the Beautiful River, Moncacht-apé encountered a tribe living in the forests in apprehension of "bearded men who come upon their coasts in floating villages, and carry off their children to make slaves of them."

The invaders were described to the Yazoo as white men, thick and short in stature with large heads covered with cloth and with long black beards that came down to their breasts. He was told, "They were always thus dressed, even in the greatest heats," and "their cloaths fell down to the middle of their legs, which with their feet were covered with red or yellow stuff. Their arms made a great fire and a great noise; and when they saw themselves outnumbered by Red Men, they retired on board their large pettiaugre, the number [of men] sometimes amounting to thirty, but never more."

In a mystifying detail that du Pratz unfortunately did not pursue, Moncacht-apé reported that the coastal tribesmen said the strangers came from the sun-setting "in search of a yellow stinking wood which dyes a fine yellow colour." He said the coastal people he was visiting "had destroyed all those kind of trees" to deter the white barbarians from "visiting them," but that two other "nations" in the area could not destroy the trees since they had no other wood. The bearded men had invaded these tribes and so "greatly incommoded" them the Indians laid plans to ambush the outlanders the next time they came ashore.

Moncacht-apé said he was curious about these bearded white interlopers who were apparently neither English, French, nor Spanish, and the following summer joined in an expedition the Pacific tribes were mounting against them.

When the time of the invaders' arrival approached, the Indians' families were sent inland so that their young women would not be captured. After this precaution, the men left their camp near the Beautiful River and journeyed five days along the coast of the Great Water to a point where two great rocks stood, from which a shallow stream issued into the sea. Near this shore, the Indians told Moncacht-apé, the yellow wood was found, and it was here the interlopers always ran their boats ashore.

"The Red men, by my advice, placed themselves in ambuscade to surprize the strangers," the Yazoo said, and after all preparations were made, the Indians waited seventeen days before spying a familiar boat heading for the beach, and four more days until the invaders were well scattered, gathering wood and water. Then the tribesmen launched their attack, killing eleven of the "strangers." During the fight, Moncacht-apé said, "An unknown number of them immediately escaped on board two large pettiaugres, and flew westward upon the Great Water."

The Yazoo studied the corpses closely and reported:

> Upon examining those whom we had killed, we found them much smaller than ourselves, and very white; they had a large head, and in the middle of the crown the hair was very long; their head was wrapt in a great many folds of stuff, and their cloaths seemed to be made neither of wool nor silk; they were very soft, and of different colors.

He said their bodies were short and thick and that instead of hats they wore cloth wound round the head and that their feet and legs were covered with long moccasins. Two of the dead carried firearms—powder and ball. "I tried their pieces and found that they were much heavier than yours," he told du Pratz, "and did not kill at so great a distance."

Soon after this adventure, he resumed his journey, traveling along the shore of the Great Water, visiting many villages on the north. Then, "on account of the severity of the climate, and the want of game," he said he returned

> by the same route by which I had set out; and reducing my whole travels westward to days' journeys, I compute that they would have employed me thirty-six moons; but on account of my frequent delays, it was five years before I returned to my relations among the Yazous.

M. Antoine Simon LePage du Pratz left no record of his reaction to the baffling but extraordinary story Moncacht-apé told, but he presumably wrote it down faithfully and had no doubt of its veracity. In 1758, twenty-four years after he returned to France, he published the account in his three-volume work, *Histoire de la Louisiane*, which became available to the English-reading world in 1763 with the English translation, published with the cumbersome title, *The History of Louisiana, or of The Western Parts of Virginia and Carolina: Containing a Description of the Countries that lie on both Sides of the River Mississippi: With an Account of the Settlements, Inhabitants, Soil, Climate, and Products.*

One hundred and thirty years after du Pratz's book appeared, the prolific American historian Hubert Howe Bancroft, in preparing his massive *History of the Northwest Coast*, adopted and defended the Yazoo's story and thus opened his chapters on the first overland expedition to the Pacific:

> The first exploring expedition across the Rocky Mountains, and thence to the Pacific Ocean, was neither that of Alexander Mackenzie nor yet that of Lewis and Clark. It was not performed by an armed band under the auspices of a powerful corporation or by army officers guarded by a posse of soldiers. We are not indebted to European intelligence or progress for the first account of the Oregon country. Prompted by curiosity, the stimulant underlying all advancement, a native of the Mississippi Valley, unassisted and unattended, found the path which Jefferson's captains sixty years later, with all their government aid, encountered such laborious difficulty in following; for brains work under red skins as well as under white.

Bancroft found Moncacht-apé "remarkable for his solid understanding and elevation of sentiments," and said, "I may justly compare him to those first Greeks, who traveled chiefly into the east to examine the manners and customs of different nations, and to communicate to their fellow-citizens upon their return, the knowledge which they had acquired."

Comparing the Indian to Plato for his love of the sciences

and to Herodotus for his "thirst for the enlightenments of travel," the historian said,

> It is a mistake to give civilization all the brain-power of the planet. Not less than Europe, America had her arts, her letters, her eloquence and diplomacy; not less than the university, the forest has its lofty contemplations, its hungerings after higher intelligence, its battlings with black ignorance and mental obscurations.

Bancroft seriously weighed the Yazoo's narrative, necessarily vague as it was, and found it completely credible:

> The mountains, the river, and the sea are there today as Moncacht-apé described them, and let it be remembered, no other person, white or red, so far as known, had ever before performed this journey between the Mississippi and the Pacific Ocean by way of the Columbia River.

As to such matters as the long-haired chief Big Roebuck telling the Yazoo that the Missouri and the "Beautiful River" flowed parallel to each other for some distance, Bancroft says, "this was in error—as was the direction given to the Columbia and the general course of the Columbia to the Great Water—the Pacific . . . we can readily excuse slight discrepancies as to direction by one without charts or compass, and the first to traverse this region and return to tell of it."

Du Pratz guessed that the black-bearded white intruders whose dead bodies Moncacht-apé had examined ("like a scientist," Bancroft wrote) were Japanese or Koreans. This fulfilled his pet theory on the Asiatic origin of American aboriginals. From the Yazoo's description of their color, dress, weapons, and the direction of their arrival on the Oregon coast, Bancroft thought the evidence "may point toward Kamchatka, or Japan."

Since it seems likely that Moncacht-apé would have been able to distinguish between "white men" and Asiatics—who may have appeared more Indian than "white"—it is likelier that the intruders were Russians. Bancroft asserts that at the time of the Yazoo's arrival on the Pacific, no Russians were known to have penetrated the coast below 50 degrees north latitude. But small hunting parties may have crossed the ocean from Kamchatka, the pendulum-like peninsula on the Russian edge of the Bering Sea, the southern tip of which lies at about 50 degrees north. Paddling and sailing their "floating villages," probably a flotilla of small boats, the Russians may have used the Aleutian Islands as stepping stones to the North American continent. (Moncacht-apé stated that the raiders wore long moccasins that covered their legs and feet, and Bancroft states these may have been Aleut Indian in origin.) It is possible that the Russians thus came to the shores of Vancouver Island from Kamchatka and the Aleutians and forayed south along the Oregon coast. The British fur trader John Meares came upon a Russian trapper's camp at Unalaska in the Aleutian Islands in 1786, and his description of these men and the boats that carried them from Kamchatka bears a striking resemblance to Moncacht-apé's account.

The mystery of the "yellow stinking wood which dyes a fine yellow colour" has never been solved. Something was lost in translation—the tongue of the coastal tribe to Moncacht-apé's Yazoo, the Yazoo to du Pratz's French, the French to English.

(Another apparent mistranslation was encountered by the Lewis and Clark expedition, which carried a copy of a 1774 English edition of du Pratz's *History of Louisiana*—as well as Mackenzie's *Voyages from Montreal*—to the Pacific. In July 1804, at an abandoned Kanza Indian village, William Clark found no cane growing in the vicinity as du Pratz had claimed was used by natives, including Moncacht-apé, to construct rafts to cross the river. Gary Moulton, a modern editor of the Lewis and Clark journals, explains: ". . . the 'canes' do not appear in the original [of du Pratz's book], which states that the Indians crossed the river in *cajeaux* ['rafts'] made of unstated materials.")

Du Pratz spent an unspecified time with Moncacht-apé gleaning the story of the Yazoo's epic journeys, but *when* these interviews took place is among the many mysteries of the remarkable story.

He arrived in Louisiana in 1718, and a modern scholar states that he returned to France in 1734 and published his three-volume work containing the Moncacht-apé account in 1758. It appears that the Yazoo told his story to the Frenchman at some point in the sixteen-year period between 1718 and 1734, very likely before 1729, the year the Yazoo and Natchez people were dispersed. And if the Indian was an "ancient aboriginal" when du Pratz first met him, *Moncacht-apé's journeys might have occurred in the last quarter of the seventeenth century—perhaps as early as the 1660s.*

Also, if Moncacht-apé was an ancient aboriginal when the Frenchman interviewed him, it is not possible, as Bancroft asserts, that the transcontinental journey was made between 1730 and 1745. Du Pratz probably met him between 1720 and 1729, and by 1734—at least according to the best evidence—du Pratz had returned to France.

Whatever the precise timing of the Yazoo's journey, he long preceded Mackenzie and Lewis and Clark and has the distinction of being the first, and only, identified and recorded pre-nineteenth-century Native American to have crossed the continent to the Pacific.

Details of du Pratz's career after he returned home are unknown except that he lived long enough—twenty-four years—to prepare his journals and notebooks of his long sojourn in Louisiana and presumably to see them in print.

Nor do we know what became of Moncacht-apé. We do know that in return for his services in telling of his great odyssey, du Pratz, whose generosity knew definite bounds, gave the Yazoo pilgrim "a present of several wares of no great value, among which was a concave mirror about two inches and a half diameter, which had cost me about three halfpence." The magnanimous Frenchman said the poor Yazoo elder "was wonderfully delighted with it, and would not have exchanged it with the best mirror in France."

"OH, HOW HARD IT IS TO DIE"

. . . This disorder . . .
always ends in decrepitude,
death, or premature
old age.

—MERIWETHER LEWIS
January 27, 1806

I

THE STAND

Forty years ago, the Western novelist and historian Vardis Fisher published a book on an American mystery that has baffled historians for nearly two centuries. The title, *Suicide or Murder? The Strange Death of Meriwether Lewis*, seemed to sum up the entire issue: How did the explorer Meriwether Lewis—the Lewis of Lewis and Clark—die in backwoods Tennessee in the late night or early morning hours of October 10 or 11, 1809? That he died violently is certain, but did he take his own life or was it taken from him?

How he died, however, is not the only issue.

There is the matter of *why*.

This we know.

Meriwether Lewis, born near Charlottesville, Virginia, in 1774, was a veteran of the First Infantry in campaigns under Gen. "Mad Anthony" Wayne in the Ohio Valley and had served as Jefferson's private secretary. He was well educated, precise, and dependable. He was also skittish, given to bursts of nervous energy, as well as to periods of illness and lassitude. He was ambitious, and so self-possessed and "serious" in demeanor, he was thought to be melancholic. Like his mentor in the White House, he had a scientific bent and on the expedition served as medical officer, botanist, zoologist, and primary journal keeper.

We know, too, from dependable accounts and Lewis's own words, that he changed radically after the great cross-continent exploration ended in the fall of 1806. Introspective by nature, he became solitary, his temperament more mercurial, his outlook more fatalistic. He seemed consumed with what he believed to be failing health and dosed himself with pills and elixirs, including laudanum, an addictive opiate in liquid form, and his quick mind appeared to have succumbed to a strange inertia, as if he dreaded to act for fear of failure. Jefferson appointed him governor of Upper Louisiana Territory in February 1807, but Lewis tarried for a full year in Washington, Philadelphia, and Virginia before taking up the post. He fell ill with "a raging fever," scouted for a publisher for the massive journals of the Corps of Discovery, hired naturalists, artists, and engravers to illustrate the work, and a mathematician to check his calculations, but could not write a line of supporting material. Instead, he sat for portraits, including at least three by the celebrated French profilist Charles Févret de Saint-Mémin. Lewis attended meetings of the American Philosophical Society of Philadelphia and fell in and out of love—at least twice, once experiencing the rejection of his proposal of marriage. He spent time with his mother at Locust Hill. He began drinking heavily—the "habit into which he had fallen" about which Jefferson later referred. And, in August 1807, by some accounts, he traveled to Richmond as Jefferson's representative at Aaron Burr's treason trial.

At some point in all this miscellaneous activity, Lewis had a falling out with his mentor when Jefferson scolded him for his failure to write the narrative for the expedition journals. The president was probably also impatient for Lewis to move on west to assume his governorship.

The explorer turned more and more to the anodyne of alcohol while fretting about his future: his chronic ill health, the loneliness of bachelorhood, the loss of the friendship, counsel, and patronage of his idol. On the eve of his departure to the Mississippi, Lewis wrote his Philadelphia lawyer and friend Mahlon Dickerson, "I never felt less like a heroe than at the present moment . . . you see already . . . the changes which have taken place in my disposition."

In March 1808, in this state of health and mind and after being governor in absentia for one year and eight days, Lewis reached Saint Louis to take up his administrative post.

His professional and personal affairs continued to decline in his eighteen months in office.

Even before he arrived in the steamy seat of governance, he fell afoul of the territorial secretary who was serving as acting governor pending Lewis's arrival. This man, Frederick Bates, a Virginia lawyer who also received his appointment from Jefferson, was a capable administrator but also a magniloquent, pettifogging, hatefully jealous bureaucrat who coveted the governorship.* After hearing the news of Lewis's death in Tennessee, Bates would insist that the explorer had been drunken and "insane" from the outset of his administration, charges the secretary had not made in his voluminous, often viciously anti-Lewis, personal correspondence *before* Lewis's death.

---

*Bates (1777–1825) won the Missouri governorship in 1824 but served less than a year before he died in office, of pleurisy. His brief tenure was remembered by his veto of a bill outlawing dueling and for his refusal to greet the Marquis de Lafayette when the Revolutionary War hero came to Saint Louis. Punctilious to the end, Bates said the Missouri General Assembly had made no appropriation for the marquis's visit.

Added to the Bates distraction, Lewis lost money in land speculations in Saint Louis and also became embroiled in a dispute with the War and Treasury departments in Washington. The governor's grievance was based on the refusal of the federal government to honor the vouchers (one for a paltry nineteen dollars) he submitted for payments made, out of his annual two-thousand-dollar stipend, for official territorial business.

These disputed vouchers became the ostensible motive for his plan to return to Washington in the fall of 1809. Another purpose was to move publication of the expedition journals off dead center, a source of contention between Lewis and the now former president for at least two years. Less than a month before he began his trip East, the explorer received a letter from Monticello in which Jefferson repeated his anxiety over the journals. "I have so long promised copies to my literary correspondents in France, that I am almost bankrupt in their eyes. I shall be very happy to receive from yourself information of your expectations on this subject. Everybody is impatient for it."

On September 4, Lewis departed Saint Louis by flatboat, accompanied by his servant John Pernier (or Pernia, who had been one of Jefferson's servants in Washington and was variously described as a Creole, Frenchman, Spaniard, and a "free mulatto") and four large trunks. These contained saddles and tack, weapons, clothing, personal belongings and papers, including his disputed expense accounts and sixteen notebooks bound in red morocco comprising the journals of the Corps of Discovery.

At New Madrid, two hundred miles below Saint Louis, Lewis had to be taken ashore to see a doctor, reportedly because of a flare-up of his intermittent fever. On September 11, during his time in the town, he wrote his last will and testament, leaving his estate to his mother, Lucy Marks. Crewmen carried him ashore again at Chickasaw Bluffs (on the site of present-day Memphis) on a muggy September 15, still quite ill and dosing himself with laudanum and "tartar"—tartar emetic, a compound used to induce sweating and vomiting.

At Fort Pickering, the town's military post to which Lewis had been assigned in 1797, he came under the care of the commander of the fort, Capt. Gilbert Russell. This officer wrote to Jefferson on January 31, 1810, three months after Lewis's death, of the governor's "intemperance" before and after his arrival "and the possibility that the free use of alcohol contributed to his suicide."

The former president, now sixty-six years old and retired to his hilltop villa overlooking Charlottesville, wrote to Russell that Lewis's death "was an act of desperation" and went on to say that Lewis "was much afflicted & habitually so with hypochondria."

Two years later, Russell wrote an account of Lewis's stay at Fort Pickering, saying the explorer was "in a state of mental derangement" and that the river boatmen who brought him to Chickasaw Bluffs said Lewis had "made two attempts to kill himself, in one of which he nearly succeeded" during the voyage. (Since Russell did not mention wounds, investigators have speculated that Lewis may have tried to jump overboard in his delirium.) The governor, Russell went on, had to be kept under close watch since he "had made several attempts to put an end to his existence" but that after six or seven days "all signs of derangement disappeared and he was completely in his senses."

E. G. Chuinard, a physician-writer who studied medical aspects of the Lewis and Clark expedition, has suggested that Lewis's recurrent bouts with malaria must be taken into account as a source for his "derangement." Chuinard stated that Lewis's "indispositions" and "violent agues"* may have been malarial in nature and that the ten days he spent at Fort Pickering was "the usual time for patients with estivo [summer] malaria attacks to recover."

(The fear of malaria and the belief that it would be the

---

*In a time when the source of malaria, the mosquito of the genus *Anopheles*, was unknown, *ague* was a common word for "the fever." It derives from the French *fièvre aigue*, "acute fever."

prevalent affliction on the journey to the Pacific accounts for the fact that one-third of the cost of the expedition's medical supplies was for "Peruvian bark," to be boiled into a medicinal tea. The main ingredient of the bark was quinine.)

During his eight days of recuperation at Fort Pickering, Lewis's mental state did not prevent him from writing a shaky but lucid letter to President James Madison explaining why he had decided to travel overland to Washington and not via New Orleans as he had originally planned. He said he felt the overland route would be less taxing on his "indisposition" in the heat of the climate and that he feared the possibility of his "original papers relative to my voyage to the Pacific falling into the hands of the British." (The British were not in or even close to New Orleans at this time, but Lewis may have depended upon erroneous information.)

Captain Russell lent the explorer $100 in gold and two horses with saddles, the total loan of $379.58 secured by a promissory note signed by both men. Then, on September 29, after leaving two of his four trunks under Russell's care, Lewis departed the fort and rode east toward the Tennessee River and after a two-day rest by the river, proceeded on and struck the Natchez Trace.

What we know of the eleven days remaining in the life of Meriwether Lewis derives from a muddle of contradictory after-the-fact testimony, *all* of it from dubious sources: an obscure Indian agent; a mysterious servant; and the terrified, probably illiterate wife of a wilderness innkeeper who told her story at least three times, each time differently.

As to the explorer's conduct on the trail into the Natchez Trace of Tennessee, the only "evidence" is that provided by John Neelly, agent for the Chickasaw Indians of the region. Of this elusive figure we know little except that he was a former militiaman commissioned as agent less than three months before he met Governor Lewis at Fort Pickering, that he was intensely disliked by

Captain Russell, and that he would be dismissed from his post by the secretary of war in July 1812, for "hostility to the Indians."

Neelly had arrived at Fort Pickering from the Chickasaw Agency in Mississippi, 150 miles to the southeast, only three days before Lewis arrived and apparently volunteered to accompany Lewis back toward Nashville. It was Neelly alone who in a letter to Jefferson, attested that Lewis appeared "deranged of mind" on the trail, and it was Neelly who first reported the secondhand account of the governor's death "by suicide."

Lewis and his little entourage—his servant Pernier, Neelly and his slave (whose name is not recorded), a few Chickasaw Indians, and a remuda of pack horses—departed Fort Pickering on September 29, crossed the Tennessee River on October 8, and made camp. On the morning of October 10, Neelly said, he discovered that two of the pack animals had slipped away during the night. He stayed behind to find them while the restless and anxious Lewis, with Pernier and Neelly's black man accompanying him, proceeded toward the Natchez Trace, about a day's ride to the north.

The Trace, an old path running north out of Natchez 550 miles through the valley of Tennessee to Nashville, had a history as a haven for "land pirates"—highwaymen and bushwhackers lurking in the brush waiting to assail unwary travelers—but the Lewis party rode into it unmolested, and on the evening of October 10 reached Grinder's Stand. This place, one of several "stands," wilderness hostelries, along the Natchez Trace, was situated in a clearing in a grove of old oak and persimmon trees and consisted of two rough-hewn log cabins separated by a narrow dog run.

Meeting the travelers at the breezeway between the cabins was Priscilla Grinder, wife of Robert Grinder, owner of the property. Lewis, wearing a white-and-blue-striped linen duster, did not identify himself as governor of Upper Louisiana, only requested lodging, telling Mrs. Grinder that he had been eleven days on the trail and was en route to Nashville.

She offered Lewis the vacant cabin and a warm meal. Pernier and Neelly's slave brought his trunks forward and then took the animals to a nearby barn, where they were instructed to remain for the night. Mrs. Grinder's servant girl took food to the barn for the two men while Lewis ate sparingly of the meal prepared for him, then threw a bearskin on the puncheon floor of the cabin, wrapped himself in a buffalo robe, and retired for the night.

Now it was twilight, October 10, 1809, and within a few hours, Meriwether Lewis would be dead.

Just as we are forced to depend upon James Neelly's testimony on Lewis's journey from Fort Pickering to the Natchez Trace, so are we at the mercy of a single witness to the last hours of Lewis's life: Priscilla Knight Grinder (or perhaps Griner—the record is unclear), who with her husband Robert came to Tennessee in the recent past from Stokes County, North Carolina.

She told her story to Neelly, to the ornithologist Alexander Wilson in 1811, and to a schoolteacher in 1838. Although her accounts varied maddeningly with each telling, these are the essentials of what she reported.

At sunset on October 10, when Lewis and the two other men rode into the stand, Mrs. Grinder's husband was away, working at their farm on the Duck River, ten miles north, leaving Priscilla to mind the cabins with two of their youngest children and a black servant girl named Malinda, about twelve years old.

After he made arrangements with her, Mrs. Grinder said Lewis took his saddle into the cabin, then asked for spirits but drank little. When Pernier came up with Neelly's black man, Lewis made a remark to them about his "powder," apparently signifying that the pistols he carried were unloaded and that he did not carry his own powder horn.

He paced nervously, she recalled, and spoke loudly, his face flushed. He ate little of the food she prepared for him, lit his pipe, drew up a chair in the dog run, and said in a kindly way to his hostess, "Madam, this is a very pleasant evening." Later, after refilling his pipe, he looked out toward the dying light in the west and said, "What a sweet evening it is."

Before he retired, she said she heard Lewis striding back and forth in the path between the cabins, talking to himself "like a lawyer."

A bit later three men rode into the stand to ask for lodging but rode on after being threatened by Lewis, who stood by his cabin brandishing a brace of pistols.

At about three o'clock in the morning of October 11, Mrs. Grinder heard gunshots and a few minutes later heard Lewis at her door saying "O madam! Give me some water and heal my wounds!" (In another account she said that after the first gunshot she heard something fall heavily to the floor of the cabin, heard the words "Oh, Lord!" then heard a second shot.)

She peered through the cracks between the logs of her kitchen and saw a man stagger and fall against a stump, crawl some distance away, and raise himself against a tree.

She was terrified, alone in the pitch-black night, and would not open her door.

She later heard the scraping of a gourd dipper in a water bucket.

She waited about two hours, then, at dawn, sent her children to the barn to fetch the two men who slept there.

Pernier found Lewis, still conscious, lying on his blood-soaked bearskin, a piece of his forehead blown away and his brain exposed, another gaping wound in his chest, and (this from a later recounting) cuts on his body seemingly made with a razor.

The explorer died about two hours later and was buried on the property, his coffin cobbled together from oak boards joined with wooden pegs. In 1811, the Scottish-born ornithologist Alexander Wilson, the first person after Neelly to speak to the Grinders about the tragedy, was shown the grave and asked Robert Grinder to fence the area to keep hogs and wolves from foraging in it. Wilson said he obtained a written promise from Grinder that the fence would be erected.

In 1838, after her husband's death, Priscilla Grinder, now in her sixties, spoke again of the incident, this time to a schoolteacher who came to visit the Lewis grave site. Mrs. Grinder's story now contained some baffling new details. She told the teacher that when she saw Lewis at sunrise, the dying man had exchanged clothes with Pernier, that Pernier said the governor had given his clothes to him, and that the servant also had Lewis's gold watch. Mrs. Grinder also recalled that as Lewis lay on his bloody bearskin he said, "Oh, how hard it is to die. I am so strong."

James Neelly rode into Grinder's Stand during the forenoon of October 11, leading one of the two strayed horses. While he left no record of what he found as he rode up to the cabins, in a letter to Thomas Jefferson on October 18, he wrote, "It is with extreme pain that I have to inform you of the death of His Excellency, Meriwether Lewis, Governor of Upper Louisiana, who died on the morning of the 11th instant, and, I am sorry to say, by suicide." He related to Jefferson Mrs. Grinder's account of the tragedy and added that Lewis appeared "deranged in mind" on the trail and that "He had shot himself in the head with one pistol & a little below the Breast with the other." He made no mention of razor wounds. Neelly said that he had possession of the governor's two trunks of papers, rifle, silver watch, brace of flintlock pistols, dirk, and tomahawk. He asked Jefferson for instructions on forwarding the trunks as well as the others left at Fort Pickering.

It appears that William Clark later collected the trunks from Neelly in Nashville and those left in Gilbert Russell's care. The hundred dollars in gold Captain Russell had lent the explorer was never found, and the dirk and pistols also subsequently disappeared. Nor was any solution found to the question of the two watches—the gold one Pernier said Lewis gave him, and the silver one Neely found in the governor's belongings.

Neely gave John Pernier fifteen dollars for expenses, and the servant, taking Lewis's packhorse with him, traveled on to Virginia and talked to Jefferson, his old employer, at Monticello on November 26. Thereafter Pernier paid a visit to Lewis's family near Charlottesville, where he attempted to collect $240 in back wages he said were owed him. The result of this visit was to convince Lucy Marks, Lewis's mother, that Pernier had murdered her son.

Six months after his return to Washington, John Pernier apparently killed himself. When Priscilla Grinder told her reconstituted story to the anonymous schoolteacher in 1838, she said she had heard that Pernier, after being rebuffed by Lewis's mother, "finally cut his own throat, and thus put an end to his existence." But a May 5, 1810, letter to Jefferson from John Christopher Sueverman, also a former presidential servant, reported that "Mr. Pirny" (Pernier), who Sueverman described as "wretchedly destitute," had died of an overdose of laudanum and was "buried neat and decent the next day."

The news of Lewis's death first appeared in print in the *Nashville Clarion* ten days after the event, the story containing the essentials of what Priscilla Grinder told John Neely. A similar account appeared in the *Washington National Intelligencer* on November 15.

In 1893, the army surgeon and naturalist Elliott Coues, a New Hampshireman who retraced much of the Corps of Discovery route and visited the site of Lewis's death, published in four volumes his vastly annotated *A History of the Expedition Under the Command of Captains Lewis and Clark*. In this work, Coues stated that the ornithologist Alexander Wilson was a precise and dependable man of science. "There is no more reason to doubt Wilson's painstaking correctness than there is reason to doubt his veracity," he wrote. But, he added, Mrs. Grinder's testimony "is not to be believed under oath" and said of her account of Lewis's death, "there is every sign that it is a concoction on the part of an accomplice in crime, either before or after the event."

Coues was the first writer of eminence to call into question Priscilla Grinder's entire story, in particular her odd behavior after hearing the pistol shots, seeing her guest staggering about the yard begging for water, then waiting until sunrise to notify the servants in the barn of what she heard and saw. "Governor Lewis may have committed the deed . . . in a fit of suicidal mania," Coues wrote,

> and the woman's incoherent story may not have been intended to deceive, but may have arisen from confused memories of an exciting night. That is conceivable; but my contention is that the testimony, as we have it, does not suffice to prove suicide, and does raise a strong suspicion that Governor Lewis was foully dealt with by some person or persons unknown—presumably [Robert] Grinder, or him and some accomplices.

He stated unequivocally his belief that "Mrs. Grinder was privy to a plot to murder Governor Lewis, and therefore had her own part to play in the tragedy, even if that part was a passive one."

Murder or suicide?

The late Stephen Ambrose held to the conviction that Lewis was a suicide and cited as the most convincing evidence that "Neither Jefferson nor Clark ever doubted that Lewis killed himself." The author of *Undaunted Courage* stated that if William Clark had any suspicion of murder, he would have gone to Tennessee to personally investigate the matter and that if Jefferson had any such a suspicion, he would have insisted the government launch an investigation. "There is simply no question whatsoever about how he died," Ambrose told *USA Today* in October 1995. "Let him rest."

But, of course, neither Ambrose nor any other investigator can slam the door on any matter so historically important as this and there *is* a question, two in fact, for this nagging, unsettling mystery: If murder, who? If suicide, why?

Writers such as Elliott Coues in 1893, Olin D. Wheeler (*On the Trail of Lewis and Clark*, 1926), John Bakeless (*Lewis and Clark: Partners in Discovery*, 1947), Vardis Fisher (*Murder or Suicide?*, 1962), Donald Jackson (*Letters of the Lewis and Clark Expedition*, 1962), and Richard Dillon (*Meriwether Lewis: a Biography*, 1965), all lean toward the murder theory. They ask if a veteran soldier and frontiersman would fail twice to kill himself with his weapons. Could he have held one of the long-barreled flintlock pistols in such a manner that the ball would penetrate his breast and exit low in his back? Could he could have blown off part of his skull, exposing his brain, then shoot himself through the chest, or vice versa, and still manage to stagger to Priscilla Grinder's door begging for water?* And would a man bent on suicide, after botching the job with guns and perhaps a razor, beg for water and for someone to "heal my wounds"?

Inevitably, the suicide doubters point to Mrs. Grinder, her ever-embroidered stories serving as the only real eyewitness account of Lewis's death, and her peculiar timidity. Here was a frontier woman, her critics say, toughened by her life in the wilderness, in a place inhabited by outlaws and thugs, who was so terrified by a gentleman guest's pacing and talking to himself that she could not sleep and would not unbar her door to the dy-

---

*Lewis's brace of pistols, which disappeared at some point after his death, are believed to have been Model 1799, .691-caliber North and Cheney muzzle-loaders. This was a smoothbore weapon with an 8½-inch barrel and an overall length of 14½ inches firing a lead ball .69 inches in diameter.

ing man begging for water and succor. Here was a woman married to a man who sold "high wine" and whiskey to the Indians,
a probable crony of the land pirates of the Natchez Trace, who
was mysteriously missing on that bloody night and morning of
October 9 and 10.

In one of her recollections, Mrs. Grinder spoke of three
men who rode into the stand but rode out again after being
threatened by Lewis. She said the men were only seeking lodging, but were they drawn to the cabins by another motive? Had
they followed Lewis there, seen that he was a man of means accompanied only by a servant and a black slave? Or did they
reach these conclusions after he chased them off, and returned
later to kill him and steal his gold and guns? A hundred or
more dollars was an ample attraction for highwaymen skulking
in the forests of the Natchez Trace, the infamous "Devil's Backbone," and no money was ever recovered among the explorer's
effects.

The idea that Lewis had been murdered was so prevalent that
in 1849, the year his remains were reburied under a monument
at Grinder's Stand, the Tennessee commission that arranged for
the memorial included the speculation in its proceedings. The
commissioners stated in their report that, "The impression has
long prevailed that under the disease of body and mind . . . Governor Lewis perished by his own hand. It seems to be more probable that he died by the hands of an assassin."

But, while even Lucy Meriwether Lewis Marks, the explorer's
mother, is said to have insisted to her death that her son was murdered (and had no hesitation in pointing her finger at John Pernier
as the killer), others close to Lewis thought otherwise.

Thomas Jefferson, Lewis's mentor and the man responsible
for his achievements as explorer and territorial governor, harbored no shadow of doubt that his admirable friend had killed
himself. On August 18 (coincidentally Lewis's birthday), 1813,
Jefferson wrote of Governor Lewis's "hypochondriac affections"
and "sensible depressions of mind," exacerbated by his "seden-

tary occupations" in Saint Louis. Then the former president wrote,

> He stopped at the house of Mr. Grinder, who not being at home, his wife, alarmed at the symptoms of derangement she discovered, gave him the house then retired to rest herself. . . . About three o'clock in the night he did the deed which plunged his friends into affliction, and deprived the country of one of her most valued citizens.

William Clark, Lewis's expedition partner, subscribed to Jefferson's conviction: "I fear O! I fear the weight of his mind has overcome him," he wrote to his brother upon reading in a Kentucky newspaper of Lewis's death.

The magnitude of Jefferson's prestige was such that his suicide verdict was regarded as Scripture, and all inquiry into the manner of Lewis's death seemed superfluous. This despite the fact that the verdict was based exclusively on what he was told by the shadowy Indian agent James Neelly, who knew only what he had been told by the even shadowier Priscilla Grinder.

The "weight of his mind," as Clark aptly put it, was a formidable factor to consider. Even discounting as suspect the testimony of Gilbert Russell, James Neelly, and Priscilla Grinder, and laying aside the postmortems of Frederick Bates, Thomas Jefferson, William Clark, and others, there remains ample evidence to suspect that Meriwether Lewis killed himself. He was sunk deep in debt, suffering from a recurrent malarial fever, perhaps addicted to opiates and alcohol, anguished over failing in love, failing in preparing his and Clark's journals for publication, failing to preserve his friendship with his great mentor at Monticello, and failing in the governorship Jefferson had bestowed upon him.

Recent medical scholarship suggests yet another motive for suicide, a diagnosis advanced by an eminent Seattle physician and epidemiologist, Reimert Thorolf Ravenholt. In May 1994, Dr. Ravenholt presented in the medical journal *Epidemiology* the hypothesis that Lewis may have killed himself because of despair over his knowledge that he was dying of paresis, the terminal phase of syphilis. The disease, from which several other expedition members suffered, was probably contracted by Lewis during an August 1913 stayover in a Shoshoni Indian village after the explorers crossed the Continental Divide, Dr. Ravenholt states. He proposes that Lewis's loss of vitality, febrile disorientation, fatalism, and drift toward self-destruction—all common symptoms of paresis—fit the last, sad weeks of Lewis's life.

Lewis himself, who had treated cases of syphilis among his expedition members, wrote in 1806, "This disorder . . . always ends in decrepitude, death, or premature old age."

Several historians say that the key to determining the explorer's manner of death is exhumation of the Lewis remains at the site of Grinder's Stand, near Hohenwald, Tennessee. Dr. Ravenholt says if, for example, Lewis ever received or self-administered a mercuric treatment to combat a venereal disease, traces of it might be found with his remains. More significant, the bone remains might contain evidence of syphilitic invasion.

Other researchers are interested in any traces remaining of gunshot wounds.

Although he takes the opposite, "it was murder" view on Lewis's death, James E. Starrs, the acclaimed forensic scientist at Georgetown University, would also like to open Lewis's grave at the Natchez Trace monument. Starrs has experience in this work: in 1989, he directed the Alferd Packer* exhumations in Colorado and also studied the remains of Jesse James in Kearney, Missouri, proving through mitochondrial DNA that the remains were indeed James's.

---

*Packer, a prospector who cannibalized five companions during the winter of 1874, said he killed the men in self-defense, but knife and hatchet blows on the bones of the exhumed proved Alferd Packer was a murderer.

Starrs, like many murder advocates, is convinced that the descriptions of Lewis's wounds do not suggest suicide, that a soldier experienced in firearms would not have failed twice to kill himself, and he believes it more likely that the explorer was accosted and shot by Natchez Trace outlaws or by a person in his entourage.

In June 1996, Starrs spearheaded plans to exhume the Lewis remains and helped convince a coroner's jury in Tennessee that the National Park Service, on whose land the explorer is buried, should allow it. In this he was joined by a University of Southern Mississippi history professor and authority on the Natchez Trace, by Dr. Ravenholt, and by other interested parties. The exhumation plan also had the overwhelming endorsement of Lewis descendants, 160 of them signing a statement supporting it. Among those opposed to the project, one calling it "a ghoulish business," were the late historian Stephen Ambrose and, more important, the National Park Service.

The coroner's jury convened at Hohenwald did not vote on the matter of suicide or murder but did recommend that the Lewis remains be exhumed. The Park Service did not agree, saying that such an act would set a dangerous precedent that could lead to national monuments being dug up all over the country, and it denied the request. After a subsequent hearing in Atlanta, Georgia, in January 1998, the NPS again denied the exhumation request.

So far at least, that jury, and the bigger one on how and why Meriwether Lewis died, is out.

11

THEODOSIA

Meriwether Lewis died 194 years ago.

What more can we possibly learn from a case so cold?

Would an exhumation of his remains solve the mystery or the manner of his death? Would forensic scientists find traces of mercury or evidence of syphilis in his bones? And if so, would such a finding close the argument over whether he was a victim of murder or, afflicted by a diseased brain, of self-murder?

And while we wait for the National Park Service to change its mind on the exhumation issue, there is an important—at least interesting—matter in the sad saga of Meriwether Lewis's death to unravel: a fine mystery within this great mystery, the tangled affair of the Theodosia letter.

To see Theodosia Burr, her male contemporaries said, was to love her; to know her was a precious privilege. To begin with, she was radiantly beautiful: small, fair, with auburn hair and mesmerizing brown eyes. She was self-confident, with a quick humor and coquettish manner, and brilliant, schooled in classical Greek and Latin, in literature, and all the arts, and sophisticated in worldly society far beyond her years and the permissions of her era.

She was the pampered daughter of Aaron Burr, Revolutionary War officer, New York attorney general, senator, third Vice President of the United States, and slayer of Alexander Hamilton. In 1782, the year Burr was admitted to the bar in New York, he married Theodosia Prevost, ten years his senior, the widow of a British officer, and in 1783, the year British troops evacuated New York, their daughter Theodosia was born in Albany.

While his wife had two teenaged sons by her first marriage, Theodosia was Burr's only child, and for all her life he was obsessively protective of her and she utterly devoted to him. A child of influence and affluence, she grew up in Manhattan, her education a rigorous program authored by her ever-looming father who tutored her tutors in what he wanted her to learn: dance, music, art, literature, languages (she spoke six by age sixteen), readings of Plato, Socrates, Homer, and Lucian; and Cicero, Vergil, Horace, and Terence, in the original Greek and Latin texts. A liberal thinker, Burr exposed Theodosia, then in her teens, to Mary Wollstonecraft's *A Vindication of the Rights of Women,* a 1792 tract in which the author demanded social and sexual equality and full educational opportunities for women. All this, Jefferson biographer Fawn Brodie says, was "destined to make his daughter a fit companion for himself." Theodosia, Brodie says, "was a beautiful and forward child."

During her formative years, with Burr in Washington more often than at the family estate in Manhattan, the light of his life, minded by a governess, became accustomed to trading letters with him—a voluminous exchange that sustained over a period of twenty years.*

---

*A sampling of which can be read in *Correspondence of Aaron Burr and His Daughter,* edited by Mark Van Doren (1929).

At age twelve, after her mother died of cancer, Theodosia became mistress of Richmond Hill, the 160-acre Burr estate in Manhattan on the banks of the Hudson River. She strengthened her father's political career by hosting parties at the sprawling mansion where Washington, Jefferson, and Hamilton were regular guests, as well as such distinguished exiles from the French Revolution as Prince Charles-Maurice de Talleyrand-Périgord and Jérome Bonaparte, and even an eminent Indian chief, Joseph Brant of the Mohawks, leader of the Iroquois League.

She had many suitors, including young Washington Irving, whose family lived near the Burrs in Manhattan, but the man who won her hand came to New York from the Southern aristocracy. He was a twenty-two-year-old, Princeton-educated rice planter named Joseph Alston, and in February 1801, the two were married in Albany, where Burr, who blessed the union, was serving in the state legislature.

Soon after the wedding, Theodosia left Richmond Hill to make her home in South Carolina, where, at Georgetown and Charleston, Alston owned busy and profitable plantations. From the instant she was separated from her father, she longed for his company, his counsel, wit, and intelligence. She pined for the comforts of Richmond Hill, writing often of the hot, muggy climate and swampy terrain of the Waccamaw region, where she now made her home, contrasting it to the cool beauty of the Hudson River Valley.

In the presidential election of 1800, with Jefferson the Republican nominee, Aaron Burr stood as the party's vice presidential candidate. He served until 1804 but was not renominated for a second term. He lost his bid for the governorship of New York that year, too, largely because of the opposition of Alexander Hamilton, a powerful force in New York politics. Burr and Hamilton had become bitter rivals and waged a war of personal insults in Northern newspapers until Burr, outraged beyond apology, challenged Hamilton to a duel. The two men faced each other on July 11, 1804, at Weehawken Heights, New Jersey, and Hamilton was killed.

Meantime, Theodosia's health declined after she gave birth to her son, Aaron Burr Alston, in May 1802, and she never fully recovered, haunting health resorts but remaining fragile and suffering various illnesses the rest of her brief life. Even so, when her father was charged with the murder of Hamilton, she rushed to his side, traveling by coach and carriage to New York several times for the long trial in which he was finally acquitted.

The embittered Burr continued to dream of political power but became involved in a scheme that rendered any political recovery impossible. He had purchased land in the newly acquired Louisiana Territory and in the summer of 1805 traveled down the Ohio River on a luxurious four-room flatboat, crisscrossed Tennessee and Kentucky on horseback, visited New Orleans, took the Natchez Trace trail back to Tennessee, and then pushed on to Saint Louis to confer with the governor of Louisiana Territory, Gen. James Wilkinson. The purpose of these peregrinations was never fully revealed, but Burr was suspected of conspiring to convince several Western states (that is, west of the Appalachians) to secede and place him at the head of a new government. It was also bruited about that he was using New Orleans as a base of operations for an invasion of Mexico.

While he vehemently denied any wrongdoing in what became known as the Burr Conspiracy, he was arrested in Mississippi on orders from President Jefferson and, in March 1807, lodged in a hotel in Richmond, Virginia, to await trial. He was accused of plotting to induce the secession of certain states and conspiring to invade a foreign country.

Once again, Theodosia joined her beleaguered father and remained with him throughout the trial, held in the Hall of the

Virginia House of Delegates with John Marshall, Chief Justice of
the United States Supreme Court, presiding.

The trial opened on August 4, 1807, and on September 1,
the jury found that "Aaron Burr is not proved to be guilty under
this indictment by any evidence submitted to us. We therefore
find him not guilty."

There is an old and persistent tradition that Meriwether Lewis
and Theodosia Burr met in Washington in the spring of 1801,
soon after his appointment as Jefferson's secretary and about a
month after her marriage to Joseph Alston. Lewis, the story
goes, fell deeply in love with the vice president's daughter. Those
who have written about this purported relationship differ on the
matter of whether Theodosia returned Lewis's love with the
same fervor he felt for her, or with any fervor at all.

Among the first, if not the first, to write of a romance between
the two was Emerson Hough (1857–1923), an Iowa lawyer who
became a popular writer of historical fiction. In his 1916 Lewis
and Clark novel, *The Magnificent Adventure,* Hough has Lewis
first meeting Theodosia at Monticello while out exercising Jefferson's favorite horse, then teaching her to ride and falling in love
with her. She admires him, calls him by the nickname Merne
(which Lewis's mother pronounces as "Mairn") and returns his
love, but, except for a parting kiss, obeys her marriage vows.
During the Corps of Discovery expedition, Lewis finds hidden
letters she has written him and had placed among his belongings.
They are passionate appeals for his safe return and clear signals
of her forbidden love for him.

Back in Washington, Jefferson greets his triumphant explorer and soon after nominates the young hero governor of Upper Louisiana Territory. But, that spring of 1807, Jefferson sees
and understands the sadness in Lewis, knows of Merne's love for
the married daughter of his old adversary, Aaron Burr, soon to
be tried for sedition in Richmond.

"But tell me, Merne, can you not tear her from your soul?" Jefferson says. "It will ruin you, this hopeless attachment which you cherish."

The president recognizes that his warning is to be unheeded and says finally, "Go to Richmond, Merne. You will find there a broken conspirator and his unhappy daughter. . . . Go to Theodosia, Merne, in her desperate need."

He goes, is reunited with Theodosia, and sits with her in the courtroom where her father is being tried, a daring thing that gives the jury the sense that the celebrated explorer is supportive of the accused traitor.

At the end of Hough's melodrama, Lewis departs Saint Louis for the trip east, suffers from his recurring fever at Chickasaw Bluffs, but after a brief stay over, rides on east into the Natchez Trace with his servant Pernier, the Indian agent Neelly, and a few other escorters. Among these is an unnamed man, "well dressed, apparently of education and of some means," who tags along, seems suspiciously interested in Lewis's baggage, and is seen in furtive conversation with Pernier.

When some of the packhorses stray from the trail, Neelly and the escort men stay behind to locate them while Lewis rides on into Grinder's Stand and takes the cabin offered to him. From his saddle case, he retrieves his watch with a portrait of Theodosia inside and is thinking of her when "his doom came to him"—three pistol shots that wound him in the forehead, throat, and chest.

His last act is to burn the letters from Theodosia that he has treasured and carried with him across the continent and to the end.

The Magnificent Adventure is fiction, a romantic novel, but Emerson Hough had researched his story of Meriwether Lewis and accurately portrayed the essentials of Lewis's life, his relationship with his mother, with Thomas Jefferson, and with William Clark. Hough had studied the mysterious circumstances of Lewis's death, knew of the suspicion surrounding Neelly and

Pernier, knew that the gold Lewis carried was never recovered, knew of the theory that Lewis was murdered and robbed by thugs infesting the Natchez Trace, knew of Theodosia's devotion to her father, knew the details of her father's trial in Richmond and of Theodosia's presence there.

John Bakeless, in his dual biography, *Lewis and Clark: Partners in Discovery* (1947), believed Hough originated the tale of a Meriwether-Theodosia *affaire d'amour,* writing that "the tale of the flaming and romantic love affair arose solely because in 1916 Emerson Hough felt the need of a little love interest for his novel, *The Magnificent Adventure.*" The author, after apparently contacting Hough, said, "The unanimous howl of rage that arose from the indignant Burr, Alston, and Lewis families appalled the too inventive scribbler" and reported that Hough admitted, "So far as I know the love affair between Meriwether and Theodosia Burr is wholly imaginary."

Hough, an inventive writer of fiction, was fully capable of inventing the whole business, but his "So far as I know" statement seems pregnant with the possibility that he *learned* of the affair somewhere and that he did not fashion it out of the whole cloth.

A more elaborate treatment of the Meriwether–Theodosia romance, and the first in an ostensible nonfiction book, appeared in 1934 with publication of the first full-length biography of Lewis, *Meriwether Lewis of Lewis and Clark,* by Charles Morrow Wilson.

Wilson described the men surrounding Jefferson in his first term of office—John Randolph, James Madison, James Monroe, Alexander Hamilton, Henry Clay, Col. Aaron Burr, the vice president, "small, dapper, and sarcastic, but withal, charming and powerful"—and the president's secretary, Meriwether Lewis.

"From the beginning," Wilson wrote,

Meriwether rather liked Aaron Burr. The Vice President treated the young captain with all courtesy. The Virginian was more than casually interested in Burr even before meeting his daughter. After that his interest gave way to silent enthusiasm.

Second only to Thomas Jefferson, Theodosia Burr Alston was locally the most talked-about person in all Washington. . . . She remained also the animated handbook for the day's fashion in feminine graces, a subject for masculine sighs and for feminine perusal and imitation . . . petite and willowy of form, gowned like a princess, handsomely featured.

Wilson claimed that Theodosia and Meriwether met at the White House during a dinner Jefferson was holding to honor the British ambassador. At the table, Jefferson, clad in bedroom slippers, riding breeches, and waistcoat of yellow linen, began a discourse on mastodons, a subject that captivated Theodosia, who asked if there might be mastodons still living somewhere in North America.

According to Wilson,

The President wagged a long forefinger toward Meriwether Lewis.

"Madam, there sits a young man who will eventually be able to tell you everything you need to know about mastodons."

Later, according to Wilson's scenario, Theodosia sought out Lewis and the two talked, not of mastodons, but of horses and of Theodosia's novice horsewomanship at Richmond Hill, where she was being tutored by a New York riding master.

This first encounter, Wilson said, occurred in "April," presumably April 1801, two months after Theodosia's marriage to Joseph Alston and a month after Lewis assumed his duties as presidential secretary. The biographer claimed that Lewis continued teaching Theodosia through the spring: "The President's secretary and the Vice President's daughter rode together over romantic hills and lanes in the mountainous outskirts of Washington, stopping sometimes at farmhouse hostelries for wine and cake, so delaying their return," and that "Theodosia apparently viewed the procedure with a mixture of humor and elation."

"The long and short of it," Wilson stated, "was that the young captain fell head-over-heels in love with Theodosia Burr Alston." That Theodosia was a married woman "meant very little, if anything at all, to the Virginian. Tongues wagged to be sure, but Meriwether Lewis was a product of a frontier wherein gentlemen did not hide behind cloaks of convention. He despised scandal-mongering and held no fear of it."

This detailed account of their relationship differed markedly from Emerson Hough's when Wilson revealed that Lewis's love for Theodosia was not reciprocated. When Lewis sought to tell her of his love, Theodosia was "pleasantly frank," Wilson said. She liked him well enough, "believed him a sterling young man blessed with a brilliant future," but she had a reputation and a husband to mind.

"That ended it," the biographer wrote. "If Theodosia could find no place for him in the locked walls of her heart, then as an officer and gentleman he would go his way. Theodosia, smiling much, had termed the affair romantic idiocy."

While not explaining how Theodosia could have absented herself from her husband in South Carolina for her liaisons with Lewis, or the origin of dinner table dialogue and other conversations, Wilson did contribute an alternative explanation for Lewis's long delay in the East—a full year—after Jefferson appointed him governor of Upper Louisiana Territory in February 1807.

In his 1969 biography of Lewis, Richard Dillon said the Virginian was "anxious" to get to Saint Louis to undertake his governorship but was detained by working on his notes and journals, visiting with publishers, sitting for portraits, falling in and out of love, and running errands for Jefferson.* Charles Morrow Wil-

---

*All these matters seem trivial except for the expected writing up the expedition papers. For all of Jefferson's belaboring him to complete this work, there is no

son, on the other hand, stated that Lewis was prepared to start out for Saint Louis soon after Jefferson announced his gubernatorial appointment but, "Thomas Jefferson, who had his own notions of order in action, explained in quiet determinedness that the time was not yet ripe for the change in territorial administration." The president, the biographer said, believed Lewis should wait to assume his duties until Congress was done with, until the incumbent Louisiana governor, James Wilkinson, could be retired "with complete grace and decorum," and finally "not until some judicial handling could be devised for a particular Aaron Burr."

The latter reference was to the Burr treason trial, which opened in Richmond in August 1807. Lewis's presence at the trial, a matter of considerable historical significance, remains an unresolved matter. If he attended the trial, his whereabouts that summer are known for the first time, and if he attended, his presence lends some credence, minor as it is, to the tradition that he encountered Theodosia Burr there. Lewis biographer Richard Dillon made no mention of his attendance in Richmond nor did such modern Jefferson biographers as Dumas Malone or Fawn Brodie. But John Bakeless, in his respected *Lewis and Clark: Partners in Discovery,* stated unequivocally, "Thither [to Richmond] went Captain Lewis to represent Mr. Jefferson. . . . Lewis watched it all [the trial] and returned to Washington." Bakeless also wrote, "Though there is not the slightest evidence that they ever exchanged a word, it is possible that, at the trial, he caught a glimpse of Theodosia Burr Alston, who was with her accused father."

In his Lewis book, Charles Morrow Wilson maintained that Jefferson dispatched Lewis to the trial since he, as "a matter of ethics," could not himself attend, and thus needed Lewis's eyes and ears.

---

evidence Lewis ever wrote a line of text for the books in the East or after he returned to Saint Louis.

Wilson wrote that Theodosia arrived from Richmond on the second day of the trial, accompanied by her son, now three years old, and that Lewis saw her when she first entered the crowded courtroom. Six years had come and gone since they had first met, and, the biographer stated, "in that six years [she] was grown old. She was thinner, and her skin browned and parched by the fury of the Southern sun." Her marriage had brought her wealth and an heir to bear her beloved father's name, "but a casual onlooker had no reason to gather that marriage had brought her either increase of health or of happiness."

She and Lewis met and talked, Wilson said. Theodosia had read of the great journey to the Pacific and had heard of Lewis's appointment as governor of Louisiana. "She was proud to have known a young man so brave and so justly famous. . . . She had always believed in him." At dinner together, "He held full conviction that this would be their last meeting. . . . Theodosia had been principal of the Virginian's one enduring love, a love which no casual passing of months and years could turn into dust." She held forth her hand. "Good-night, Governor—until we meet again," she said. Lewis touched the outstretched hand and said, "We will never meet again."

On his final journey into the Natchez Trace, Wilson had Lewis "come to think well of death . . . Now he rather wanted it, wanted it worse than he had ever wanted anything before—even more than he had wanted Theodosia."

Wilson's account of Lewis's death at Grinder's stand was an equivocal patchwork of old sources, many of them specious, newspaper stories, and quotations from Jefferson on the nobility of his Virginia friend.

Charles Morrow Wilson was an Arkansas newspaperman, magazine writer, and novelist of the Ozarks. For all the use made of his book by subsequent writers, he is not a credible source on the life of Meriwether Lewis. Vardis Fisher, in his *Suicide or Murder?* (1962), calls Wilson's biography a "farrago of errors" and of the Meriwether–Theodosia story states,

Emerson Hough, in a trashy novel, has Lewis madly infatuated
with the married daughter of Aaron Burr, whom so far as we
know he never met. This stupid "romance" was a calumny on
both persons, and had been exposed as a piece of nonsense before Wilson wrote his book.

No modern writer on Meriwether Lewis has used Wilson's
book and for good reason: With his concocted dialogue and
mind-readings, the author was far more novelist than historian,
and with a few fugitive exceptions, he documented nothing,
added no meaningful footnotes, endnotes, or bibliography.

A far more credible writer than Emerson Hough or Charles Morrow Wilson perpetuated the story of the Meriwether–Theodosia
romance. Claude Bowers (1878–1958), an Indiana native, had
a distinguished career as newspaper editor, columnist for the
New York World and *New York Journal,* ambassador to Spain
(1933–1939) during the Spanish Civil War, ambassador to Chile
(1939–1953), and historian-author of books on the Jefferson
and Andrew Jackson eras of presidential politics. Among these,
his *Jefferson in Power* was published in 1936, two years after
Wilson's concoction on Meriwether Lewis.

In the opening chapter of this book, "Mayfair in the Mud,"
about the city of Washington in Jefferson's time, Bowers wrote
of "the gorgeous scintillating Theodosia, daughter of Aaron
Burr, and but recently married to a South Carolinian," who
came visiting her father. "And how the tongues clatter over the
advanced views and unconventionality of the beautiful young
woman!" Bowers said, and told of tongues also clattering "over
the card-tables about the infatuation of young Meriwether
Lewis, the brilliant and elegant young secretary of Jefferson!"
Bowers had the two dancing and dining together and cantering
on horseback over the Virginia hills. "And she a married woman!
How the country town would have rocked had it then known

that he had declared his passion, and the wise Theodosia, un-shocked, had dismissed it as 'romantic idiocy' and remained his friend!"

Bowers, who supplied no source for his exclamation-laden anecdote about the two, appears to have taken Wilson's *Meriwether Lewis of Lewis and Clark* more seriously than any modern historian has.

In 1994, the late David L. Chandler, a Pulitzer Prize winner, published *The Jefferson Conspiracies,* subtitled "A President's Role in the Assassination of Meriwether Lewis." The book is an undocumented and altogether impossible speculation on the roles played by President Jefferson and Gen. James Wilkinson (Lewis's predecessor as governor of Louisiana, and a key figure in the Aaron Burr conspiracy) in Lewis's death. As a minor sidelight to his overly complex conspiracy theory, Chandler states that "He [Lewis] was supposed to have been in love with one of the famous belles of the day, Theodosia Burr, daughter of Aaron Burr" and that "Legend has it that when Meriwether arrived in Washington to take up his assignment [as Jefferson's secretary], he intended to propose marriage to her." But, the author said, after Lewis learned that Theodosia had wed the South Carolinian Joseph Alston, he did not pursue her further.

Chandler supplies no source for the "legend."

In 1941, another novelist took up the Meriwether–Theodosia story and added some new elements to it, including a letter that was to have a significance beyond even a novelist's imagining.

My Theodosia was the first novel of Anya Seton (1904–1990), daughter of English-born naturalist, author, and illustrator Ernest Thompson Seton. In her "Author's Note" preceding the opening chapter of the novel, Seton wrote that while the story "is a fictional interpretation of Theodosia's life," she, the author, consulted "all the Burr biographies, many contemporary newspapers, and have read unpublished Burr letters in the New York and Congressional libraries as well as a few which are privately owned." She cites Matthew Davis's *Memoirs of Aaron Burr* as furnishing the "backbone of my plot," then adds this tantalizing tidbit: "with the exception of the Meriwether Lewis romance for which there are three separate sources."

She does not cite these sources, but we can guess who they were: Hough, Wilson, and Bowers.

My Theodosia opens in midsummer 1800, with Theodosia's seventeenth birthday, during which she gets her first kiss—from young Washington Irving, the future author. In Seton's reconstruction, Theodosia does not love the Carolina planter Joseph Alston but becomes engaged to him to appease her father who sees the marriage as politically helpful.

She sees Meriwether Lewis for the first time at an opera. He is a captain of the First Regiment of Infantry, and she calls him Merne (the nickname also appearing in Emerson Hough's novel and Charles Morrow Wilson's pseudobiography. They fall in love, and after learning of the affair, Burr uses his political power to have Lewis sent out of Washington for army service.

The lovers meet again when Lewis is preparing to leave Washington for the expedition to the Pacific with his friend "Billy" Clark and again when he returns from his explorations. The two pledge their love and later, in Richmond for her father's trial, they have a painful final reunion.

After Theodosia returns to South Carolina, a Sioux chief named Wabasha brings her a letter, dated Saint Louis, September 1, 1809, and signed *"Merne."*

"I am going to die, Theodosia," Lewis says.

I cannot tell you how I know it, but I do. I might tell you of a vision I had, the second-sight of my Scotch forebears. I might tell you of a prophecy of a Mandan woman. These Indians see many things we do not, and they often see the future true. This may be folly and superstition. But for me, I know the trail is nearly ended.

He concludes the letter, "I want to see you once again first. I shall be with you in mid-October. I shall not embarrass you; it will be but for a few hours." He says he is en route to Washington to try to clear his name over expenditures he has made as governor and which President Madison has questioned. "He questions my honor. It seems that I have made many enemies, who do not scruple to slander me."

He writes of his loneliness—"I am thirty-five, yet I feel old and finished"—and his need to see her once again, as "a yearning of the spirit." He and she were, he believes, "Meant, by Heaven or destiny or what you will to be together . . . the result of the strange compulsions of the human heart."

Theodosia discounts his premonition of death. That morbidity, she believes, is born of loneliness, and perhaps of illness.

Then, some days after receiving the letter, Theodosia's husband returns from a trip to his plantation and brings some newspapers from Columbia. In one she reads:

GOVERNOR MERIWETHER LEWIS
OF THE NORTH LOUISIANA TERRITORY
MOST FOULLY MURDERED

Three years later, facing death herself, Theodosia dreams of dancing with Merne, thinks of her father, of her son, dead from a fever, and of waiting with her son and Merne, presumably in heaven, until her father joins them.

The "I am going to die" letter Anya Seton employed in her 1941 novel, a letter Lewis allegedly wrote to Theodosia forty days before his death in the Tennessee wilderness, turned up again a year later in a serious, scholarly, nonfiction book. The letter, and the assertion of a love affair between the two appeared in *Saint-Mémin in Virginia: Portraits and Biographies* by Fillmore Norfleet, a respected Virginia-born historian.

Norfleet's book, published in Richmond in 1942, is a biographical study of Charles Févret de Saint-Mémin (1739–1852), a French aristocrat from Dijon who emigrated to New York in 1793 and set up a portrait studio. Among clients who had their profiles (the popular form of portraiture in that day) rendered by Saint-Mémin were John Adams, Thomas Jefferson, John Marshall, Oliver Hazard Perry, and Pierre Lachaise. The artist established a studio in Richmond during Aaron Burr's trial in the summer of 1807 and made pictures of such luminaries as Commodore Stephen Decatur, General of the Army James Wilkinson, the explorers Meriwether Lewis and William Clark, and Aaron Burr and his daughter, Theodosia Burr Alston.

Norfleet stated that Burr's "beloved Theodosia forgot momentarily the pall of marital unhappiness and hurried up with Joseph Alston [her husband] from the swamps of South Carolina to renew her father's courage and help him reorganize his thwarted plan for a western empire."

In a footnote on the portraits Saint-Mémin made of Meriwether Lewis, Norfleet wrote that Lewis resigned from the army on March 2, 1807, was appointed governor of Louisiana Territory the following day, and was sent by Jefferson to Richmond sometime during the Burr trial. During the trial, the author said, Lewis "saw Theodosia Burr Alston, for whom his love had never waned despite her marriage and her father's antipathy for him." Then, " 'Merne,' as Theodosia called him, wrote her from Saint Louis on September 1, 1809: 'I am going to die, Theodosia, I cannot tell you how I know it but I do. I might tell you a vision I had, the second-sight of my Scotch forebears . . ." Norfleet was quoting the letter, foreshortened and with ellipsis points added, precisely as it appeared in Anya Seton's *My Theodosia.*

Norfleet's source for the letter remains unclear; since the citation itself appeared in a footnote, he supplied no source for it.

The mysterious letter was given yet another exposure by another respected historian, Eldon G. Chuinard, M.D., in his *Only One Man Died: The Medical Aspects of The Lewis and Clark Expedition,* published in 1969. Chuinard wrote that "A short time before Lewis started east and met his death on the Natchez Trace, he wrote a morbid prophecy to his 'old flame,' Theodosia Burr Alston, daughter of Aaron Burr, in which he said 'I am going to die, Theodosia. . . .'"

The author acknowledged Norfleet as his source for the information.

What, then, can we make of the "tradition" that Theodosia Burr and Meriwether Lewis were romantically paired, and what of the mysterious "I am going to die" letter? If authentic, the letter would add immeasurable weight to the finding of suicide in Lewis's unaccountable death at Grinder's Stand. It would even add to Dr. Reimert Ravenholt's theory that Lewis was suffering from the terminal stage of syphilis and knew he was dying.

Theodosia's first biographer, Charles F. Pidgin, in his *Theodosia: The First Gentlewoman of Her Time* (1907), makes no reference to Lewis. Her most recent biographer, Richard N. Côté (*Theodosia Burr Alston: Portrait of a Prodigy,* 2003), stated that Lewis could not have courted her, because he was serving on the Indian frontier in 1800, did not arrive in Washington as Jefferson's secretary until March, 1801, by which time Theodosia had married and removed to South Carolina. And, Côté said, when she visited Washington in October 1803, Lewis was en route to Saint Louis to rendezvous with Clark and begin the great exploration.

Côté mentioned, but did not seem to endorse, what two of Lewis's biographers (Charles Morrow Wilson and John Bakeless) claimed, that Lewis was in Richmond at the time of Aaron Burr's trial, and also quoted, but called "unfounded gossip," Claude Bowers's story in his *Jefferson in Power* that Lewis and Theodosia "dance together, dine together, and together they canter over the Virginia hills on horseback." (This, as has been established, is Bowers borrowing from Wilson's fictionalized biography of Lewis.)

There is no mention of Lewis being dispatched to Richmond by Jefferson, or being there of his own accord, in Richard Dillon's standard biography of Lewis or in any of the reputable biographies of Jefferson or Burr.

Unfortunately for the romantics among us, the evidence—or rather the lack of it—tells us that neither the Richmond interlude nor any other pairing of Theodosia and Meriwether ever took place. And since they were never romantically involved—and probably never met—Bakeless, incorrect on Lewis's presence in Richmond, appears to have been correct about the origin of all Meriwether-Theodosia mischief.

It began with Emerson Hough's 1916 novel, *Magnificent Adventure* and that invented romance was embroidered in 1934 by the Ozark novelist Charles Morrow Wilson in his fiction-posing-as-biography, *Meriwether Lewis of Lewis and Clark.* That "farrago of errors" as Vardis Fisher called it, was the source of the perpetuation of the story that was written two years later by the respected diplomat and historian Claude Bowers in his *Jefferson in Power*.

In 1941, in her novel *My Theodosia,* Anya Seton ran the story up a rung or two, adding forbidden passion, clandestine liaisons, Lewis's thoughts on the thwarted destiny of their relationship, and the "I am going to die, Theodosia" letter.

After these writers created and added elaborate layers to Hough's pipe dream, the historian Fillmore Norfleet gave the story credibility by quoting Seton's invented letter in his 1942 book, *Saint-Mémin in Virginia,* as did Eldon G. Chuinard in his *Only One Man Died* in 1979.

There remains a question about Emerson Hough and his confession, "So far as I know the love affair between Meriwether and Theodosia Burr is wholly imaginary." Does he imply there might be something to it but his own researches failed to find the evidence? And how and where did he stumble on the idea for the romance to begin with? Doesn't it seem likely he read something about the two while preparing to write his novel? And if he did, what did he read, and when?

If Emerson Hough was not the author of the entire idea of a Meriwether–Theodosia romance, who was?

Theodosia did not love Meriwether Lewis, but she certainly loved her father—probably more than any other man. In fact, her love for Aaron Burr ended in tragedy and mystery.

Burr sailed for Europe in June 1808 and remained in self-exile until 1812. Toward the end of that year, Joseph Alston was elected governor of South Carolina, but whatever joy Theodosia had as the state's First Lady was offset by her declining health and depressed state of mind over her father's fate. Both her physical and mental state deteriorated further after the death of her ten-year-old son, Aaron Burr Alston, from an undiagnosed fever, in June of the year. After this tragedy she wrote her father, "There is no more joy for me, the world is a blank. I have lost my boy. My child is gone forever."

When Burr returned to New York in May 1812, he urged Theodosia to come home to Richmond Hill for the holidays. It would be her first visit there in five years, but Alston appears to have been opposed to such a journey. An overland trip by carriage was out of the question—two weeks of travel on rough roads for a woman in fragile health. A voyage north by sailing ship had its hazards, too—the war with Britain was on, there were rumors of pirate activity along the Outer Banks of the Carolinas, foul weather was commonplace—but at least the sea journey took less than half the time of one on land.

Theodosia could not be persuaded to stay at home and recover her health, so Alston wrote a letter to the commander of the Royal Navy warships blockading the coast, asking for safe passage for his wife, and Burr sent a trusted friend, the Boston physician Timothy Green, south to serve as escort for Theodosia.

On December 30, 1812, her trunks stowed, she boarded the coastal schooner *Patriot,* Capt. William Overstocks commanding, in Georgetown harbor. Theodosia, attired in a silk frock trimmed in lace and carrying a sewing basket, was accompanied by her French maid, perhaps one other servant, and Timothy Green.

The *Patriot* turned out to be no ordinary passenger vessel. It had a history of privateering in the West Indies and had recently been hired by the American government to harass British shipping along the Atlantic coast. To conceal its identity, the captain had its name painted over and its guns stowed in a hold below decks.

The schooner set sail late in the afternoon of December 30 and vanished somewhere off the Outer Banks.

The sea journey from Charleston to New York normally took five or six days, and when that time passed with no news of the *Patriot*'s whereabouts, Burr and Joseph Alston frantically sought information on the ship. After two weeks of waiting, hope dwindled further when Alston wrote to Burr of rumors of a great gale off Cape Hatteras, North Carolina, that might have claimed the schooner. Burr walked the docks of New York Harbor and sent letters of inquiry to port officials as distant as Nassau and

Bermuda. In Charleston, Alston also failed to turn up a clue, and the two desperate men hurried letters north and south describing their despair and their reluctant conclusion that Theodosia was dead.

A single scrap of dependable news eventually emerged: the British fleet had stopped the *Patriot* off Cape Hatteras on January 2, 1813, but allowed her to continue on. Later that night, a gale blew up and scattered the fleet. A natural and widely accepted theory was that the same gale destroyed the schooner and that all on board perished in the sea.

Joseph Alston died in 1815 at age thirty-seven, still in mourning for his beloved wife. Aaron Burr died on September 14, 1836, still mourning his beloved daughter.

Naturally, there were other reports about the fate of the *Patriot* and its passengers.

In June 1820, a New York newspaper carried a story about two men serving on a privateer who were captured after their ship lost a fight with United States revenue cutters off the Dry Tortugas. The men, subsequently found to have been sailors on the *Patriot* at the time it sailed from Georgetown, were sentenced to hang after confessing to the murders of the schooner's passengers and crew. The condemned men claimed to have mutinied, overpowered captain and crew, and confined them and the passengers belowdecks. After looting the ship, the mutineers said they scuttled it and escaped in a boat while the *Patriot* sank with all aboard.

The story was never verified.

In 1833, a Mobile, Alabama, newspaper reported that a local citizen, a confessed pirate, admitted on his deathbed to participating in the plunder of the *Patriot* and the murder of all on board. Theodosia, the man said, was forced to "walk the plank" to her death in the Atlantic coastal waters.

Seventeen years later, another self-proclaimed former pirate,

"Old Frank" Burdick, a resident of a Michigan poorhouse, told a similar story. He claimed to have actually held the plank that Theodosia was forced to walk, that she was dressed in white, clasping a prayer book, and begged her captors to notify her father of her fate. Burdick said that after the crew and passengers were murdered, the ship was looted and abandoned under full sail.

Another oft-told fantastic tale had Theodosia taken captive by the pirates who overwhelmed the *Patriot* and spirited it to Galveston Island, off the Texas coast. There, after a storm wrecked the ship, she was rescued by a Karankawa Indian chief and died of deprivation a short time later. She was buried, this egregious tale went, near the mouth of a river just west of Galveston Bay.

The most intriguing story of the aftermath of the loss of the *Patriot* is that of the Nag's Head Portrait, a painting, believed to be of Theodosia, that turned up in 1869 on the Carolina coast.

That year, William G. Pool, a physician in Elizabeth City, North Carolina, was called to the bed of an ailing old woman in Nag's Head, on the state's Outer Banks. The woman was related by marriage to a "wrecker" family that plundered vessels washed ashore on the coast. Poole noticed a portrait on the wall of the woman's shack, that of a beautiful young woman dressed in white, and was told the story behind it. One night in 1813, during the "English war," the woman said, a pilot boat drifted ashore near Kitty Hawk, a few miles north of Nag's Head, at the height of a winter gale. The boat had been abandoned with full sails set, the name on its bow painted over. In the main cabin were found trunks, a sewing basket, women's clothing and belongings, and the twelve-by-eighteen-inch portrait the physician was examining. The old woman, a teenaged girl when the ship ran ashore, married one of the wreckers who had ransacked the vessel and was given the portrait by her husband.

The painting, in oils on a wooden panel by an unknown artist,* is no crude, amateur rendering but a notable, professional work of portraiture, a waist-up likeness depicting a strikingly beautiful young woman—dark-eyed, auburn-haired—in a frilly white gown. Dr. Pool must have noticed the quick intelligence in the subject's eyes and the enigmatic half-smile on her lips and wondered how so fine a work, with such a captivating subject, ended up on the beached coastal schooner described by his patient.

The undeniable artistic quality of the painting and the similarity of its subject to physical descriptions of Theodosia Burr Alston by contemporaries have satisfied many authorities that the work is indeed a portrait of her—this despite the fact that the picture is untitled, unsigned, and undated. Dr. Pool, who was given the portrait by his Nag's Head patient in payment for his medical services, spent years trying to authenticate it. He sent photographs of the portrait to Burr and Alston family descendants, and while many of the Burrs pronounced it authentic, none had ever seen the living model, Theodosia herself. Of the Alston descendants, none are on record as commenting on the work.

Did Theodosia commission a portrait of herself as a gift for her father and have it with her belongings aboard the *Patriot*? If so, when was it painted? (The woman in the picture is pink cheeked and healthy, and Theodosia was said to be wan, ill, even emaciated, following the death of her son in June, six months before she boarded the schooner.) Was the *Patriot* the ship that ran aground at Kitty Hawk, and did it run aground in January 1813—a time that would fit the ship's whereabouts after it departed Georgetown in late December 1812?

---

*It is owned and displayed today by the Lewis Walpole Library at Yale University.

To those who learn Theodosia's story and ponder the mystery of her fate, the Nag's Head portrait is especially poignant. That enigmatic, Mona Lisa–like smile symbolizes all the secrets she took with her when she died.

SAM HOUSTON'S DILEMMA

*The storm will soon sweep by,
and Time will be my
vindicator.*

—SAM HOUSTON
April 1829

Until January 22, 1829, Sam Houston had every reason to be pleased with the course of his life. He was a hero of the War of 1812, governor of Tennessee, a crony of the newly elected President Andrew Jackson—his commanding officer in the Creek War in Alabama—and was only thirty-six years old. Few of his contemporaries, not even David Crockett, could match his Roman candle rise in backwoods politics. And, after January 22, 1829, the day he married and the day his marriage fell apart, none could guess how far the candle would fall or imagine that it could rise again.

He was the fifth son of nine Houston children and was born on March 2, 1793, on the family's farm near Lexington, Virginia. His father, Samuel Houston, had served as a rifleman in the Revolutionary War, and in 1788 married Elizabeth Paxton, about whom little is known except that she was of British ancestry.

Young Sam had a rudimentary frontier education: six months in a country school and the rest gleaned from his father's library. Samuel the father died in 1806, and soon after, the widow Houston sold the family's land and livestock, loaded the household necessities in three wagons, gathered her six sons and three daughters, and crossed the Alleghenies into Tennessee. The Virginia property had produced enough money for Elizabeth to buy a small farm near Maryville, just south of Knoxville, and there Sam rusticated for a time, working in the fields and in a general store his mother opened. But plowing and clerking and following the orders of his older brothers had no appeal to a boy whose skills lay in shirking work and skipping school. By age fifteen, he was two or three inches over six feet tall, militarily erect with a lean, strengthy body and a handsome if often frowning face. His gray eyes were deep set behind a shelf of brow, later described as "heavy and thundering"; he was high of forehead and large-nosed with a grim saber-slash of a mouth that belied a sharp sense of ironic humor.

Such was the man of sixteen when in 1809 he let his itchy feet guide his dreamy brain and ran away from home. Fifty years afterward he remembered the running: "It was a moulding period of life, when the heart, just charmed into the feverish hopes and dreams of youth, looks wistfully around on all things for light and beauty. . . ."

He crossed the Tennessee River into Cherokee country and lived for three years with the band of Chief Oolooteka, whose name was said to have translated to "He Puts the Drum Away" and who was known to non-Indians as John Jolly. Sam learned the Cherokee tongue and, being a serious yet engaging lad, earned the respect of his surrogate family, especially Oolooteka, who gave him the name Colonneh ("Raven").

At age eighteen, Sam returned to Maryville and, to pay his debts, set up a school teaching frontier children the rudiments of reading and writing. For two years in this strange endeavor—being a chronic school truant himself—he was successful, but after news of the war against the British reached Maryville, he enlisted, in March 1813, as a private in the army of the United States.

He quickly rose from the ranks. In training in Knoxville, he was promoted to drill sergeant, then to ensign in the Thirty-ninth Infantry, commanded by Col. Thomas Hart Benton, later the expansion-minded senator from Missouri. Early in 1814, Sam and the Thirty-ninth joined Gen. Andrew Jackson's campaign against the Creek Indians—the "Red Sticks," so called from their red-painted war clubs—who were being supplied by the British and were attacking settlers in the Tallapoosa River region of Alabama. The key battle of the Creek War was fought on March 26, 1814, at Horseshoe Bend on the Tallapoosa, with Jackson's force of two thousand men overwhelming and killing most of the nine hundred Creeks defending a strong entrenchment.

Jackson's casualties were fifty-one men killed and a like number wounded, among them Sam Houston, who fell at the head of his company with a brutal arrow wound in his thigh, inches from his groin. A fellow officer wrenched the barbed arrow free, bringing with it a ragged ball of flesh and a gout of blood. The regimental surgeon plugged the gaping wound with rags and with the battle still raging, Sam gathered a few men and hobbled back toward the Red Stick barricade and into a hail of musket balls. He was hit twice, in his right upper arm and shoulder, and was carried back to the surgeon's tent. There, one ball was removed but the other, buried in bone chips, was left alone. The arm and shoulder wounds yielded bone splinters for years afterward; the thigh wound never fully healed and suppurated regularly. Houston's close friend and family physician, the Yale-educated Ashbel Smith, said, "the [thigh] wound remained a running sore to his grave"—this close to a half-century after the Battle of Horseshoe Bend.

Sam was promoted to second lieutenant during his convalescence and while stationed in Nashville in 1817 was assigned as subagent to the Cherokees. The reunion with his "Indian father" Oolooteka was a sad one for the Raven, whose mission was to assist the chief and his clan in their removal to Indian Territory west of the Mississippi.

He resigned from the army in 1818 and, with his health restored, studied law in Nashville and opened a law office in the town of Lebanon, Tennessee. His association with Andrew Jackson, now a major general and victor in the Seminole campaign in Florida, paid dividends. Upon Jackson's recommendation, Sam was appointed adjutant general of the state, then was elected at-

torney general. In 1823, he moved to Washington as the newest
Tennessee congressman.

Ever the Jackson loyalist, Houston devoted much of his first
term in the House of Representatives working on the general's
presidential campaign. Jackson's popular vote was forty-five thousand over that of John Quincy Adams of Massachusetts, but the
electoral voting was close, and since no candidate had a majority,
the election fell to the House for resolution. Adams was elected.

After a second term in Congress, Houston returned to Tennessee and in 1827 won election as governor of the state.

That year, at age thirty-four, he also fell in love.

Eliza Allen was half Houston's age when he met her after getting
to know her congressman brother Robert in Washington. Sam
often visited the Allen family, occasionally in company with
General Jackson, whose home was in a neighboring county, and
with the general's entourage. Sam took notice of Eliza on every
trip.

She was born in Gallatin, Sumner County, Tennessee, in
1809, the daughter of Col. John Allen, a wealthy planter and
horse breeder whose Allendale property, on a bend of the Cum-
berland River north of Nashville, included a handsome two-
story house and quarters for thirty-nine slaves.

Although no likeness of her has survived, Eliza was said to
have been blond, delicate, and dignified. One friend remembered
her as "queenly" and as a fine horsewoman. The Allens, if not
Eliza herself, must have been honored when Samuel Houston,
General Jackson's protégé, war hero, congressman, and in 1827,
governor of Tennessee, approached them for permission to court
Eliza and ask her hand in marriage. John Allen was well-to-do,
well-connected politically and socially, and ambitious—the match
appealed to him.

While there is no record of the engagement or its duration, it
appears to have been brief. Two snippets of correspondence sur-

vive that indicate this, and also show a squall brewing in their
relationship.

In November 1828, Houston wrote to a cousin, "I am not
married but it may be the case in a few weeks." Then, on December 4, in a letter to his friend, the Tennessee congressman
John Marable, he said, "I have as usual had 'a small blow up.'
What the devil is the matter with the gals I can't say but there has
been hell to pay and no pitch hot!" He ended the letter, "May
God bless you and it may be that I will splice myself with a rib."

The pitch may not have been hot but it was at least tacky
when Eliza and Sam were married in a candlelit ceremony at Allendale on January 22, 1829. She was nineteen, he thirty-five,
just a year younger than Eliza's mother.

The couple spent their wedding night at the Allen home, apparently in separate bedrooms. Something occurred between
them that night—but it was not the consummation of the marriage.

The next morning the newlyweds started toward Nashville
on horseback and stayed the night of the twenty-third with a
friend of the Allen family, Martha Martin, on the Gallatin Pike.
In the morning, as Sam and Mrs. Martin's daughters were throwing snowballs at one another and he getting the worst of it, Eliza
told Martha, "I wish they would kill him."*

They rode on into Nashville, and since there was as yet no
official residence for the governor, the two took up lodgings at
the Nashville Inn, a hostelry quite familiar to Sam but not a place
to please Eliza. The inn, called by Houston biographer Marquis
James "the political vortex of the state," consisted of a warren of
public rooms and large private suites, porches, and galleries.
These places swarmed with militia officers, minor politicians,
and other "persons of consequence"—most of them Gen. (now
President) Andrew Jackson's former war comrades, friends, and

---

*This stands, says novelist and historian Elizabeth Crook, "as Eliza's only re-
ported comment about her husband during their eleven weeks together."

hangers-on. These patrons made the inn a gathering place for war stories, arguments, and gossip over cigars and whiskey.

Sam felt at home at the Nashville Inn and comfortable with its occupants. He was governor of Tennessee, the biggest Jackson Democrat of all those foregathered, and he could hold the spotlight and drink other men's whiskey to his heart's delight. Now, especially, he had a lot on his mind. He was campaigning for a second term in office and had married a woman who appeared to despise him, so, after depositing Eliza in his suite, he probably joined the inn crowd and got drunk.

Eliza Allen Houston appears to have made an effort to keep the marriage together, even to attending some social functions as Tennessee's First Lady. She could not keep up the pretense, however, and after writing her father of her distress, on April 9, 1829, Colonel Allen came for her. She had her bags packed and departed for Allendale and the arms of her family.

Except for one letter, to Eliza's father, and a hint or two to others, Houston never explained the nearly instant failure of the marriage, and Eliza went to her grave thirty-two years later without uttering or writing a word about it. Others who knew them both left only nebulous clues for future investigators to puzzle over.

Houston's contribution to the mystery was a rambling, barely coherent letter to John Allen, written on the day Eliza departed, in which he all but confessed to jealousy, to quizzing Eliza about her virtue, and of serving as her judge and jury. He began:

> Mr. Allen: The most unpleasant & unhappy circumstance has just taken place in the family, & one that was entirely unnecessary at this time. Whatever had been my feelings or opinions in relation to Eliza at one time, I have been satisfied & it is now unfit that anything should be averted to.

Then, in a welter of overwrought and confused verbiage, said, "Eliza will do me the justice to say that she believes I was really unhappy. That I was *satisfied & believed her virtuous* [Houston's emphasis], I had assured her on last night & this morning."

He said he would rather "have prevented the facts ever coming to your knowledge, & that of Mrs. Allen" and mysteriously confessed that only "one human being knew anything of it from me, & that was by Eliza's consent and wish."

The matter of Eliza's "virtue" seemed obsessive: "I would have perished first & if mortal man had dared to charge my wife or say ought against her virtue I would have slain him." He said that as for his love for Eliza, "none can doubt,—that she is the only earthly object dear to me God will witness."

He suggested that "The only way this matter can now be overcome will be for all of us to meet as tho it never occurred, & this will keep the world, as it should ever be, ignorant that such thoughts ever were." As if his wife and her virtue had been on trial, he made the astonishing statement that "Eliza stands acquitted by me. I have received her as a virtuous wife, & as such I pray God I may ever regard her, & trust I ever shall."

In a chaotic but key final paragraph of his letter, Houston may have inadvertently indicted himself if, as it seems, he questioned Eliza about her virtue:

> She was cold to me, & I thought did not love me. She owns that such was one cause of my unhappiness. You can judge how unhappy I was to think I was united to a woman that did not love me.

He desperately wanted to put the whole matter to rest. He assumed no blame for the issues that had ruined their wedding day, but was hopeful that he and Eliza could make their marriage work. "This time is now past," he wrote,

& my future happiness can only exist in the assurance that Eliza & myself can be happy & that Mrs. Allen & you can forget the past,—forgive all & find your lost peace & you may rest assured that nothing on my part shall be wanting to restore it. Let me know what is to be done.

John Allen must have read the letter a dozen times, in palpable fury and confusion, attempting to decode it. What did Houston *mean* by saying the "unpleasant & unhappy circumstance" was unnecessary *at this time*? That it might have been necessary later? And what of the repeated words about her virtue and the implication that somebody might impugn it and be slain for it? Who was the "one human being" Houston said "knew anything of it" and what was the *it* to begin? What did the Allens have to forgive and forget? And if, as Houston as much as confessed, he quizzed Eliza at length, presumably about her "virtue," then magnanimously "acquitted" her, could there be any wonder that she was "cold" to him?

Sam must have felt Eliza's departure temporary, perhaps was confident that he could talk her into returning, since, two days after she left, he gathered his wits and debated William "Billy" Carroll, his opponent in the governor's race, in Gallatin. At about that time, when he was urged to offer some explanation about the separation, he told his longtime friend Willoughby Williams, "I can make no explanation. I exonerate the lady fully, and do not justify myself."

But he learned the finality of her decision after the April 11 debate when he managed to meet with John Allen. No clue about their conversation has endured, but the meeting must have been taut as a bowstring, as neither man was known for his governable temper. Probably after considerable begging, Sam was permitted to see Eliza in the Allendale parlor. One of Eliza's aunts was present and later recalled that Houston, on his knees, begged his wife to return with him to Nashville "and with tears streaming down his face implored forgiveness." She refused, and Houston rode back to Nashville, shut himself up at the inn, and, with a whiskey bottle for companionship, wrote a letter resigning the governorship of Tennessee.

In light of how quickly news of his and Eliza's separation spread, Houston's decision to quit the office he had campaigned for only a few days earlier was not as abrupt as it seemed. Gallatin, near where he had debated Billy Carroll on April 11, was Eliza Allen's birthplace, and the townspeople there seem to have known of the "scandal," as it was already being called, two days after Eliza's departure from the Nashville Inn. This was made clear by a man named Charles J. Love, a mutual acquaintance of both Houston and Andrew Jackson, who knew Sam's plans in startling detail. On April 15, Love wrote to President Jackson: "Our old friend Houston has separated from his wife; and will resign tomorrow and leave the state Immediately for the Arkansas Territory to reside among the Indians. There is a hundred reports about the cause of the separation." Love added that Sam gave Eliza's father "a certificate that she was virtuous" and said that the governor's "hope for happiness in this world are blasted forever, his effigy burned in Gallatin on Saturday night last." The Saturday referred to was the eleventh, the day of the Houston-Carroll debate.

Love had the facts. On April 16, Houston wrote his letter of resignation, and it appeared in the *Niles Register,* the Baltimore-based political weekly, on May 9, together with the editor's comments on the governor's "deeply wounded spirit." In the letter, Houston spoke of being "delicately circumstanced . . . by my own misfortunes, more than by the fault or contrivance of any one," and being "overwhelmed by sudden calamities" as the motive for his resignation.

Besides Charles Love, Houston confided his decision to a few others, notably Tennessee Congressman David Crockett, who afterward wrote that Houston "was going to leave the country and go up the Arkansaw and live with the Indians, as he calls them his adopted Brothers, the balance of his days."

Sam left Nashville in disguise on April 23, 1829, taking the river steamer *Red Rover* south to the Arkansas River country, now the home of his old Cherokee "father" Chief Oolooteka. Many years in the future, Houston told Baptist minister Rufus Burleson that on board the steamer he thought of "the bitter disappointment I had caused General Jackson and all my friends and especially the blight and ruin of a pure and innocent woman who had entrusted her whole happiness to me." He confessed, "I was in an agony of despair and strongly tempted to leap overboard and end my worthless life."

He also told Reverend Burleson of an encounter with two of the Allen brothers as the steamer made a freight stop at Clarksville, Tennessee. The brothers, heavily armed and angry, boarded the boat, found Sam, and proceeded to upbraid him for the scandal he had caused, the wild rumors flying around Nashville, and demanded that he publicly deny the accusations against their sister. Burleson wrote in his 1901 memoirs that Houston told the Allens to "publish in the Nashville papers that if any wretch ever dares to utter a word against the purity of Mrs. Houston, I will come back and write the libel in his heart's blood."

The Allens did publish in the Nashville papers—they published Houston's bizarre letter of April 9 together with details on the failure of the marriage, placing all blame on the then ex-governor, and announced the formation of a "committee" to investigate the slanders against Eliza. How she felt about her family's airing the details of her brief marriage and repeating all the "slanders" about her virtue is unknown, but the Allen investigators made a report in April 1830, and it, too, occupied space in the Nashville paper and others more far-flung. Samuel Houston, committee members not surprisingly said, was a "deluded man" who rendered his wife alienated by his unfounded jealousies and allegations of "coldness."

To all this, Sam coolly congratulated the committee on its work in vindicating Eliza's character.

From Little Rock on May 11, 1829, he wrote to a friend in Nashville that he was "setting out for the Cherokees" and expected to be hunting buffalo before midsummer. On the same day he wrote to President Jackson describing himself as "an unfortunate, and doubtless the most unhappy man now living. . . . An Exile from my home and my country, a houseless, unshelter'd wanderer, among the Indians!"

In an 1846 campaign biography of Houston, he is quoted as having his final word on the subject of his brief marriage to Eliza Allen: "This is a painful but it is a private affair. I do not recognize the right of the public to interfere in it, and I shall treat the public just as though it never happened." He added, with theatric chivalry, "it is no part of the conduct of a gallant or a generous man to take up arms against a woman. If my character cannot stand the shock, let me lose it. The storm will soon sweep by, and Time will be my vindicator."

The "What happened?" theories on the seventy-seven days of the Sam Houston–Eliza Allen marriage have been accumulating for 175 years.

A recurring scenario among Allen family descendants was that on their wedding night Eliza was repelled by the suppurating arrow wound in Sam's groin area, inflicted in the fight at Horseshoe Bend in 1814. This idea was also posited by Houston's physician, W. D. Haggard (who later married one of Eliza's daughters by her second marriage). That the wound never healed was confirmed by Dr. Ashbel Smith, Houston's friend and confidant.

While the sight of the wound might well have repulsed the innocent eighteen-year-old Eliza, the problems between the two were, without doubt, graver. Many of Houston's friends, as well as his political enemies, theorized that she was an unwilling bride at the outset. According to this speculation, the Allens were flattered that the governor of Tennessee was interested in their daughter and John Allen's "ambition" blinded him to the fact that the two were not compatible. The union would gain for Colonel Allen access not only to the state house, but also to the even headier world of Houston's great friend Andrew Jackson. Thus he pressured Eliza to marry Sam.

One of Eliza's relatives, who wrote under the initials M.B.H. in a New Orleans newspaper in 1871, said that Eliza had a former beau in the Nashville area, one "William T———," who was a consumptive. This man, researchers believe, was William Tyree, a young lawyer who came to Missouri to start a practice and who some time thereafter died of tuberculosis. The implication seemed to be that Eliza loved Tyree and was either hoping to marry him or mourning his death at the time she and Houston were wed.

Another of Eliza's supposed loves was Dr. Elmore Douglass, a Gallatin physician whom she later married.

While he was serving in the United States Senate, Houston himself allegedly told his pastor, Dr. George W. Samson, that on his wedding night he elicited a confession from Eliza that "her affections had been given and pledged to another" before they met and that she married Sam out of "filial duty." Upon hearing this, Houston said, he "retired from the wedding chamber."

Houston's enemies and fair-weather friends said he was an opportunist who married for money and the Allen family prestige. He was infatuated with Eliza but grew infuriated when he learned she had loved another. These people said he was "a maniac on the subject of female virtue" who upbraided Eliza on their wedding night, quizzed her mercilessly on the other men in her life, and relentlessly questioned her virtue until she fled from him.

Virtually everything written in the post-1829 accounts of the Houston–Allen relationship—postmortem recollections of family members, erstwhile friends of both parties—is "alleged" to have been said or done. Eliza left no written record—letter or diary—expressing herself on the matter, and Houston's comments on the record, most of them quoted by others, are vague and unhelpful.

After escaping Tennessee in April 1829, Sam settled among his old Cherokee friends on the Arkansas River near Cantonment Gibson, then the westernmost military fort. He proclaimed himself a citizen of the Cherokee Nation, dressed in beaded buckskins, had his hair plaited in a long queue decorated with turkey feathers, and renewed his fluency in the Cherokee tongue. With borrowed funds he set up a trading post he called Wigwam Neosho, after the nearby river that flowed into the Arkansas, and began making a dent in the post's whiskey stock ("buried his sorrows in the flowing bowl, gave himself up to the fatal enchantress" as he wrote of himself in third person). His succumbing to his insatiable thirst earned the Raven a new name among his Cherokee hosts, *Ootsetse Ardeetahskee*—Big Drunk.

He also soon found a mixed-blood Cherokee widow, Tiana Rogers Gentry to move into Wigwam Neosho with him. Their log house lay a short horseback ride to the road that led to the Red River and Texas.

As an unofficial Cherokee ambassador, Houston regularly traveled to Washington to visit President Jackson, to seek contracts and assist in resolving tribal grievances. In his Indian garb, adding bright woven blankets, a ruffled shirt sewn with jingling metal ornaments, and an elaborate, bright turbanlike hat, he cut somewhat of a comic figure in the executive mansion and especially in the halls of Congress, where many of his former colleagues remembered him in more sedate and sober times.

One notorious Houstonian incident occurred in the spring of 1832, when Sam challenged an Ohio congressman named William Stanbery to a duel. This man had the temerity to accuse the Cherokee-garbed former Tennessee governor of fraud in winning an Indian ration contract. Stanbery refused to meet Houston on a field of honor, but Sam found a way to redress the grievance when he met Stanbery on Pennsylvania Avenue on the evening of April 13. Houston called the congressman "a damned rascal" and caned the terrified lawmaker with a hickory staff. Stanbery, who managed to draw a pistol—which failed to fire—vowed revenge. He reported to the Speaker of the House that he had been "attacked, knocked down by bludgeon, severely bruised and wounded by Samuel Houston, late of Tennessee, for words spoken in my place in the House of Representatives" and had Sam arrested and charged with assault and battery.

From political friends Houston scraped together the funds to hire the distinguished lawyer Francis Scott Key to defend him. The highly publicized trial lasted a month, one of its highlights the testimony of Sen. Alexander Buckner of Missouri, who said that Houston, when he finished caning Stanbery's head and shoulders, lifted the congressman's feet in the air and "struck him elsewhere."

Sam was sentenced to be reprimanded by the Speaker and to pay five hundred dollars in fines for the assault. He was later acquitted of fraud after a House committee investigated the Indian contract and found nothing illegal in it. To his credit as an honorable man, the canee, Congressman Stanbery, chaired the committee.

Marquis James, author of a colorful, fictionalized, 1929 Houston biography, said that after the Stanbery affair Sam decided to do something grand: "He would capture an empire and lay it at his old Chieftain's [Jackson's] feet," James wrote. "Texas, or the new Estremadura, as Houston used to say when his poetic fancy was on the wing" was his objective, and in the summer of 1832 he crossed the Red River as a presidential envoy. The mission was to determine how Texans felt on the issue of the "acquisition of Texas" by the United States. To this, Houston reported, there could be no doubt. "Such a measure is desired by 19/20ths of the population of the province," he reported.

He settled in the old Mexican frontier city of Nacogdoches, close to the Louisiana border, and there practiced law and maneuvered for a position of prominence in Texas affairs, the opportunity for which arrived in the fall of 1835, when war between the Texan-Americans and Mexico seemed certain. Houston, with his military background and experience in Tennessee politics, was commissioned commander in chief of the "Armies of Texas"—a grandiose term for scattered bands of settler volunteers.

When news arrived that a Mexican army of seven thousand men under Gen. Antonio López de Santa Anna had invaded Texas and was moving on Bexar (San Antonio), Houston met the crisis decisively. He ordered all the town's fortifications, including the Alamo, to be demolished, all their cannon removed to safety, and Bexar abandoned. Lt. Col. William Barret Travis, in command of the "regular" Texas troops in San Antonio, flew in the face of this prudent plan by occupying the Alamo with a force of 182 men, including Houston's friends David Crockett and James Bowie.

Travis and all the Alamo defenders died in the battle of March 6, 1836, and its aftermath.

Houston fell back to build up his force of volunteers, and after long and complex maneuvering turned his men toward Harrisburg, the provisional capital, then to Lynch's Ferry, at a point where Buffalo Bayou flowed into the San Jacinto River. There, twenty miles east of the city later named for him, Houston placed his army, 783 men, and two small iron cannon, in a grove of oaks.

At 4 p.m. on April 21, 1836, forty-six days after the Alamo fell, Houston ordered an advance on Santa Anna's camp. The Texans, with a fife and drum band playing "Come to the Bower," marched while the Mexican regulars were relaxing at their cook fires, their arms stacked, their commander comfortable under his carpeted marquee.

The battle lasted fifteen minutes and resulted in a rout seldom seen in warfare: 630 Mexicans were killed, 208 wounded, and 730 taken prisoner, including Santa Anna. The Texans suffered six killed and twenty-five wounded, including Houston, his left ankle crushed after his horse was shot and fell on him.

The year of the great victory, he ran for the presidency of the Republic of Texas and was overwhelmingly elected—he was "Old Sam Jacinto," after all. His main order of business was Texas statehood, an uphill fight since Northern politicians did not want a state admitted to the Union that sanctioned slavery.

He served twice as president of the Republic, 1836–1838 and again 1841–1844. (The town of Houston was founded in 1836 and served as capital of the Republic during his first administration.) With Texas admitted to the Union in December 1845 as the twenty-eighth state, Sam returned to Washington as United States Senator. He served nearly fourteen years, his great fight trying to persuade his colleagues not to join the Confederacy. "I wish, if this Union must be dissolved, that its ruins may be the monument of my grave," he said. Then, when the Texas legislature took away his senate seat because of his pro-Union stand, he recovered and won election as governor in 1859, continuing to campaign against secession. When, despite his heroic efforts, Texas seceded in 1861, Houston refused to take an oath of allegiance to the Confederacy and was deposed.

The sad and inexplicable events of January 22 through April 9, 1829, had to be lived over again, if briefly, when Sam obtained a divorce from Eliza Allen Houston in 1837 while serving his first term as president of the Texas Republic. Now, with his Cherokee wife, Tiana Rogers Gentry Houston, deceased, he was free to marry again, and in May 1840, Margaret Moffette Lea of Marion, Alabama, became the third and last Mrs. Houston. She was twenty-one years old, the pretty, shy, somewhat gloomy daugh-

ter of a Baptist minister, well educated in private schools and described as "spiritual minded."

Sam met her during a garden party while on a business trip
to Mobile, and he fell hard. From all accounts, Margaret saw
Sam as the Ivanhoe of her Sir Walter Scott dreams, and their
marriage was a good one. It produced four daughters and four
sons, chased Houston from hard liquor, and converted him to
the Baptist faith. (After his baptism, the story goes, a friend said,
"Well, General, I hear your sins were washed away." To this Sam
replied, "I hope so, but if they were all washed away, the Lord
help the fish down below.")

According to her relative, the anonymous M.B.H., Eliza Allen
Houston lived in seclusion for a "year or two—a picture of perfect woe" following her ordeal, or whatever it was, as a newlywed.
"She never uttered a harsh or reproachful word of the General,"
wrote M.B.H., and lived a retired life.

While there is no dependable evidence that Eliza and Sam
ever met after the April 1829 separation, Houston asked of her
welfare among Tennessee friends and received occasional tidbits
of information. One of these morsels came from John Campbell,
another Allen family relative, who had passed through Lebanon,
Tennessee, in October 1836, en route to visiting a brother. Campbell wrote to Houston that Eliza was residing in Lebanon "about
the time the news [arrived] that you had gained the victory over
Santa Anna." Campbell said she "showed great pleasure at your
success and fairly exulted" and added that "Some of her friends
wanted her to get a divorce; and she positively refused; and said
she was not displeased with her present name; therefore she
would not change it on this earth; but would take it to the grave
with her."

She did change her name—rather added to it—when, in November 1840, six months after Sam married Margaret Lea, Eliza

wed Dr. Elmore Douglass, a widower with whom she would have four children.

She died of cancer at the age of fifty-one in March 1861, the month Houston was deposed as governor of Texas after refusing to pledge his allegiance to the Confederacy.

Eliza was true to her word about taking the name of her first husband to her grave. The stone over her remains read

><+<>-O-<>+<

ELIZA ALLEN HOUSTON DOUGLASS
DAUGHTER OF JOHN AND LETITIA ALLEN
DEC. 2, 1809—MARCH 3, 1861

><+<>-O-<>+<

Samuel Houston survived her by two years and five months.

He lived long enough to learn of the battles of Gettysburg and Vicksburg, dying of pneumonia at age seventy on July 26, 1863, at his home in Huntsville. His last words were "Texas . . . Texas . . . Margaret."

MEAGHER OF
THE SWORD

You true Sons of Erin, awake from your slumbers!
No longer leave tyrants your valleys invade.
Let the long silent Harp vibrate its loud numbers;
Now Meagher is leading the Irish Brigade!

—AUTHOR UNKNOWN CA. 1862

I

IRELAND AND BEYOND

When the Irish patriot, once exiled felon, late major general of the Union Army, and former acting governor of Montana Territory, fell off or was pushed off a steamboat moored at Fort Benton on the night of July 1, 1867, he vanished without a trace. A few hours before he died, he wrote a letter to his friend and fellow expatriate Richard O'Gorman, a Limerick man and a New York lawyer. O'Gorman never divulged the contents of the letter, but when he learned of his friend's apparent drowning wrote, "He is gone. The pitiless Missouri has enwrapped him in a watery shroud and dug him a lonely grave beneath its turbid waves." The *New York Sun* waxed even more eloquent: "There is a hint of the mystic in that disappearance from the steamer as if an unearthly hand had stretched from the fairy depths to draw him down as the hand snatched Excalibur when it was to be wielded in battle no more."

The Excalibur image was especially appropriate for the man embraced by the fairy depths of the river. He was Thomas Francis Meagher—"Meagher of the Sword"—and the Missouri never claimed a more extraordinary victim or created a greater mystery.

Meagher (rhymes with *star*) was born in August 1823 at Waterford, located on the Suir River on the south coast of Ireland, the town chartered in the thirteenth century and celebrated for its manufacture of superior glass. Thomas Senior, a wealthy merchant, became mayor of Waterford in 1829 and later represented his county in the House of Commons.

Young Tom benefited from his family's position and influence, receiving a rigorous Jesuit school education in the classics, mathematics, history, and literature, and from traveling on the continent. By the time he turned up in Dublin in the mid-1840s, attending nationalist meetings and associating with the writers, orators, and activists of the Young Ireland movement, he had grown into a striking figure. He stood a few inches under six feet tall with a handsome, boyish face, languid blue eyes, and thick, unruly dark hair. On his family estate and in his European travels, he had become an accomplished horseman, fencer, and marksman. His body was muscular, his walk and manner imperious, his character somber yet ardent.

In July 1846, Tom Meagher's gift for oratory was instantly and startlingly recognized when he made his maiden independence speech at a meeting of Young Irelanders and the Lord Mayor of Dublin. The rhetorical debut came at a perilous time, in the opening year of the Great Hunger, Ireland's potato blight and famine that would leave a million dead in five years. The firebrand from Waterford, not yet twenty-three years old, designed his remarks to drive the moderates out of the Free Ireland movement and to denounce the 1800 Act of Union under which England's parliament joined the two islands under English rule and law.

Meagher called for repeal of the act and left no doubt that, failing diplomacy and reason, he advocated ending English hegemony by arms—with the sword his favorite metaphor.

He directed his words to the Lord Mayor:

> The soldier is proof, my lord, against an argument but he is
> not proof against a bullet. The man who will listen to rea-
> son—let him be reasoned with; but it is the weaponed arm of
> the patriot that can alone avail against battalioned despo-
> tism. . . . I look upon the sword as a sacred weapon. And if,
> my lord, it has sometimes reddened the shroud of the oppres-
> sor with too deep a dye, like the anointed rod of the High
> Priest, it has, at other times, and as often, blossomed into ce-
> lestial flower to deck the freeman's bow!

Meagher of the Sword was thus publicly born and destined
to remain public in Ireland for two more years.

At Young Ireland rallies in Cork, Killarney, and Dublin, he
championed violent revolution and was twice jailed for sedition.
He also took part in the 1848 rising in Tipperary, which fizzled
out after a squad of English riflemen fired on the rebels, forcing
them to withdraw and to leave their dead and wounded behind.
For this and an accumulation of charges, in the fall of 1848
Meagher was again arrested. Charged with sedition and treason-
ous activity, he was sentenced in October in Clonmel, County
Tipperary. The punishment was ancient and ghastly: he would be
hanged, drawn (eviscerated), and quartered.

Meagher's parting words to the court that sentenced him
were of the same studied eloquence that awed and angered the
Lord Mayor of Dublin:

> Judged by the law of England I know this crime entails the
> penalty of death; but the history of Ireland explains this crime
> and justifies it. . . . I hope to be able with a pure heart and per-
> fect composure to appear before a higher court, a tribunal
> where a judge of infinite goodness, as well as justice, will pre-
> side, and where, My Lords, many—*many*—of the judgements
> of this court will be reversed.

Seven months after the trial, his death penalty was commuted by Queen Victoria, and he was resentenced to "transportation"—forced exile—and penal servitude at Van Diemen's Land. This big shield-shaped island, 150 miles south of the Australian continent, had become a favored dumping ground for convicts from across the British Empire. Discovered in 1642 by the Dutch explorer Abel Tasman, who named it after his patron, the island had been charted by English navigator James Cook in 1777, and a British settlement called Hobart had been founded there in 1803.

Meagher sailed on the six-gun brigantine *Swift* from the port of Kingstown, not far from his birthplace of Waterford, on June 9, 1849, and spent much of the four-and-a-half-month voyage reading—Petrarch's *Lives,* Shelley's essays, Carlyle's *Sartor Resartus,* and the other books he had stowed in his baggage.

On October 27, 1849, he stood at the rail as the *Swift* slid into Hobart harbor and saw that the hills of Van Diemen's Land were as lush and green as his cherished homeland.

His "Convict Profile" listed him as prisoner number 1613: Age, twenty-three; Trade, law student; Level of Literacy, "Can read and write" with the added note that he had been transported for "High treason," his sentence, "Life, a commutation." He was described as five feet nine inches tall with a fair complexion, round head, brown hair, light blue eyes, and a clean-shaven "long visage."

Except for being a half a world away from Ireland, Meagher's twenty-eight months' exile turned out to be light punishment for a man originally condemned to be hideously executed. He was sent to the village of Ross in the Vandemonian midlands and on November 6, 1849, given a "parole" or "ticket of leave," allowing him the freedom of the district upon his pledge not to attempt to escape. Since he was a moneyed parolee, he rented a lakeside cottage, took long horseback rides, hunted (having a rifle was apparently not against the rules for privileged ticket-of-leave men), managed to meet other Irishmen banished to the island, and plotted his escape to America.

He even married and fathered a child during his exile. His wife, Catherine Bennett, daughter of a New Norfolk farmer, he met during an excursion to a village near Ross and wed in February 1851. She was pregnant when he escaped—"absconded," as was noted on his Convict Profile—on January 3, 1852.

The escape was engineered with the help of Irish-American sympathizers in New York, and villagers, fishermen, and sailors who knew the sailing ship traffic off the island's northern shore. These conspirators, some of them paid for their services, smuggled Meagher to the mouth of the Tamar River, where a fishing party rowed him out to Waterhouse Island in Bass Strait, the passageway between Van Dieman's Land and the south Australian coast. With his few possessions, some matches, and a tin cup, he spent ten Robinson Crusoe–like days there, subsisting on gull's eggs and shellfish and building huge signal fires. At last the merchant ship *Elizabeth Thompson*, flying Australian colors, sent a boat ashore and picked him up.

In six weeks, the *Thompson* worked its way around Cape Horn and up the South American coast. At Pernambuco, Brazil, the Irish absconder took passage on the American brig *Acorn* and reached New York Harbor on May 28, 1852.

Meagher of the Sword had escaped!

This was electrifying news to the great Irish community in New York, thousands of whom had but recently poured into the city off immigrant ships from their famine-stricken homeland.

John Dillon and Richard O'Gorman, old friends and revolutionary compatriots, welcomed him warmly and by midday a great hail-the-conquering-hero mob had gathered in front of Dillon's home in Brooklyn, clamoring for a speech from the Irish idol as a band of the Sixty-ninth Regiment of the New York militia marched past.

The *New York Herald* heralded his appearance and good looks ("always a favorite with the ladies") and compared his oratory to that of the Hungarian patriot, Kossuth; Boston offered him the freedom of the city; rallies and receptions were held in his honor and Meagher clubs formed; invitations poured in from all over New England and west to Ohio and Indiana; Tammany Hall politicians planned a banquet for him, with a parade and lavish ball; Fordham University, the Jesuit college in the Bronx, awarded him an honorary law degree.

He sought respite from the commotion and found a place at Glen Cove on Long Island to make plans. There he received a letter from Van Diemen's Land. His wife, Catherine, wrote that their baby son Henry had died and that she had fallen ill. She said she would soon embark for Ireland to stay for a time with Tom's father while she recuperated; then the two would join him in America.

Meagher did not long dwell on these matters; he was too eager to make up for the two years lost in exile.

He lectured on Australia at Metropolitan Hall in New York to standing-room-only crowds, each attendant paying fifty cents to see him, earned a quick thousand dollars, and launched a profitable lecture tour. While speaking in Philadelphia, he received a letter inviting him to the inauguration on March 4, 1853, of President-elect Franklin Pierce. In Washington he met the new president, Pierce's secretary of war, Jefferson Davis, and such national luminaries as Senators Sam Houston of Texas, Stephen Douglas of Illinois, and William H. Seward of New York.

That spring Catherine arrived from Ireland with Tom's father, and the family spent some tranquil months in Manhattan and at Glen Cove before Meagher, forever fitful, departed on another lecture trip, visiting twenty-five states from the Deep South to California. In his absence, his wife and father returned to Ireland, and when he returned to New York he learned of Catherine's death, from typhus, in Waterford.

Between 1855 and the opening of the Civil War, Meagher took American citizenship, studied law, earned admission to the New York bar, and remarried. The second Mrs. Meagher was Elizabeth "Libby" Townsend, the pretty young daughter of a wealthy owner of a New York ironworks.

As founder and editor of the weekly *Irish News,* in 1856 he used the paper to support such varied causes as the filibustering expedition of William Walker into Nicaragua to free the country from Costa Rican rule, and to support the presidential candidacy of Irish Democrat James Buchanan against the Republican nominee, the Western explorer John C. Frémont.

Meagher himself explored in the lull before the war. He tramped through Costa Rica, Nicaragua, and Venezuela; wrote enthusiastic articles for *Harper's* magazine on his impressions and experiences; and made a valuable report on the feasibility of a canal through the Central American isthmus by way of Nicaragua.

In his final prewar public act, in April 1859, he assisted in the defense of Congressman Dan Sickles, a powerful Tammany politician and friend of the Irish cause. Sickles had shot and killed United States District Attorney Philip Barton Key, grandson of the author of the National Anthem. Key had been having an affair with Sickles's wife, and the jury was sympathetic to the cuckolded congressman and found him not guilty.

Despite some Southern sympathies, at the outbreak of the Civil War, Meagher formed a company of Irish Zouaves for the Union Army and marched them down Broadway with troops of the Sixty-ninth New York Regiment. By the summer of 1861, his company had become an official unit of the Sixty-ninth and part of Col. William Tecumseh Sherman's brigade in the advance into Fairfax County, Virginia. On July 21, the brigade reached Bull

Run Creek and the opening battle of the war. Shouting *"Erin go bragh!"* ("Ireland Forever!"), Brevet Major Meagher's Zouaves, in green uniforms dazzlingly embroidered and betassled in gilt, made three headlong charges against Confederate positions and were repulsed each time as the Union forces were routed. He lost thirty-eight of his men dead, many others wounded, had his own horse blown to bits beneath him and was carried on an artillery caisson to a Washington hospital to recover.

He spent the next six months preaching to his countrymen to "fight today to preserve America, tomorrow to liberate Ireland," while gathering volunteers for an Irish Brigade. From New York, Boston, and Philadelphia, he and his loyal aides recruited five regiments, five thousand men, to be trained and bivouacked at Fort Schuyler, New York. Meagher was confirmed as a brigadier general of volunteers on February 3, 1862, with his brigade attached to Gen. Edwin V. Sumner's II Corps in the Army of the Potomac. As the corps was ordered to Warrenton, Virginia, forty miles west of Washington, the "Sons of Erin," as the newspapers called Meagher's brigade, wore green plumes in their kepis and carried green flags embroidered in gold with a sewn harp, shamrock, and sunburst, and a streamer proclaiming "Clear the Way!" in Gaelic.

Riding conspicuously in the van wearing a green tunic set off with a yellow scarf, Meagher led the brigade into its first battle, Fair Oaks, Virginia, on the Chickahominy River, a few miles northeast of Richmond. The fight raged on between May 31 and June 1, 1862, with neither side gaining ground but leaving a combined eleven thousand casualties on the field.

They fought in the bloodiest day of the war, September 17, 1862, in the Bloody Lane of Antietam Creek, Maryland, a day when the Confederates lost nearly fourteen thousand men (2,700 killed) and the Union twelve thousand (2,108 killed) and Meager's brigade was reduced by five hundred casualties.

They fought in the second wave at Fredericksburg, Virginia, on December 13, 1862—1,300 of the Irish Brigade singing "The

Wearin' of the Green" and marching at double-step up a slope into the ferocious wall of fire from the rebel-held Sunken Road at the foot of Marye's Heights. In one of the war's countless ironies, Meagher's men charged that part of the Confederate line held by other Irishmen—the Twenty-fourth Georgia Regiment commanded by Col. Robert McMillan. (When one of McMillan's officers saw through his binoculars the Irish Brigade advancing, he remarked, "What a pity. Here comes Meagher's fellows.") Five hundred and thirty-five of the brigade were killed or wounded among the eighteen thousand casualties on both sides. A pro-South London correspondent, who expressed regret that the Irish fighting spirit was not "exhibited in a holier cause," wrote, "Never at Fontenoy, Albuera, or Waterloo was more undaunted courage displayed by the sons of Erin."

They fought in the Wilderness Campaign, Chancellorsville, Virginia, on May 1 through 6, 1863, during which each side lost over twelve thousand casualties. Meagher returned from the battle with less than a regiment of infantry, what he called his "poor vestige and relic of the Irish Brigade," and on May 19 resigned his command in protest over the plan to distribute the survivors among other units.

The remnant, without Meagher but with some new recruits, fought in the Seven Days' Battle at Gaine's Mill (June 27, 1863), Savage Station (June 28, 1863), White Oak Swamp (June 30, 1863), Malvern Hill, and Harrison's Landing (July 1, 1863), the engagements resulting in fifty-six thousand combined casualties and spelling the end of the Irish Brigade.

No unit of the Union Army had fought harder and sacrificed more. After the war, Robert E. Lee said of them, "Never were men so brave."

Early in 1864, after a period of boredom in New York, Meagher sought a new command and was assigned to duty in Tennessee. He spend the rest of the war in minor posts there and in Georgia and North Carolina.

He was accused repeatedly of drunkenness. In the retreat

from Fair Oaks on June 1, 1862, he was placed under "twenty-four hour arrest" but the reason for the punishment was never divulged, and the arrest did not appear on his service record. At Antietam, after his horse was shot and he fell from the saddle, one of Gen. George McClellan's staff officers reported that Meagher had fallen down drunk, but the officer was nowhere near the Irish Brigade during the battle. There were other stories of Meagher's inebriation, but one of the brigade chaplains said the general never drank during a battle and when he did imbibe did so only in the spirit of camp conviviality. He admitted there were occasions when the spirit "led him too far."

Some of the accusations derived from the rampant anti-Irish, "All Irishmen are drunks" sentiment of the day, some from the fact that between battles, the Irish Brigade's camps were popular and crowded with war-weary men relaxing with songfests, dances, horse races—and whiskey. The drink flowed from a makeshift tavern that seemed to appear out of nowhere wherever Meagher's men bivouacked despite the scoldings of a brigade Temperance Society organized by one of the Irish chaplains.

Still, while his own staff officers denied his drunkenness and remained loyal to him throughout the war and afterward, Meagher was not always innocent. In January 1865, aboard a transport vessel in Chesapeake Bay, an officer delivered papers to Meagher, assigning him to duty in New Bern, North Carolina. After handing the papers over and awaiting a reply, the officer reported to his superiors that the general was too drunk to understand the orders. The report reached commanding Gen. U.S. Grant, and three weeks later Meagher was relieved of further duty and returned to New York.

He served in the honor guard at the lying-in-state ceremony for President Lincoln a few days after the April 14, 1865, assassination, and a month later resigned his commission.

He was four months from his forty-third year, and his future seemed bleak. He could return to the lecture circuit, adding the Irish Brigade and the war to his repertoire of Irish independence,

Van Diemen's Land adventures, and explorations in Costa Rica, but there was something dreary about such a prospect. The travel, being away from his Libby, and the fact that lecturing represented no challenge and no step up for an ambitious man, nagged him.

He had long dreamed of the diplomatic service, a post in which his education, oratorical gift, persuasiveness and status as war hero and leader of men could be put to significant use. In 1857, he had petitioned President James Buchanan for a consular post in either Central or South America; at the beginning of the Lincoln administration, he asked for a diplomatic appointment, perhaps in Venezuela, but nothing came of these appeals.

Then, in the summer of 1865, President Andrew Johnson offered him the position as Military Secretary of Montana Territory, an ill-defined post as second-in-command to the territorial governor. This was no minister's office, but it was a step on the federal ladder to something more important—perhaps a senatorship when Montana reached statehood—and so Meaghar accepted, saying he "hoped to prove useful in that capacity."

11

MONTANA

When Thomas Francis Meagher—Irish patriot, former exiled felon, and late major general of the Union Army—stepped off the Virginia City stagecoach in September 1865, Montana had been a territory of the United States for just a year, and only sixty years had passed since Meriwether Lewis had passed through upon returning from the Pacific coast. In all his world travels, Meagher had never seen a land like it: Ireland, Europe, Van Diemen's Land, the eastern United States, Central and South America—no place was remotely comparable.

The sheer vastness of the place was breathtaking; indeed, it was so immense that most of it remained unexplored, at least by white men, and there were very few of those. In 1860, there were fewer than a hundred settlers in Montana; only after the gold discoveries in 1862 and '64 did the population make a leap, to about fifteen thousand, virtually all in the mountainous western third of the territory. It was this region, the northern and middle Rockies west of the Continental Divide, that gave rise to the territorial name—from the Spanish *montaña,* "mountain"—a name that seemed to ignore the fact that the eastern two thirds of Montana's 147,000 square miles of land were pristine grasslands, a buffalo's paradise.

In truth, except for the teeming gold towns and camps, all clotted into a tiny pocket of mountain foothills in the western territory, the Montana that Meagher saw in the summer of 1865 had changed little from the misty past. For centuries the Blackfeet, Northern Cheyenne, Sioux, Crow, Gros Ventre, Flathead, Kalispel, Kootenai, and Assiniboine, buffalo hunters migrating with the vast herds that flourished in the grasslands, made up the human populace of the primitive, untrammeled land. Montana's great river valleys and mountain slopes were still blanketed with trees—fir, spruce, pine, hemlock, larch—and a gorgeous profusion of wildflowers. The place teemed with deer, elks, and bears, bighorn sheep, mountain goats, mountain lions, moose, wolves, beavers, fishers, lynx, bobcats, wolverines; all manner of game and songbirds and raptors; and rivers and streams alive with walleye, salmon, trout, grayling, bass, perch.

But it was not this Eden of the Great West, where the outside world was "the States," that brought men—mostly men—into Montana; not the vastness and emptiness of the place or its intrinsic beauty or its limitless potential for hunter, farmer, and stockman. Gold brought them, as it had to California in 1849.

The first important Montana gold discovery occurred in 1862 at a place called Grasshopper Creek, two years before Montana was carved out of Idaho Territory and just three years before Tom Meagher's arrival there. The camp at Grasshopper Creek, named Bannack, grew to a population of three thousand within a few months.

Unfortunately the Bannack placers were thin, soon worked out, and while boomtown became ghost town, seventy miles east, new and richer bonanzas were being worked at Alder Gulch. There, the story goes, in 1863 a prospector named Bill

Fairweather and his party were on their way to the Yellowstone Country from Bannack when they were waylaid by a band of Crow Indians. While hiding in a coulee, Fairweather and his partners kicked up some gold-bearing gravel and, after the Indian scare ended, named the place after the alder trees lining their hiding place.

Alder Gulch, among the greatest gold producers on earth, gave rise to the miners' settlement of Virginia City (originally named Varina, for the wife of Jefferson Davis, president of the Confederacy), where a sudden population of ten thousand lived in windblown tents and flimsy shacks and where a saloon accounted for every third building constructed. The rise of Virginia City opened the era "When the territory was filled with gold, Indians, whiskey, and fugitive Rebels," wrote Montana historian Joseph Kinsey Howard.

During these wild times arrived two men who were to cross and recross Meagher's forthcoming path through the territory. Sidney Edgerton, an Akron, Ohio, lawyer and Radical Republican had been appointed federal judge for Idaho Territory, and at his side stood his young, dynamic, and ambitious nephew and law partner. This was Wilbur Fisk Sanders, a thirty-year-old former Union army colonel, a New Yorker who, like his uncle, had studied law in Ohio. They reached ramshackle Bannack in September 1863, a propitious moment for both, as they were to witness the dying months of a period of lawlessness and terrorism and the rise of a powerful force in territorial life: vigilante justice.

The Montana vigilantes and lynch law rose to combat a gang of road agents issuing from their "Robber's Roost" headquarters between Bannack and Virginia City and preying with merciless abandon on individual miners, mine camps, and stagecoach gold shipments. The leader of the cutthroat crew—he called his companions "the Innocents"—was the handsome, well-spoken, and engaging Henry Plummer. Born in Maine, New York, Connecticut, or Wisconsin in about 1832 (details of his early life are spotty), he first appeared in public records in the California gold country in 1852, where he was known as a gambler, saloon habitué, and pistoleer.

None of these activities, however, prevented him from being elected city marshal in 1857 in the thriving California gold town of Nevada City. He held office briefly, was sent to San Quentin in 1859 for murder, and upon his release drifted to the Oregon country, then to Idaho Territory following the gold frenzy. He organized his bandit crew in Bannack from the nest of drifters and petty criminals contaminating the mine camps, but seemed to be such a charming and upstanding citizen, he was elected sheriff of the town in May 1863, and the following September, of Virginia City.

For a time the badge was a perfect cover for his principal occupation as bandit chief. Although no names were ever chronicled or bodies found, some contemporary accounts claim that more than a hundred miners and other innocents were murdered or disappeared during Plummer's tenure as sheriff and that an untold amount of gold was stolen and cached.

Helping organize the Vigilance Committee that brought Plummer and his gang to the noose was Sidney Edgerton's nephew, Wilbur Sanders. Upon arriving in the territory, he set up a practice in Bannack and joined other influential men there and in Virginia City to end the road agent's rule. Vigilante justice was swift and sure: after a Ferreting Committee identified the miscreants and condemned them to death, Plummer and two of his deputies were hanged in Bannack on January 10, 1864, on a gallows Plummer himself had built. Twenty other members of the gang were lynched from cottonwood trees or from the rafters of unfinished buildings eighteen months before Meagher arrived in Virginia City.

Since he was a member of the territorial judiciary, Sidney Edgerton's involvement in the Vigilance Committee had to be covert, but he was nonetheless active, and with the end of the Plummer gang and a new era of law (even if vigilante law) he envisioned the need to split a new territory out of sprawling Idaho.

He returned to Washington that January after Plummer's execution, and there, with Wilbur Sanders's assistance and that of other influential Western politicians, he helped persuade President Lincoln and Congress to create the Territory of Montana. The bill passed on May 24, 1864, and Lincoln named Edgerton Montana's first governor.

Edgerton returned to Bannack that summer and contrived to have the town—more Republican than its rival Virginia City—named the territorial capital. He convened the first legislature there in December at a time when the riches of Alder Gulch were drawing the mining populace from Bannack. Inevitably, in 1865, the territorial capital was moved to Virginia City.

By then, Montana's millions in raw gold were being sent down the Missouri by steamboat from Fort Benton. The first of these to reach Benton was the *Yellowstone,* which had departed Saint Louis on March 20 and after two months and eight days, traveling nearly three thousand miles of river with 250 tons of freight, reached the fort on May 28, 1865. There, the steamer loaded twenty-nine thousand buffalo robes, assorted furs, and over eleven thousand pounds of gold sent there by stagecoach from Virginia City, 265 miles to the southwest.

How much Tom Meagher knew about Montana before he arrived there is unknown. He had been visiting a friend on Long Island when he received the letter from President Johnson offering him the territorial secretaryship, and he must have gathered up government documents and maps before his departure. The maps would have depicted with some accuracy the great river systems of the territory, particularly the Missouri and its headwaters and the river's greatest branch, the Yellowstone.

In planning his westward journey, Meagher must have given some thought to traveling the Missouri route. He probably did not know of the *Yellowstone*'s May-to-June voyage up the river to Fort Benton, and in any event, no steamboat was destined to Benton at the time he needed. He could travel on the river to Fort Union, the American Fur Company post near the confluence of the Missouri and Yellowstone, two thousand miles from Saint Louis. But even this leg of the trip would probably take five or six weeks, depending upon the depth of the river, stoppages to load and offload freight and passengers, and the time needed to run the notorious Missouri obstacles. The river was a twisting, muddy gauntlet of looping switchbacks, fallen trees, sandbars, and islands, and at Fort Union, he would still have two weeks or more to travel to reach Benton and Virginia City, there to rendezvous with Sidney Edgerton before the governor's departure.

Meagher opted for an overland journey. Among its advantages: he could travel some distance in the comfort of a railway car, and he could make a few speeches along the way.

In late August, he traveled by rail to Atchison, Kansas, and caught a stagecoach for the bone-jarring journey into Montana via Denver, Salt Lake City, and Pocatello, Idaho. In Bannack, weary and bedraggled, he met Edgerton, who was eager to return to the eastern seaboard. The governor, a former two-term Republican congressman, Civil War colonel, and Idaho Territorial jurist, turned out to be an amiable man and seemed quite willing, in his haste to return East on an extended leave, to turn his responsibilities over to his new territorial secretary. He thrust a handful of documents into Meagher's hands, gave him a few words of advice, and was out the door of his makeshift and now abandoned governmental office.

Meagher had thus risen in the space of a few days from territorial secretary to acting governor. He was an Irish Roman Catholic, a Democrat, and a former Union general in a territory ruled by Protestants, members of the Masonic Order, and some of Edgerton's Republican cohorts. Also conspicuous in his immediate future were a number of erstwhile vigilantes, a cadre of influential Southerners, including Confederate army veterans who had fled west after the war, and three or four thousand Sioux warriors under the Oglala chief Red Cloud, who had announced that he was prepared to evict white settlers from the territory.

Such were the weighty matters on his mind when he reached the raucous, clapboarded shanty town of Virginia City in late September and found the governor's residence to be a log cabin with a bearskin nailed to the wall.

He took comfort in the knowledge that his beloved Libby would be coming out to join him in the spring and that he still hoped "to prove useful" in his assignment—even more useful now as de facto governor in a place desperately needing governance. The first territorial legislature under Edgerton had been useful but had dissolved without arranging for future sessions. Another assembly was needed to pass laws, appoint territorial officials, arrange for a militia, discuss means of protecting settlers from Indian depredations, negotiate Indian treaties, bring real law and order to the territory, and end the influence of the Vigilance Committee. Such a program, and the convening of a constitutional convention, would be necessary to push Montana toward statehood.

Or so Acting Governor Tom Meagher thought.

In late October, six weeks after his arrival in the territory and with a party of five men and a string of pack mules, Meagher started out on horseback to Fort Benton to oversee a treaty being made with the "Chiefs, Head Men and Delegates representing the several tribes of Indians of the Blackfeet Nation." Meagher's associates were Montana territorial Chief Justice Hezekiah L. Hosmer, Associate Justice Lyman E. Munson, and a young Harvard-educated lawyer named Cornelius Hedges—later a Republican state senator. Two deputy United States marshals accompanied the party: John X. Beidler (known as X. Biedler, or simply X in vigilante chronicles), a short, sinister Pennsylvanian, one-time John Brown partisan, and locally famed as the vigilantes' chief hangman; and Neil Howie, originally from Wisconsin, the son of Scotch'immigrants, a former Virginia City sheriff and Vigilance Committee member.

In a frozen camp along the Missouri north of Helena, the party discovered a Jesuit priest, Father Francis Xavier Kuppens, a twenty-seven-year-old Belgian-born missionary to the Blackfeet out of the Saint Peter's mission near Great Falls. With the temperature plummeting to 40 degrees below zero in an intermittent blizzard, Meagher and the others, welcomed by Kuppens, set up their tents, laid down pine boughs to sleep on, and for two days huddled in their buffalo robes and blankets, waiting out the storm.

The acting governor, educated by Jesuits, struck up a friendship with Father Kuppens. The priest later recalled their campfire talks about the Young Ireland movement, the Irish Brigade, and Indian problems, which Kuppens knew intimately and about which the acting governor was eager for education. The priest also spoke at length on "the wonders of the Yellowstone," which he had apparently seen firsthand. These wonders had first been sighted in 1810 by the mountain man John Colter, a Lewis-and-Clark expedition member. His stories of a high, broad volcanic plateau pierced by hundreds of titanic geysers and hot springs, waterfalls, and tinted canyons bordered by primeval forests, were treated as amusing tall tales for forty years. Not until another Belgian Jesuit, Father Pierre-Jean De Smet, explored and described the region in 1852, were the stories proved true—and if anything, understated.

During a lull in the storm, Kuppens received another visitor who substantiated all the priest's descriptions. The man, named Viell, was a Canadian married to a Blackfeet woman who "had come over to see the distinguished visitors," the priest said. He described to Meagher and the others the Yellowstone phenomena "in a most graphic manner." His audience hung on his words: "None of the visitors had ever heard of the wonderful place," Kuppens said. He added that "General Meagher said if things were as described the government ought to reserve the territory for a national park. The others agreed that efforts should be made to explore the region and that a report of the exploration be sent to the government."*

The object of the Fort Benton visit, the treaty with the Black-feet Nation, was signed on November 16, 1865, after which Meagher and his companions returned home.

During that winter, in Virginia City and Helena, the gold town a hundred miles north, where he had rented a place in anticipation of Libby's arrival, Meagher received a string of visitors. These were miners, businessmen, citizens with problems, and several of the territory's judges, lawyers, and other of Edgerton's Republican cronies. Of the influential callers, Wilbur Fisk Sanders among them, several informed "The Acting One," as they called Meagher, that under the Organic Act that had created the territory, he had no authority to convene a legislature and certainly not a constitutional convention.

Meagher had read the Organic Act, and at first agreed he was powerless to call either body into session; then in a sudden about-face, Meagher notified President Johnson that "it was within the scope of my prerogatives," and that he decided to do both.

The special session of the legislature, "for the transaction of business as well as to give legislative sanction and validity to the constitutional convention," convened on March 5, 1866, in rented rooms in Virginia City and ran until April 14. Meagher's opening remarks were surprisingly murky for such a daring and auspicious occasion: "We are going to have nationality without sectionalism, we are going to have an enlightened civilization, religion without puritanism and loyalty without humiliation."

During the forty-day session some bills were written, budgets

---

*In 1870, Cornelius Hedges, the young lawyer in Meagher's party, served as correspondent for the *Helena Herald* on a Yellowstone expedition and became an advocate of the national park idea. Yellowstone, the nation's first national park, was created by an act of Congress in January 1872.

set, appointments made, a draft of a constitution written by a separate body convened in Helena in late March, but all the work was to no avail.* A month after adjournment, Massachusetts-born and Yale-educated Lyman Munson, a member of the Fort Benton party seven months past and now the territory's senior federal judge, issued a decision declaring the entire legislative session, all its bills and decisions, to be null and void. Meagher was furious but could not have been much surprised. Munson had warned against the validity of the legislature while it was in session and received a blow to his judicial pride from "the Acting One" that had been printed in Virginia City's *Montana Democrat*. Meagher announced that he did not hold himself "in the least accountable" to Judge Munson for any "official acts."

In October, Edgerton's replacement, Green Clay Smith of Kentucky, arrived in the territory. A distinguished Kentucky lawyer, barely forty years old, the new governor had served as an infantry lieutenant in the Mexican War and, like Meagher, a brigadier general of volunteers in the Civil War. He had served two terms in Congress when breveted a major general "for meritorious service in the late war" and offered the Montana office. Acting and governor became friends at once despite obvious differences. Smith, an evangelical Baptist and temperance advocate was affable and appreciative of Meagher's work under strained conditions. Meagher described Smith as "a genial, lighthearted, high-minded young fellow."

Smith was to stay in Montana for only a few weeks, to acclimate himself to the territory and to the office. He had made arrangements before leaving Washington to return there on an extended leave to settle business affairs before returning to Virginia City as the full-time chief executive. For his part, Meagher had intended to resign as secretary and return East with Elizabeth and begin a new career, perhaps in Congress. However, Smith

---

*Montana was admitted to the Union as the forty-first state in November 1889.

persuaded him to stay on, and when he departed the territory in January 1867, Meagher became, once again, the Acting One.

That winter, before Smith's departure, Meagher rode out again from Helena for a second visit to Fort Benton, this time to witness the arrival of a detachment of soldiers being towed on barges up the Missouri for assignment at Benton and Camp Cook, 120 miles downriver. He waited, roaming the mile-long levee, where not too many years past, keelboats, canoes, bullboats, and mackinaws tied up each fall with their cargoes of beaver skins and buffalo robes bound for Saint Louis.

The river was low, and the flatboats, it turned out, had run aground at the mouth of the Judith River, seventy miles east of Benton.

With some difficulty, again traveling in blizzard weather, Meagher returned to Helena and Virginia City.

After a single year in Montana, Meagher had collected an impressive array of enemies, many of whom sent slandering letters about him to Washington. Chief among the charges against him was incessant drunkenness, but he was also accused, in a rat's nest of frontier slanders, of madness, being "beastly and filthy" in his habits, rendezvousing with "vile prostitutes," using territorial funds to finance his debauchery, and conniving with certain villainous Democrats, including former Confederates, in his attempt to rise to power in the territory.

Meagher wrote to Secretary of State William Seward of the "conspiracy of scandalous misrepresentations, base calumnies, and dastardly spite" being leveled against him by "Republican officials, radicals, and extremists," but reserved most of his communication for more serious business. He pelted Washington with telegrams and letters, minutes, and urgent appeals, sent them to Secretary of State Seward, President Johnson, and a host of bureaucrats, appealing for salary funds, appointment of a surveyor general, and a postal system.

To his old chief, Gen. W. T. Sherman, now commanding the Army's Department of the Missouri, Meagher requested a military force of a thousand men and a permanent garrison for the territory to protect its settlers, miners, and citizens against Indian raids. There were plenty of disturbing signs. A band of Bloods (a Blackfeet tribe) had attacked some settlers on the Musselshell River; two prospectors had been killed by hostiles in the Bear Paw Mountains, fifty miles downriver from Fort Benton; there were widespread rumors that Red Cloud intended to lead four thousand Sioux, Cheyennes, and Arapahoes into the Gallatin Valley to expel all white settlers there. Even such a veteran frontiersman and Indian fighter as John Bozeman, who had led wagon trains into Montana along a trail he blazed, asked Meagher for protection.*

Sherman was unmoved, and called the acting governor a "stampeder." The general did partially acquiesce to one request Meagher originally made to Secretary of War William Stanton: permission to raise a citizen militia to defend settlers against Indian attacks. Sherman authorized the raising of the First Montana Volunteer Militia for eight months' service, the men to furnish their own horses and be paid forty cents a day. Meagher was able to enlist 475 volunteers, most with their own Civil War–era muskets, but only about two hundred could be mustered at one time, and these men spent their time on patrols in the Gallatin River Valley and never engaged in an Indian fight. Meagher wrote a friend to say that he was commander, not of an "invincible" militia but of an "invisible" one.

In June 1867 he butted heads for the final time with his judicial nemesis Lyman Munson. The case involved one James B. Daniels, a ne'er-do-well gambler who had knifed and killed a man in a Helena saloon fight in the winter of 1865. In Montana's rude legal system, Daniels's fate rested in the hands of se-

---

*Bozeman was killed by Blackfeet at a crossing of the Yellowstone River on April 20, 1867.

nior Federal Judge Munson, who found some extenuating circumstances in the case, declared the gambler guilty only of
manslaughter, and sentenced him to three years in prison.

After receiving petitions from Daniels's friends and an appeal signed by thirty respectable citizens who believed the man
had been provoked and the murder committed in self-defense,
Meagher pardoned him. This odd act may have been in retalia-
tion for Munson's decision to throw out all the legislative proceedings Meagher had masterminded, or it may have been based
upon the testimonials and evidence of provocation. Whatever the
case, the verdict had been overturned, the judge was furious and
demanded the pardon be voided, and Meager refused.

(Munson later claimed that when he confronted Meagher,
he found the man "still in his debauch," and said Meagher had
acted "while under the influence of an unfortunate habit," the
judge's euphemism for drunkenness.)

Daniels did not long enjoy his freedom. The still-active and
still potent Vigilance Committee claimed that he openly threatened to wreak vengeance on those who had testified against
him, and so, on March 2, 1866, Daniels was lynched at Dry
Gulch, on the outskirts of Helena. According to the newspapers,
"angered citizens" strung him up with his pardon in his coat
pocket. Pinned to the coat was the message, THE ACTING ONE IS
NEXT.

Nathaniel P. Langford, a member of the Vigilance Committee's executive council, said the Daniels killing was "an irrepara-
ble error" but that the pardon was due to a "mistaken sense of
his [Meagher's] own powers," and that the gambler was "one of
the worst ruffians whose careers I have passed under review."
Langford said Daniels was a career criminal who had killed another man in California before drifting to Montana but dis-
avowed the story that the Vigilance Committee sanctioned or
took part in the execution.

Daniels's funeral drew a huge crowd. Montana historian

Joseph K. Howard quotes a contemporary as saying of the case that the gambler "was indicted for a crime he did not commit, tried by a court without jurisdiction, reprieved by a governor by mistake, and lynched by a mob."

III

FORT BENTON

In late June 1867, the Daniels matter still fresh, Meagher departed Virginia City with a militia escort. Following a Sioux raid on northern territorial settlers and in his capacity as both acting governor and territorial secretary, he dispatched a message to the War Department pleading for 2,500 rifles, powder, and ammunition to defend the territory. After notification that the arms were en route, he elected to travel to Fort Benton to meet the steamer coming upriver from Saint Joseph.

Named for Thomas Hart Benton, the eminent Missouri senator, the fort lay among red bluffs on the Missouri River 120 miles northeast of Helena and eighty miles south of the Canadian border. The locale had been visited by Capt. Meriwether Lewis in 1806, when the explorer was headed toward the Marias River to the north. The fort was erected during the winter of 1846–1847 as headquarters of the American Fur Company, which conducted a lucrative trade with the Blackfeet and other tribes. The trade was principally in buffalo robes, the AFC paying an average of a dollar each for them and shipping the supple, hairy hides to Saint Louis, where they were resold in the East to serve as carriage and sleigh lap warmers. American Fur sold out in 1864, but the fort survived as a Blackfeet Indian Agency, a military fort, a thriving inland trade port three thousand river miles from Saint Louis, and the terminus of steamboat traffic on the river. It was a rowdy, lawless, and, some in Meagher's time said, a vigilante town.

After a brief visit with Libby in Helena and a six-day march with a small escort of militiamen, he reached Benton on July 1, weak with dysentery, and learned that the arms shipment had not yet arrived. He met some friends as he toured the levee fronting the fort's shops and while at the home of Isaac G. Baker, the fort's leading merchant, Baker offered Meagher some black-berry wine as an antidote for the "summer complaint" and said later that while the governor "may have gotten on a bender" en route to the fort, he was "stone sober" when he got there.

One who later testified that the governor suffered only from a six-day bout with dysentery and not with a hangover was the Irish-born John T. "Johnny" Doran, pilot of the steamboat *G. A. Thompson,* which had arrived at Benton from Saint Louis two days earlier. The pilot learned that Meagher was not only ill, but also concerned for his own safety, telling Doran that he had heard "whispering" around town leading him to believe vigilantes were threatening his life as they had in the James Daniels case.

Doran offered his friend a berth on the steamer to rest and recuperate.

After writing a letter to his New York friend Richard O'Gor-man and another leisurely walk along the riverbank, Meagher climbed aboard the *Thompson* and enjoyed a cigar and chat with Doran before retiring early. To Doran he probably men-tioned the two-*Thompson* coincidence: the ship that rescued him after his escape from Van Diemen's Land was the *Elizabeth Thompson.*

Between nine and ten that night of July 1, 1867, the governor awoke and walked out onto the upper deck. Within minutes, somebody yelled, "Man overboard!" and Thomas Francis Meagher, age forty-three years and eleven months, was never seen again.

There were witnesses, but nobody could testify with certainty what had happened or why.

Ferd Roosevelt, a Wells-Fargo agent, said he saw Meagher fall from the *Thompson* and disappear under the keel of a neighboring boat.

A man named W. S. Stocking said the general made a "misstep," signifying that Meagher had tripped and fallen into the river.

A watchman on the boat said Meagher appeared to be vomiting when he lost his balance and fell overboard.

A barber said Meagher "let himself down to the lower deck and jumped into the river without saying a thing."

In 1892, Capt. Patrick J. Condon, a veteran of the Irish Brigade, was working on a bridge over the Missouri at Omaha when he met a soldier who had been on sentry duty on the *G. A. Thompson* the night of Meagher's death. The soldier's story so impressed Condon that he took the man, whose name the captain did not reveal, to a magistrate, where an affidavit was prepared. The sum of the witness's testimony was that Meagher had been ailing with dysentery—the "summer complaint"—several days by the time he reached Fort Benton and took to bed at I. G. Baker's home to rest. Meagher, the witness said, drank four glasses of blackberry wine through the evening and toward nightfall agreed to be escorted to the pilot's stateroom aboard the *Thompson*. Then, while on sentry duty the night of July 1, the soldier said he heard a noise toward the stern of the vessel and saw somebody moving about in white clothing—presumably longjohn underwear—on the port side of the stern. A minute or two later, he heard a shout, then a splash, and shouted "Man overboard!" after which the deck came alive. The witness said that life buoys were flung into the water, and lanterns lit as crewmen on the boats ran ashore and followed the current, hoping to find Meagher swimming or, if knocked unconscious, floating.

He said the river ran at ten miles per hour in the summer, sometimes faster at Fort Benton, and that it must have carried Meagher downriver quickly. Darkness prevented the body from being found that night.

Except for the question of how he knew Meagher had drunk four glasses of blackberry wine, the sentry's testimony seemed authentic to Captain Condon. Even so, it did not help in explaining how and why Meagher fell or if anybody "assisted" in his death. He was too faithful a Catholic for suicide to be seriously considered.

The other great unanswered question—what became of the body?—was particularly bothersome. While the river was high at Fort Benton that summer night, and flowing swiftly, still it was a braided and oxbowing waterway with plenty of nearby sandbars, islands, and impediments to snag a floating corpse. One theory is that the "shout" the sentry heard was the sound of Meagher striking his head on the rail or some deck projection, and that he was unconscious when he fell into the river, was sucked under the keel of the boat, and drowned. Then during the night as he floated downstream, his body hung up on a sunken tree below the river's surface.

Whatever happened, no trace of his body was ever found, despite a two-thousand-dollar reward for the person who discovered it, half put up by Governor Smith, who had just returned to the territory, and half from "Helena Citizens."

Drunkenness, the familiar old charge, promptly reared its head. Meagher himself seems to have admitted to a friend that he had too much to drink when he and his escort camped on the Sun River en route to Fort Benton. Granville Stuart, an eminent Montana miner, rancher, and settler, while not present in Benton at the time of the tragedy, claimed that Meagher had joined a bunch of hard-drinking friends at the fort and "may have overindulged." The *Eureka Journal,* sixty years after the event, implied delirium tremens: "It is agreed by all who have investigated the events leading up to his death that the general was temporarily mentally deranged. In such a condition his death could have come either voluntarily or involuntarily. No one but God knows for sure."

Some hinted that dangerous men, maybe vigilantes, were responsible.

"Montana was restive under the iron command of Meagher, its first dictator," wrote Joseph K. Howard in his 1943 book, *Montana: High, Wide, and Handsome.*

> He was one of the greatest soldiers of fortune who ever lived. A strikingly handsome and effective Irish patriot at twenty-four, in the space of twenty years his adventures carried him around the world and ended with his mysterious death in the rough river town of Fort Benton, Montana Territory, where as late as 1882 visitors were warned, "Walk in the middle of the street and mind your own business; this is a tough town!"

There was even a far-fetched "Fenian theory" that Meagher had somehow fallen victim to radical Irishmen angered by his failure to support their activities. The Irish Republican Brotherhood, popularly called the Fenians (from the *féinne,* a legendary band of second century Gaelic warriors), was a secret Irish-American revolutionary society whose members were bound by a sworn oath of allegiance to Irish republican ideals and pledged to take up arms when necessary to promote and defend them.

Meagher had been inducted into the Fenian Brotherhood in the summer of 1863, at the time he was attempting to have his resignation from the army rescinded. From the beginning, while sympathetic to the order's philosophy, he was not comfortable with the organization, especially after a denunciation of it was made by the Catholic church. He did not participate in any Fenian meetings or plans, stoutly defended the Union cause (a dubious position in Fenian thinking), and was accused by the brotherhood of being a "Lincoln man," a phrase of censure. Even so, he had many Fenian friends, including several influential ones in Montana.

The theory that the vigilantes killed him also lacked plausible foundation. The idea was based upon several coincidental facts: Meagher was anti-vigilante, a proponent of organized law and order. Meagher's pardon of James Daniels rankled the vigilantes, who had apprehended the man. Meagher had disputes with the notable Vigilance Committee member Wilbur Sanders. In vigilante circles, Meagher was regarded as a newcomer, a Democrat, a usurper of authority, a troublemaker. Fort Benton was known to be a vigilante stronghold, and Meagher had heard, according to Johnny Doran and others, vague, whispered threats as he entered the town.

However, the vigilante speculation failed to include such critical matters as motive and opportunity. What would the vigilantes have gained by murdering a man whose time in Montana was close to ending? Whose offenses against them were political and minor? Whose murder, if bungled, would have brought the wrath of the federal government down on the territory and shone a bright light on every vigilante, current and former, until the culprits were identified and punished?

Even renegade vigilantes, or ordinary hoodlums, whose motives cannot be guessed, would have had no opportunity to board the *G. A. Thompson*, kill Meagher, drop him into the river—or kidnap and murder him elsewhere—and escape unnoticed. More than one man would have been required to subdue the vigorous and fearless Irishman, and not a single witness saw suspicious men on the boat or anybody *with* Meagher when he emerged on the deck.

∽

The two best sources of Meagher's final hours of life were his Irish friend Johnny Doran and, ironically, a man Meagher regarded as an enemy, Wilbur Fisk Sanders.

In 1870, Capt. William F. Lyons, who served with Meagher in the Irish Brigade and later joined the editorial staff of the *New York Herald,* published his *Life of Brigadier General Thomas Francis Meagher.* He accepted the story of his former commander's accidental death and included as an appendix in the book a letter dated December 16, 1869, from the pilot of the *G. A. Thompson,* John T. Doran, then living in Saint Louis. Doran idolized Meagher and intended to protect the general's reputation, but his story contained many valuable and believable details of the night of July 1, 1867.

While pilot on the steamboat *Ontario,* Doran met Elizabeth Meagher in the spring of 1866 when she was en route to Fort Benton to join her husband, and he subsequently became friends with her and her husband. Doran said he was with the general "constantly" on July 1 and "was the last man that spoke to him on earth." He told of being pilot on the *Thompson,* which left Saint Louis in early April 1867 and arrived at Benton on June 29. There he found two other steamers, the *Guidon* and *Amelia Poe,* about a hundred yards apart on the levee, and anchored between them. Doran said he went fishing off the deck of the *Poe* on July 1, saw a troop of about a dozen men riding into town, and learned they were General Meagher and his staff.

That afternoon Doran walked to the I. G. Baker store and found Meagher in a back room reading a newspaper. They greeted each other warmly and "engaged in a long conversation." Meagher told his friend that he was very sick on the six-day ride to Benton and explained his mission, saying he had just learned that the expected arms and ammunition had been off-loaded at Camp Cook and that he planned to proceed there the next day.

"He also spoke in the most tender and affectionate terms of his wife, residing at Helena," Doran recalled, "saying that in their mountain home they were as happy as two thrushes in a bush."

After dinner the two men walked around the riverside town, during which, Doran said, Meagher was "invited to partake of the hospitalities always urgently extended to strangers in this section of the country" and that Meagher "firmly refused" the offers and that "his experience at Sun River had given him a distaste for such amusement."

Toward evening they returned to the boat "for tea," Doran said, and at sunset took chairs out to the deck railings and lit cigars. As they relaxed in the humid night, the pilot gave Meagher a copy of the 1828 novel *The Collegians* by the beloved Limerick writer, Gerald Griffin. After perusing the book for a time, then "suddenly closing it," Doran said, "he turned to me and said very excitedly, 'Johnny, they threaten my life in that town! As I passed I heard some men say 'There he goes.'" Doran said he tried to persuade his friend that his fears were groundless, but Meagher pushed on and after asking if Doran was armed, the pilot produced two navy revolvers. "The general, seeing that they were capped and loaded, handed them back to me."

At length Meagher retired to his berth. "By this time it was pitch dark, the hour being about half past nine," Doran remembered. "He begged me not to leave him, but I assured him that it would only be for a few moments and I would return and occupy the other berth."

He said he had been on the lower deck but a short time when he heard a splash followed by the cry "Man overboard!" and rushed to the rail where the *Thompson*'s engineer saluted him and said "Johnny, it's your friend."

Doran said he thought of jumping in the river to attempt a rescue but realized such an act would be useless and deadly—pitch dark, the river twelve feet deep at the levee and running at nine or ten miles an hour. He and others aboard the *Thompson* rushed ashore toward the *Guidon,* moored nearby, and heard two agonizing cries, one short, "the last prolonged of heart-rending description."

Crew members and townspeople searched along the shore through the night, and the next day cannons were fired, the river levee dragged. "The river below is dotted with innumerable small islands," Doran said, but the presence of hostile Indians downstream prevented a prolonged search.

Doran's story appeared in 1869, sixteen months after the tragedy; Wilbur Sanders's account appeared in the *Butte Inter Mountain* in March 1902, nearly thirty-five years afterward.

As has been seen, Sanders, called "Colonel" for his Civil War service, reached Montana territory in 1863 with his uncle, the future Gov. Sidney Edgerton, and proved to be a courageous young attorney. At the trial of George Ives, first of the road agents and murderers of the Henry Plummer gang to be tried for his crimes, Sanders was appointed by the miners' court to represent the territory. He successfully prosecuted Ives in Virginia City in December 1863, despite threats of reprisal by Plummer cohorts and, after the conviction, moved that the death sentence be carried out immediately, even though darkness had fallen. Ives was taken to a partially completed house selected for the execution and hanged that same evening.

Soon after this event, Sanders became one of the founding members of the Virginia City Vigilance Committee.

By the time of his death in 1905, Sanders had made his mark on Montana. He served in the territorial legislature for six years; ran for and was defeated four times—he was a Republican—for the office of Territorial Delegate to Congress but became one of the new state's first senators in 1889. He organized the Montana Bar Association in 1865 and was founder and president for twenty-five years of the Montana Historical Society.

Despite the benevolent, occasionally saccharine tone of Sanders's memoir, he and Meagher were not friends. The Irishman considered Sanders one of the recalcitrant old guard of Montana politics, and in a letter to Secretary of State Seward he called the attorney "the most vicious of my enemies, an unrelenting and unscrupulous extremist." For his part, Sanders considered Meagher a blatant opportunist interested in Montana statehood only if he could become its senator—a seat Sanders himself coveted (and eventually won).

Sanders added some significant details to the events of July 1, particularly on Meagher's state of mind, and despite the contrived amiability of his recollections, gave what appeared to be an honest account.

Sanders wrote that he was at Fort Benton on the day of the tragedy, had known the acting governor in Virginia City, and said he was a "most genial and interesting companion." After Meagher and his escort arrived, "The afternoon was delightfully spent in social visits. . . . General Meagher seemed at his best in a conversational way, but he resolutely and undeviatingly declined that form of hospitality [drinking] with which Fort Benton then abounded."

On that July 1, there were six or seven steamboats tied up at the river levee, "among them a somewhat cheap and rude old craft named the *G. A. Thompson*," which he described as a freight boat "but had cabins for perhaps a dozen persons."

Sanders said he met James Doran, the *Thompson* pilot, who "showed the general much deference and attention and wasted on him his not inconsiderable blarney" and learned that Doran had invited the general "to become his guest on his voyage down the river as far as Camp Cook."

At dusk, the attorney was seated in front of the I. G. Baker store when he heard a loud voice and saw that it came from the general himself, in the company of the other men of his escort:

> As the party came to the place where I was, and I had listened a moment, it was apparent that he [Meagher] was deranged. He was loudly demanding a revolver to defend himself against the citizens of Fort Benton who, in his disturbed mental condition declared were hostile to him.

Sanders and several others who greeted Meagher "sought to allay his fears and by all the means in our power to restore to sanity his disturbed mental condition."

He said, after Meagher's "nautical friend" (Doran) suggested that the general rest in his stateroom on the boat, "three or four of us accompanied him." Meagher, he said,

> was still insistent that the people of Fort Benton were hostile to him and was importunate for a revolver. He was induced to retire to his berth, which was on the starboard side of the boat next to the bank, and in the hope that he would sleep we all went on shore, seeking to allay his anxiety by getting him a revolver.

After he left Meagher, Sanders walked to the office of the Fort Benton Indian agency opposite and some fifty yards distant from the *Thompson,* and there he wrote and dispatched a letter for the outgoing mail to Helena. He said he was in the office perhaps thirty minutes when he heard the stagecoach agent in the office shout, "General Meagher is drowned!"

"I dropped my pen and hastened out the door and rushed across the gangplank and across the lower deck of the steamer," he recalled.

> There was a colored man, the barber I believe, who, replying to my interrogation, said a man had let himself down from the upper to the lower deck and jumped into the river and gone down stream. I immediately returned to land and ran down the river bank, repeating the alarm until I reached one of the lower steamers, the *Guidon,* I believe, where I went across the boat to the river side to watch for the general.

Meantime, he said, boats were lowered, and "many anxious eyes were peering into darkness at the swift rolling waters of the great river, that never seemed so wicked as then." But the river "gave no wished-for sight nor sound. The search was kept up all night and for two or three days thereafter, down to south of the Marias River." Sanders provided the interesting touch that "Loaves of bread were cast on the turbid waters in obedience to a belief that they would cause a drowned body to rise to the surface of the stream," and said a cannon was brought forward for the same purpose, "but the mighty river defied all our solicitudes and kept its treasure well."

Since there was no telegraph line out of Fort Benton, news of the incident was dispatched by a mail coach the next morning. Sanders said he wrote a letter to Mrs. Meagher, informing her of the sad events of the day.*

He summed up: "No person, as far as I know, save the colored man, saw General Meagher go into the river, and he related to me the circumstances I have told." Some of the officers on Meagher's staff told Sanders that their report would call the drowning an accident and asked the attorney not to mention any "mental aberration," to which he agreed: "I could see no imputation upon the general nor cause of humiliation to his friends," he wrote piously, "if eager devotion to his duties in hand had brought upon him so great an affliction."

As to the charges that Meagher was drunk when he went aboard the *Thompson,*

> Those who were with him on that last day of his life will join me, I know, in denying his death could be attributed to any convivial habit. I was with him most of the afternoon, and he was as resolutely abstemious as the most devout anchorite, and it is cruelly unjust to repeat such an accusation.

In a florid envoi to his recollections of the event, Sanders wrote of his old adversary,

---

*Elizabeth "Libby" Meagher accepted that her husband died accidentally. Soon after his death, she returned to New York and died there forty years later. She never remarried.

His form was manly, his manners cordial, his demeanor gracious, his conversations instructive, his wit kindly, his impulses generous, and I agree with Horace Greeley, who once said that General Meagher was one of the finest conversationalists and extemporaneous speakers he had ever known.

In May 1913, the *Missoula Sentinel* carried the headline, PLAINS MAN CONFESSES MURDER OF GOVERNOR MEAGHER. The story concerned an old man named Pat Miller (also known as Frank Diamond) who had collapsed after a drunken binge at Jack Thompson's Camas Saloon in the town of Plains. Believing he was dying, Miller had Thompson write down his confession. He said he had killed Governor Meagher forty-five years ago and had been paid eight thousand dollars by a group of vigilantes to do the deed. Thompson reported the confession to police, and Miller was taken to Missoula under arrest.

The *Sentinel,* depending upon hearsay information, claimed Miller was an old army scout who had lost an eye in Indian fighting and was an "intimate" of Montana vigilantes. He was said to have been living at Fort Benton, cutting wood for the steamboats and hauling freight for I. G. Baker at the time of the general's disappearance.

In a large-type, three-column box in the Missoula paper, Miller was quoted as saying, "I killed Thomas Francis Meagher near Cow Island on the Missouri River. Meagher was governor of Montana and the Vigilantes had to get rid of him, and Axel Potter gave me $8,000 for the job. I killed him on the steamboat and threw him in the river and swam ashore."

But when the old drunk recovered from his alcoholic attack, he repudiated the confession, saying, "All I know of Governor Meagher is what I have read. I never killed a man in my life and was never arrested, even for fighting."

Another newspaper identified Miller as a tall-tale artist who had been spinning the Meagher story in Montana barrooms for years.

Miller's hallucination might have died overnight but for the intervention of an eighty-seven-year-old Butte man who came forward to say that the tale "had a shade of truth." David McMillan Billingsley, known by the name Dave Mack, was a Tennessean who had ventured into Montana Territory in 1865 and found work as a drover and miner. He claimed in the *Anaconda Standard* a few days after the Miller revelation appeared that the "shade of truth" in the story was that Meagher had been murdered, but not by one man and not on the *Thompson*. The general, Mack said, had been taken from the boat by an assassination squad of ten vigilantes, hanged, and secretly buried.

The vigilantes "had a quarrel with Meagher" over the Daniels matter, Mack insisted. He said that after the Daniels hanging, the general had been sent a small length of rope and a warning: "It don't take a bigger rope to hang the governor of Montana than it does to hang a horse thief or a murderer." Following this, a "committee of ten" ordered Meagher to be killed, whereupon the ten went to Helena to find him, discovered that the governor had departed for Fort Benton, and followed him there.

Mack added the creative detail that there were two big dances being held at Benton the night of July 1, one "by white people, the other an Indian dance," and in the midst of the excitement, he said, "well, Meagher disappeared." He told the *Standard,* "Do I know where Meagher's body was buried? Yes, I was told the location by the men who buried him. They told me it was within a mile of Fort Benton, in a southwesterly direction."

The Mack story, in conjuring a posse of ten vigilantes invading the *G. A. Thompson*, trussing Meagher up and carrying him off the boat unwitnessed, matches Miller's yarn in credibility. Miller claimed to have personally killed Meagher, dropped the body in the water, then "swam ashore" from a boat already moored at the shore.

Somewhere in the stream, his manly form sleeps in as serene repose as it would in classic Arlington, but the jealous waters guard their secret well, and the rushing waves from unfound streams seem destined forever to be his monument and his grave." So wrote Wilbur Fisk Sanders in his mellow old age, with all ill will ancient, with friends and foes dead and dying, remembering a man with whom he might truly have formed a friendship had either made an effort.

Both men are remembered in Montana—Sanders for a lifetime of service to the territory and state, Meagher as a famous man who came to Montana and died there under mysterious circumstances. Historian Joseph Kinsey Howard wrote in 1943 that while "Dictator Meagher" was virtually forgotten in the state, "in Ireland they still sing of a gallant fighter from a fighting race who died on his way to get more guns to do more fighting."

In fact, Montanans do remember him, and correctly, with an imposing equestrian statue in front of the capitol building in Helena. There rides Gen. Thomas Francis Meagher, face to the enemy, heels dug in the stirrups of a straining horse, arm raised and bearing a great cavalry saber.

In Montana, as in Ireland and Van Diemen's Land, and on the battlefields of the Civil War, he is forever Meagher of the Sword.

UNDER THE WHITE SANDS

I'm not going to show the white feather. I'll go on.

—ALBERT JENNINGS FOUNTAIN
February 1, 1896

I

FOUNTAIN AND FALL

The Tularosa Basin of southwestern New Mexico is two hundred miles long by thirty miles wide and is hemmed by the Rio Grande on the west and timbered mountains to the east. This valley, running south from the lush greenery of the Cibola National Forest to the stark wastelands of the Jornada del Muerto—"Dead Man's Journey"—and the Chihuahuan desert of Old Mexico, is a place of startling contrasts. The mountains bordering and penetrating the valley have lovely Spanish names—the Sacramentos, the San Andrés Range, the Caballos, Sierra Oscuras, Fra Cristobals, Magdalenas, and Capitáns—with pines and thick grass on their slopes. The air is clean, the mornings crisp to bitter in winter, warm to brutally hot in summer. There are intermittent cloudy days, and often a foggy mantle on the mountains, but mostly the skies are blue and cloudless and rainless.

The Tularosa country is alluring, mysterious, and strangely beautiful, as untamed lands always are, but it is contrary country, Apache and Comanche country, much of it dry, forbidding, inimical to all but the hardiest forms of life. Off and on there have been springs and secretive waterways in these lands, giving rise to *tules*—cattail reeds—and the name *tularosa,* "a reedy place." But the reeds are rare; the valley is a place of parched earth and sand, alkaline flats, dunes and hummocks bristling with thorny mesquite and gray-green tumbleweed, flatlands where stands of yucca, greasewood, prickly pear, lechugilla, rabbit brush, pincushion cactus, ocotillo, and desert willow clutch the ground with tentative roots.

The primitive splendor of the Tularosa country can be seen in the Organ Mountains, jagged outcrops at the southern end of the valley, which some romantic thought resembled a colossal, heaven-reaching pipe organ. It can be seen in the north, up around the town of Carrizozo, in the black lava flows and jumbles of sharp volcanic cinders called the *malpaís*—"bad land." And it can be seen between these ancient formations in the 275 square miles of blinding, shifting, cresting, slumping, eastward-drifting sahara of gypsum known as the White Sands.

A shallow sea covered the whole valley 250 million years ago, and at the bottom of it gypsum-bearing marine deposits were thrust up into a immense dome; this when the Rocky Mountains were formed, about seventy million years ago. Then, a mere ten million years ago, the dome collapsed, creating the Tularosa Basin, while the sides of the dome formed the San Andrés and Sacramento mountain ranges that today ring the valley. Rains and snows dissolved the gypsum in the rocks and carried it into the basin, and with no river to carry it to the sea, the mineral, hydrous calcium sulphate was trapped.

The Sands are blinding white under the customarily cloudless, palette-defying blue skies of the Tularosa country. At twilight and daybreak, as the sun dips and rises behind the San Andrés range, the wind-sculpted dunes, with their spots of saltbush, yucca, and spear-grass, are bathed in an orangish light. At these times the tracks of the rare animal species that find sustenance enough to live there—two species of lizard and a tiny white mouse—are detectable.

But it is difficult to detect anything else, living or dead.

On a late-January morning in 1896, Col. Albert Jennings Fountain stepped out of his big adobe home in Las Cruces, New Mexico Territory, and ducked into the bitter wind to load up his buckboard. The three-horse team had been watered and fed and was blowing steam into the frosty air as he placed his dispatch box, leather grip, blankets, bag of food, small keg of water, Winchester rifle, and cartridge belt into the four-wheeler.

He was a tall, fit, blue-eyed man of substance and influence and was vainly aware of it. In his fifty-eight years, he had been a soldier of fortune, legislator in Texas and New Mexico, judge, frontier lawyer, newspaper editor, miner, Indian fighter, colonel of territorial militia (a title he preferred), and lately, nemesis of New Mexico's cattle thieves. It was in the latter capacity, as attorney for the Southeastern New Mexico Stock Association, that he was heading to the town of Lincoln, 150 miles northeast of Las Cruces.

Inside the house, Mariana Pérez Fountain, the colonel's wife of thirty-four years, bundled up their nine-year-old son Henry, youngest of their nine children, who was accompanying his father to court in Lincoln. Others of the family were there to see them off, including Albert Jr., married and with a family of his own, who came over from the mining town of Hillsboro the night before.

Little Henry, his father's favorite, was excited about the trip; Mariana had proposed he go along with his father for company. This idea would later be questioned, since the colonel had received death threats over his relentless pursuit of cattle thieves. Even so, her friends said Mariana probably figured that no assassin would harm her husband while a child was with him. Certainly not even an assassin would harm a child. "In the code of the West," as New Mexico historian Marc Simmons wrote, "the one unforgivable crime was harming women and children."

The two-day trip proved uneventful, but the streets and saloons of Lincoln were soon buzzing with news of Fountain's latest foray against the rustlers in Doña Ana and neighboring counties. With his satchel stuffed with depositions, affidavits, letters, and boilerplate-filled documents, he presented the Lincoln grand jury the evidence that resulted in thirty-two indictments. Seventeen of these were for crimes against members of the stock association Fountain was representing. Named in several of the indictments, for "larceny of cattle" and "defacing brands," were the prominent ranchman Oliver Lee and two of his cowboys, James R. Gililland and William H. McNew.

Colonel Fountain knew the grand-jury work was but a step toward a jury trial, and he was in no celebratory mood when he collected his son from the home of the friends they had roomed with, loaded the buckboard again, and departed Lincoln on January 30. He drove the eighteen miles to the Apache Agency at Mescalero, and there an Apache friend of the Fountains presented Henry a little pinto mare.

Father and son set out on the Tularosa road again on the morning of January 31, the pony tethered to the rear of the light rig. They were making good time, greeting some other travelers on the trail south, and stopping at wells along the route to stretch their legs, eat a cold snack, and feed and water their horses.

Before they reached the town of Tularosa, Colonel Fountain began to notice that some of the wayfarers on the road—two, sometimes three, men on horseback—appeared to be shadowing him.

They spent the night at the settlement of La Luz, just east of the White Sands. At Charley Meyer's general store, Fountain gave Henry a quarter to buy candy. The boy bought a dime's worth and pocketed the change.

On Saturday morning, February 1, 1896, the Fountains waited in Meyer's store for a local resident, Miss Fannie Stevenson, who had asked for a lift to Las Cruces. She was consumptive, and when she felt the cold wind blowing, thought twice about the open-air trip and sent word that she had decided against it.

The colonel, now wary and carrying his Winchester across his lap, snapped the reins over the team. They were in no hurry since they could easily make it home by dark, and so proceeded in a leisurely trot southwest into the valley on the Tularosa–Las Cruces road with the San Andrés Range on the right and the taller, snowcapped Sacramentos on the left.

At Luna's Well, a mail stagecoach station about midway between La Luz and the southern end of the White Sands, Fountain paid the customary twenty-five cents per head to feed and water his horses and talked to stage driver Antonio Rey. Rey later said the colonel seemed worried as he warmed his hands at the stove and asked Rey if he had seen three men riding by the station. Yes, the driver said, he had seen three horsemen in the distance and advised the colonel to stay at the station until morning before proceeding to Las Cruces.

According to Antonio Rey, Fountain said that the riders had been trailing him all day and, "If they're after me, they'll get me sooner or later and I'm not going to show the white feather. I'll go on."

With Henry wrapped in blankets in the seat next to him, Fountain drove the team on downtrail. The eastern edge of the White Sands was grown over with greasewood and mesquite brush, some of it, witnesses said, tall enough to hide a man on horseback while a horseman atop the sand ridges could be seen ten miles away.

In the mid to late afternoon of February 1, Fountain pulled his team to a stop at a point about three miles east of Chalk Hill, a small cactus- and brush-covered ridge with exposed white outcroppings at the southern end of the Sands. There he had a brief conversation with Saturnino Barilla, another mail stage driver whose route took him from Luna's Well to Las Cruces. Barilla pointed out three riders off in the distance and told Fountain that he should come back with him to Luna's Well. The colonel said he had to be in Silver City on Monday and that Henry was "under the weather" with a cold, so he chick-chicked his horses and drove on. "I'll push on and take my chances," he told Barilla.

It was very cold with a keen wind blowing as the buckboard bounced down the road toward Chalk Hill.

Albert Jennings Fountain, the son of a sea captain, his mother descended from a French Huguenot family, was born on Staten Island in 1838 and educated at Columbia College. In his footloose teens, he traveled to California and worked as a reporter on the *Sacramento Union*. From his own allusions on the matter, in about 1855, he was dispatched by his paper to Nicaragua to cover the filibustering expedition of the Tennessee adventurer William Walker. Fountain claimed to have been arrested in the Central American country and sentenced to death by firing squad. He said he managed to escape disguised as a woman and, after many adventures and perils, returned to California.

Back in Sacramento, he served as clerk and read law with a leading attorney and was admitted to the California bar in 1861. That year he enlisted in the First California Infantry Volunteers, commanded by Col. James H. Carleton, and advanced from private to lieutenant in the regiment as it marched from San Diego to Tucson and up to the Rio Grande in 1862 as part of the Union's occupation force in New Mexico and Arizona territories. He commanded New Mexican volunteer cavalry troops in skirmishes with Mimbreño and Chiricahua Apaches, was wounded at least once in the battles, and hospitalized at Fort Bliss in El Paso, Texas. After the end of the Civil War, Fountain, now married, made his home in El Paso, establishing a law practice and involving himself in Reconstruction-era Texas politics as a militant Republican party organizer.

For the rest of his life, politics, specifically Republican politics, animated Albert J. Fountain. In law, the military, newspaper work, the judicial bench, civic leadership—whatever he pursued—politics lay at its root. Politics consumed him.

In 1868, he was elected vice chairman of the Radical Republican convention at Corpus Christi and helped draft the party's platform. He won election as state senator from the El Paso district, then in 1870 became majority leader of the Texas Senate. He commuted by stagecoach the grueling seven hundred miles between his home and the capital, worked tirelessly on reconstruction programs and in reactivating the Texas Rangers, advocated woman's suffrage in Texas, and spoke eloquently for the incorporation of his adopted home of El Paso.

Depicting him as the "Political kingpin of West Texas," the *Austin State Journal* called Fountain the "dashing young Senator from El Paso" and said he was "a gentleman of great courtesy and demeanor . . . well fitted by his gentlemanly characteristics for any society."

His courtesy and gentility did not mean he could be trifled with, as a political enemy named Frank Williams discovered in December 1870, when he called Fountain a "son of a bitch" in Ben Dowell's Saloon in El Paso. Fountain warned the man to "curb his tongue," and when Williams continued his rant, the colonel palmed a derringer in one hand and with the other swung his cane. Williams got off three shots then ran out the door. Wounded in his arm and from a bullet that grazed his head (the third shot penetrated five letters and a watch inside his coat), Fountain and a friend ran into the street, yelling for help. Williams, now running toward his rooming house, turned toward his pursuers and fired a double-barreled shotgun, killing Fountain's friend. The colonel coolly leveled his derringer and shot Williams, knocking the man off his feet. In the melee, another of Fountain's allies rushed forward and fired a coup de grâce shot into Williams's head, killing him instantly.

Fountain moved to La Mesilla, New Mexico Territory, forty miles north of El Paso, in 1874. There, on the east bank of the Rio Grande, he built a fine adobe home just twenty miles from the Organ Mountain foothills. He established a law practice, joined the Masons, and threw himself into a campaign to revive the county's moribund Republican Party.

The territory had never experienced a man so indefatigably ambitious.

In 1877, he launched the weekly *Mesilla Valley Independent,* with a Spanish-language edition, and campaigned against the comfortable corrupters of the clique-ridden legislature in Santa Fé.

He organized a *posse comitatus* of militiamen to drive horse and cattle thieves from the Mesilla Valley.

He organized the "Mesilla Scouts" in 1879 and joined the campaign against a band of Mimbreño Apaches under Chief Victorio, protégé of the greatest of all Apache generals, Mangas Coloradas. Victorio's raiders had attacked the mining settlements of Hillsboro and Lake Valley, killing several settlers.

In the spring of 1881, Fountain was appointed as defense attorney for Henry McCarty, known by the alias William "Billy the Kid" Bonney, when the outlaw was tried in a makeshift courtroom in La Mesilla for several murders. Despite Fountain's spirited efforts, the Kid was convicted, delivered to the custody of Lincoln County sheriff Pat Garrett, and sentenced to hang on May 13, 1881.

By the time Fountain moved his family to the frontier town of Las Cruces in 1885, he had built a reputation as the finest trial attorney and most powerful Republican politician in southern New Mexico. He was a skilled orator, handsome, impeccably groomed, and colorful, in court often wearing a gold-braided military uniform, complete with a saber banging against his leg. He seemed unstoppable. In November 1888, he was elected to a seat in the Territorial Legislature, later became Speaker of the House and the loudest voice in Santa Fé clamoring for New Mexico statehood.

Political power being both attractive and repellent, he collected enemies. His outspoken newspaper columns lambasting the legislature he now served, his campaigns against the rampant, organized cattle-rustling activities of certain southern ranchmen, and his unsettling radical Republican ideas created a vocal anti-Fountain faction. Among these foes none was more implacable in his hostility to the upstart Fountain than another Albert, another upstart, Albert Bacon Fall, the very man Fountain had defeated for the Doña Ana seat in the legislature.

Born in Kentucky in 1861, Fall had drifted to Texas as a young man and married Emma Morgan, the daughter of a Texas lawyer. Soon after their marriage, he took his bride to New Mexico and labored by day as a mucker in the silver mines in the Black Range foothills while reading law books at night. In 1887, he and Emma and their two children moved to Las Cruces, where he opened a real estate office and legal practice.

The two Alberts were at loggerheads from the start. Fall, as fierce a Democrat as Fountain was a Republican, began organizing his beleaguered party in Doña Ana County and, as Fountain had done in Las Mesilla, launched a newspaper, the *Independent Democrat,* to further his party's aims. He also rashly met Fountain at the polls when Fall ran for the Doña Ana County seat in the legislature, and lost the November 1888 election— but by the slim margin of forty-two votes out of two thousand cast.

If they met during the campaign, they were probably cordial. They had some things in common: both were eloquent, gentlemanly when the occasion called for it, but ruthless when it better served. They were both dynamic, vigorous men, and Fountain, twenty-three years older, may have seen something of his own youthful restlessness, drive, and ambition in Fall—and something of his own lust for party politics.

But they were mortal political enemies, and for eight years walked across each other's shadow.

Fall lost his maiden political race but helped scuttle Fountain's beloved cause, the statehood movement, as well as Fountain's brief tenure as territorial legislator. In October 1890, in a bitterly fought election, the state constitution and a bid to join the Union were defeated soundly. Fall and his party campaigned against them on a premise scary to the small rancher and farmer of the territory: that statehood would place their land titles in jeopardy.

In that same election, Fall and Fountain squared off again for the legislature, and this time Fall won the seat, despite the efforts of the Republican press, which called him "a pygmy and a baby beside Colonel Fountain." The paper also claimed that the election was crooked, fortified with Democrat whiskey and won by ballot-box stuffing.

Fall was reelected in 1892, and the next year he won an appointment as judge of the three-county Third Judicial District. This political plum elicited from Colonel Fountain a volley of frontier slander in which he described Fall as "an absconding debtor from Texas" who had defrauded clients of money, a "ward politician," a tyrant, vindictive toward his enemies and utterly unfit for the bench.

The tyrant and debtor took office anyway, and among his first acts was to appoint some cronies, men who had served as his political bodyguard, as deputy U.S. marshals. These men, all Texans and all suspected cattle rustlers, were Oliver Milton Lee, James Gililland, and William McNew.

Lee was a native of Buffalo Gap (a settlement south of Abilene, Texas) who migrated to New Mexico in 1884, when he was nineteen, in search of open range country. He set up his first cattle spread on the edge of Dog Canyon in the western slopes of the Sacramento Mountains in Doña Ana County, and soon had other outfits in the Sacramentos and the San Augustín plains west of Las Cruces. He was a handsome, steely-eyed cowman with a brushy soup-strainer mustache. A staunch Democrat, among Albert Fall's closest confidants, he was a bad man to cross. His rancher neighbor and friend Eugene Manlove Rhodes, later the acclaimed author of *Pasó por Aqui* and other classic New Mexico fiction, claimed Lee had killed at least eight men while carving out his cattle kingdom.

William Henry "Bill" McNew and James Robert "Jim" Gililland were leathery, grim-faced nondescripts, stamped from the same template that produced a thousand other Bills and Jims slapping sweat and dirt off their hats on remote Southwestern cow outfits. Each had taken up land near Oliver Lee's, and each worked more for Lee than for themselves. Gililland stood out in a crowd: He was about six feet six inches tall, even taller than his forthcoming nemesis, Pat Garrett. He and McNew were handy with guns and were also said to be artists with the "running iron"—the iron rod used by rustlers to change or deface brands.

Three years after Lee, Gililland and McNew were appointed deputy marshals. All three were among those indicted for cattle rustling after Albert J. Fountain—who came up to Lincoln from Las Cruces with his young son Henry—presented the evidence against them.

While the colonel's territory-wide political influence dimmed and Fall's brightened, Fountain did not retreat quietly when he came home from Santa Fé after his defeat in 1890. He served as chief investigator and prosecutor for the Southeastern New Mexico Stock Growers' Association and wrote, spoke, lobbied, and fought for new laws and stronger enforcement of existing ones to protect stockmen from rustlers. Nor did he fail to point out that his Democratic opponent, Albert B. Fall, had gathered around him a number of dubious characters, Oliver Lee chief among them, suspected of thieving cattle from their neighbors.

The two Alberts were now embarked on a two-year collision course.

In the 1894 territorial legislative race, Fountain's oldest son, Albert Jr., ran against Fall's handpicked candidate and won election by two hundred votes. Fall was furious, engineered a recount and stationed Oliver Lee and other armed cohorts at the ballot boxes. The recount overturned the vote in favor of the Democratic candidate, but the elder Fountain did not retreat. He gathered evidence against Fall's misuse of his powers as district judge and fired off letters, affidavits, and other documents to the Cleveland administration in Washington and forced Fall's resignation in January 1895. Soon after, Lee, McNew, and Gililland lost their deputy marshal commissions.

The colonel persevered. He aimed next at the Doña Ana County sheriff's office, won, he said in district court, by fraud and coercion by Albert Fall's armed lackeys. Fall, equally belligerent, fought the suit and was able to frustrate Fountain's effort until March 1896—by which time the colonel was no longer a problem.

A final Fountain–Fall clash occurred on September 14, 1895, when Fall and his brother-in-law Joe Morgan engaged in a gunfight on a Las Cruces street with a Fountain associate named Ben Williams. Williams and Morgan fell wounded in the fight, and Fall and Morgan were arrested. Fall claimed that his life had been threatened, that assassins were lurking in the town, waiting to ambush him, and that only faithful friends such as Joe Morgan were keeping him alive. He said that Albert J. Fountain had hired Ben Williams to kill him.

Fall, a slippery lawyer with a long run of luck, got Morgan off and escaped indictment himself, as did Fountain and Williams, who had been charged with assault with intent to murder.

Four months after this incident, Fountain, his eight-year-old son Henry accompanying him, drove his buckboard from Las Cruces to Lincoln, there winning grand-jury indictments for "larceny of cattle" and "defacing brands" against Albert Bacon Fall's associates Oliver Lee, Bill McNew, and Jim Gililland.

II

VANISHED

Mariana Pérez Fountain expected her husband and son Henry home in the evening of Saturday, February 1, 1896, and waited to hear the snorting horse team and the crunch of the big buckboard wheels as it made its way up to the front of their adobe in Las Cruces. As the evening wore on with no sign of Albert or Henry, she fretted and walked the floor. Her husband had enemies . . . there were those death threats . . . still, no one would do him harm with an eight-year-old boy at his side. He was probably delayed with legal business in Lincoln.

She waited with growing fear all day Sunday, her family gathered around her. Then, at sundown, stage driver Saturnino Barilla came to the house and asked if the colonel had reached home. He explained that he had last seen his friend and the boy a short distance from Chalk Hill on Saturday afternoon, only a few hours' drive from Las Cruces. Barilla said he was worried because the colonel had been followed by three riders. He said he tried to talk him into returning to Luna's Well but that the colonel had said, "I'll push on and take my chances."

Upon hearing this, Mariana fainted, but Barilla's news galvanized Fountain's sons, Albert Jr. and Jack, and together with some neighboring friends, they gathered up a search party and rode out to San Augustín Pass and down the long slope to Chalk Hill, where they made camp. Barilla sounded the alarm in Las Cruces, and within hours a posse rode out for Chalk Hill to camp with the Fountain sons and await daybreak.

At first light on Monday, February 3, the searchers found the tracks of three horses and followed them up an old road toward the Jarilla Mountains where, about twelve miles east of Chalk Hill, they came upon the colonel's buckboard. His cartridge belt lay on the seat, his cravat was tangled in the spokes of a wheel, his dispatch box had been opened and its papers scattered. There were pieces of harness lying around, a broken whiskey bottle, tracks of a child's shoe, the imprint of blanket on the sand. Everything else was missing: Fountain's Winchester and cartridges, the horses, water, food, spare clothing. No other traces of the colonel and his son were found.

The volunteers followed five sets of horse tracks toward the mountains and found a camp where a big fire had been built. They found cans, sticks used to cook meat, boot tracks, cigarette papers. Not far from the camp there were pony tracks headed north (Henry's gift mare was later found to have wandered back to Luna's Well), hoofprints of a heavily laden horse bearing south, and others of horses headed for Dog Canyon, location of one of Oliver Lee's ranches.

That evening the posse from Las Cruces arrived, led by Maj. William Henry Harrison Llewellyn, a prominent lawyer and former Mescalero Indian agent. He was satisfied that the trail led east to Wildy Well, an Oliver Lee ranch, and that cattle had been driven over the tracks to deface them.

Eight days later, another posse, led by Fountain's friend Eugene Van Patten, rode out, "fully armed and provisioned," that "will not return until they discover the living or dead bodies of Colonel Fountain and his son," a Las Cruces newspaper reported.

Van Patten gathered some depressing news from a La Luz settler named John Meadows, who said he had done some trailing on his own. This desert veteran found a pool of blood, which he described as "twice or three times as large as a spittoon," and several cartridge shells at a place where a buckboard stood, hidden in tall brush near Chalk Hill. He said he found blood sprayed all around, "And I found fifteen cents, a nickel and a dime," this being the change Charley Meyer had given Henry at Meyer's store in La Luz. The coins were later said to have been tied in a blood-soaked handkerchief.

After meeting with the Las Cruces posse, Meadows heard Llewellyn say that Colonel Fountain had been "killed by Oliver Lee or his men." Meadows openly disagreed with this rash judgment but Llewellyn hired him anyway to continue searching the Chalk Hill area. He spent several days following horse trails, one of a heavily loaded animal, another of a pony, a trail that led to Lee's ranch at Wildy Well, and another that disappeared in the dust, where a herd of cows had crossed it.

Meadows offered a theory on what might have happened to the Fountains: "East of the White Sands, in that big lava bed, is an old crater," he said. "Once I dropped a heavy stone into it, as heavy as I could lift, and I never did hear it strike bottom. A body could've been dropped in there and it never could've been found."

Van Patten's party pushed on and found a white horse, one of the colonel's buckboard team, the animal jaded, dried blood on its flanks, its back ulcered from carrying a heaven burden.

On February 14, two weeks after the Fountains were last seen, Oliver Lee rode into Las Cruces, stopped at the sheriff's office, and said he had heard there were charges against him. When told there were none, he rode away.

News of the Fountains' disappearance swirled through the territory like a desert dust devil. MURDER! in huge type was bannered on page one of the *Albuquerque Daily Citizen* on February 4. The smaller lines beneath the heading announced: "Col. Fountain of Las Cruces is missing. He was probably murdered by cattle thieves." The *Rio Grande Republican*, also on February 4, issued an extra edition headlined WANTED—ONE JUDGE LYNCH and stated, "Although many friends hope against fate for the return of an honored friend while others search the plains for his living or dead body . . . criminals . . . have undoubtedly murdered an honored and respected citizen and an innocent child." The paper repeatedly characterized the disappearances as "murder," and the *Santa Fé New Mexican* joined in, calling for the discovery and "adequate punishment of the cruel and cowardly perpetrators of this awful crime."

Republicans accepted Major Llewellyn's theory that Oliver Lee was the culprit, with his cowboys McNew and Gililland as the probable assassins.

Democrats said the whole thing was a frame-up to slander and ruin the career of Albert Bacon Fall.

Fall himself went on record: "Fountain might have been killed, as he had many enemies, but there is no proof that a murder has been committed," he said. He posted stories in his *Independent Democrat* that Fountain and his son had been sighted as far away as Chicago, Saint Louis, San Francisco, and Mexico City. The paper quoted Fall supporters offering ludicrous theorizing: that Fountain has "voluntarily absented himself" because he was tired of supporting his big family, that he probably took his favorite son and rode into Mexico where "he spoke the language like a native."

New Mexico Gov. William T. Thornton came down to Las Cruces from Santa Fé and announced a reward for the solution to the disappearances and called upon citizens to aid the authorities. A total of twenty thousand dollars in reward money was accumulated from the governor's office, stock growers' associations, Doña Ana County commissioners, and various Masonic Lodges.

Enter Pat Garrett.

Despite the animosity toward him held in many quarters of New Mexico Territory, Patrick Floyd Jarvis Garrett was called out of retirement. Governor Thornton invited the ex-lawman to come to Santa Fé and take a job as private investigator, at three hundred dollars a month, to look into the Fountain case. Garrett, then scratching a meager living on his farm in Uvalde County, Texas, said yes, no doubt delighted to escape the drudgery of his patch of hardscrabble land and houseful of children.

Born in 1850 in Alabama and raised in Louisiana, Garrett had been a trail driver, a buffalo-hide skinner out of Fort Griffin, Texas, and had tried hog farming at Fort Sumner, New Mexico, before he put on the badge. He married Apolinaria Gutiérrez in 1880 and that year was elected sheriff of Lincoln County, then in the throes of a bloody range conflict known as the Lincoln County War. Garrett made a niche for himself in Southwestern history by forcing the surrender of a minor but notorious figure in the war, Billy "the Kid" McCarty, also known as William Bonney, and some of his compatriots. After Bonney killed two deputies and escaped from the Lincoln jail, Garrett trailed him to Pete Maxwell's ranch house at Fort Sumner and on July 14, 1881, killed the twenty-one-year-old outlaw.

Garrett and a clumsy ghostwriter produced a book, *The Authentic Life of Billy the Kid,* in 1882, but the book, neither authentic nor much in the way of a "life," failed financially, and the lawman, who decided not to stand for reelection, left the territory. He chased rustlers in the Texas Panhandle for a time then moved on to Uvalde where he lived and farmed quietly until hired by Governor Thornton.

Garrett arrived in Santa Fé on March 3, 1896, and after a conference with the governor, moved on to Las Cruces, where he instantly centered his Fountain investigation on Albert B. Fall and Fall's disciples, Lee, Gililland, and McNew. The former deputies, Garrett was told, were walking around town armed and threatening people not to talk about the Fountain case.

At the same time he hired Garrett, Governor Thornton contacted the Denver office of the renowned Pinkerton National Detective Agency and made arrangements for an "operative" to be assigned to the case. When the Pinkerton agent, J. C. Fraser, arrived in Santa Fé, Thornton made it clear—as he had to Garrett—that the chief suspects in the crime were Lee, McNew, and Gililland, whom he called the "gang of cattle thieves." He also named Albert B. Fall as "the attorney for these cattle thieves."

Fraser and Garrett met in Las Cruces but did not collaborate. Garrett resented outside help and Fraser, a shrewd and thorough detective, probably perceived that attitude in the once-acclaimed lawman and went his own way. He questioned Fall, found him friendly and anxious to help and quite candid about the enmity between himself and Albert Jennings Fountain. Fall said he was at Sunol, a gold camp a few miles south of Chalk Hill at the time the Fountains vanished, and had no information on their alleged murder. Nor did Oliver Lee and the others Fraser interrogated. The Pinkerton man determined that Lee and others he questioned were hiding the truth of their whereabouts on the day of the disappearances.

Fraser continued his investigation through May 1896, then returned to Denver. "I feel satisfied that this entire matter will come home to Oliver Lee," the operative wrote in his report. He said he was satisfied that Albert Fall was not actually present at Chalk Hill on February 1, but he remained unconvinced by Fall's claim that he took no part in the conspiracy.

Garrett agreed with most of Fraser's findings. From the outset, he had no other suspects than Fall, Lee, and company. So confident was he in their guilt, he questioned none of them and followed no other leads.

The territorial balloting in the fall of 1896 revived the fading Fountain investigation. Maj. W. H. H. Llewellyn, one of the original posse leaders who followed trails out of Chalk Hill, was elected to the Territorial House, Albert B. Fall to the State Council, Oliver Lee as delegate to the Democratic Party Convention, and Pat Garrett, running as an Independent Democrat, won his race for the office of sheriff of Doña Ana County.

Even more important to the Fountain case was the election of Saint Louis–born Miguel Antonio Otero II, a Republican, as governor of New Mexico Territory. Following his inauguration, this dynamic lawyer's first act was to send a message south from Santa Fé that he expected a grand jury to be convened and the Fountain case to be pursued vigorously.

Even so, a year passed before any significant development in the case surfaced. A grand jury did convene, in March 1898, but adjourned without issuing indictments. Garrett then gathered his fat file of affidavits and on April 3 appeared before a district court judge asking for bench warrants for the arrests of Lee, McNew, Gililland, and another of Lee's employees, Bill Carr. The sheriff's deposition stated that he could show that these men "are the parties who murdered Colonel Albert J. Fountain and his son, Henry Fountain."

McNew and Carr were the first to be arrested and jailed in Las Cruces. Carr was released for lack of evidence, but McNew remained behind bars while Garrett and his deputies searched for Lee and Gililland. Lee now made himself scarce, explaining that if Pat Garrett were to arrest him, "he will shoot me in the back . . . and will claim it was self defense."

On July 11, two of his deputies rode up to Garrett's ranch a few miles north of San Augustín Pass to tell him they had spotted Lee and Gililland heading toward Lee's place at Wildy Well, a few miles east of the Jarilla foothills. The sheriff gathered four deputies, mounted up, and led them forty miles east, arriving at

Lee's spread at daybreak on the twelfth. They tied their horses some distance away and walked toward the flat-roofed ranch house, guns drawn, each man edgy in the gray dawn silence. The adobe house had a wagon shed next to it. There were a couple of other lean-tos, a corral with two horses inside, ears up and wide-eyed, and a big water tank on squared supports, its windmill groaning in the morning breeze.

As the lawmen advanced into the Lee compound, Garrett saw a man signaling toward the roof and concluded that Lee and perhaps Gililland were up there. He stationed two men under the water tank while he and Deputy Kent Kearney, a cowboy and former schoolteacher from La Luz, set out to climb to the roof from the wagon shed. What happened next remains disputed, but it appears that Lee and Gililland were sleeping atop the house when Kearney reached the roof parapet, followed by Garrett, who yelled to the fugitives to throw up their hands. Kearney may have seen, or imagined, one of the men reaching for a gun, and so fired a shot in their general direction. Oliver Lee then grabbed his rifle and shot Kearney off the roof, Garrett falling with him, unharmed. Gililland now had his Winchester in hand and in concert with Lee opened fire on the sheriff and his deputies below, their bullets hitting Kearney again, as well as holing the water tower and drenching the men crouched beneath it.

"You're a hell of a lot of fellows," Lee shouted, "to order a man to throw up his hands and shoot at the same time."

After some loud conversation, Lee said he would come in to Las Cruces and surrender if Garrett would promise to fix bail for him until he had to appear in court. He did not trust Garrett or his deputies to escort him to town.

Deputy Kent Kearney died of his wounds the next day, and Lee and Gililland were charged with his murder as well as for the Fountain killings. However, while the grand jury was handing down its indictments, sans the Kearney killings, which was set aside for a separate trial, the two accused went "on the dodge" and evaded capture. As Southwestern historian C. L. Sonnichsen wrote in his *Tularosa,* the two "prowled the mountains and deserts of their homeland, determined not to give up unless they were sure of an even break."

Albert Fall was also temporarily absent, departing Dona Aña County as a captain of New Mexico volunteers for the Spanish-American War. He hoped to join Theodore Roosevelt's "Rough Rider" regiment in Cuba, as had Maj. W. H. H. Llewellyn, but the war ended too quickly. Fall got no farther than Fort Whipple, Arizona, where he was mustered out after seven months' service. He returned to New Mexico on the eve of the trial of the accused Fountain murderers.

Meantime, Lee and Gililland, who had friends willing to hide them, kept on the move in the immense, thinly populated territory and managed to evade Garrett and his deputies for eight months. They spent time at a ranch in the Jornada del Muerto, a two-day ride north of Las Cruces, and at another in the San Andrés foothills owned by Eugene Manlove Rhodes, who later moved east, gave up cowboying, and became one of the Southwest's greatest authors. Rhodes had an affinity for desperadoes: he had once harbored Thomas E. "Black Jack" Ketchum, a train robber and killer who, in 1901, was beheaded in a botched hanging at Clayton, a town in the far northeast corner of the territory.

After spending time in San Antonio, Texas, and getting married there, Lee returned to the Tularosa Valley early in 1899, in time to take advantage of some clever gerrymandering that had taken place in his absence. A new county had been created out of the eastern half of Doña Aña County and the White Sands, site of the Fountain disappearance (by now, as most called the case, the Fountain *murders*) fell within it. Albert Fall had a hand in promoting the idea and Gov. Miguel Otero liked it, especially since it would be named for him. To nobody's surprise, George Curry, a friend of Oliver Lee's, was appointed the first sheriff of Otero County.

This slippery piece of geographical engineering meant that the fugitives could surrender to a law officer other than Pat Garrett. That, and the provision that they would not be incarcerated in the Dona Aña County jail, they insisted on in a letter to Governor Otero. He agreed to the demands, as did District Judge Frank Wilson Parker in Las Cruces.

On March 13, 1899, Oliver Lee and Jim Gililland rode a train south from Santa Fé to Las Cruces and surrendered at Judge Parker's house. Sheriff Curry took them and Bill McNew into custody and escorted them to the jail in Socorro, a town on the southern edge of the Jornado del Muerto, to await trial.

III

JUSTICE

The murder charges against the three men were grounded in the flimsiest of circumstantial evidence, principally the tracks leading from the Chalk Hill area toward Oliver Lee's Wildy Well ranch, and the well-known rancor between Colonel Fountain, Lee, and his cohorts. There were no corpus delicti and little else to tie the defendants to the Fountains' disappearance.

In April 1899, Judge Parker convened his court in Silver City and dismissed the charges against Bill McNew for lack of evidence—a ruling the prosecutors did not pursue, since they were determined to concentrate on convicting Lee and Gililland. In addition, two of the three indictments against these defendants were inexplicably dropped, leaving a single charge: the murder of *Henry* Fountain on or about February 1, 1896. Colonel Fountain's murder was thus submerged as the Code of the West bobbed to the surface—it was far worse to harm a woman or a child than to kill a man.

While Parker wanted to hear the case in Las Cruces, the defense attorneys argued successfully that Dona Aña County was Fountain country and therefore prejudicial. Otero County, considered Oliver Lee country, was also eliminated. Finally, all agreed on a change of venue to Hillsboro, a mining town with a population of two hundred on the eastern slope of the Black Ranges.

The trial opened on May 26, 1899, with Judge Parker announcing, "Gentlemen coming into court will kindly leave their guns outside." Despite the absence of rail service to the town, Hillsboro's population had doubled by opening day with the visitors lodging at Sadie Orchard's amusingly named Ocean Grove Hotel and, when the rooms ran out, bivouacking under the trees. Reporters from El Paso, Albuquerque, and Santa Fé came in to cover the proceedings; the Associated Press and the Hearst papers sent correspondents. Ninety witnesses had been summoned, although most failed to show up. Sierra County sheriff Max Kahler and his deputies kept the prisoners well guarded in Hillsboro's adobe *calabozo* while Fountain and Lee partisans roamed the town. There was speculation that the Lee partisans might try to spring their friend; there was speculation that the Fountain people might try to lynch him.

District Attorney Richmond P. Barnes of Silver City led the prosecution, assisted by two prominent Republicans: William B. Childers of Albuquerque and Thomas Benton Catron of Santa Fé, later a United States Senator and another territorial worthy to have a county named after him. Both volunteered to serve the prosecution without pay.

Defending Lee and Gililland were Democrats Harvey B. Fergusson of Albuquerque, Harry Dougherty of Socorro, and Albert Bacon Fall of Las Cruces. As to who would lead the defense, the smart money fell on Fall.

Three days were occupied in seating a jury, then the indictments were read, and when it became clear that Lee and Gililland were to be tried solely for the murder of Henry Fountain,

Lee whispered to his lawyer, "My God, Fergusson, they are accusing me of the murder of the child!"

The prosecution fared poorly from the first day of the proceedings. Fifteen of its witnesses failed to appear, and many of the others offered confusing and unconvincing testimony.

The territory's star witness, a cowboy named Jack Maxwell, whose spread was near Lee's Dog Canyon ranch, had earlier claimed to have been staying at Lee's place on February 1, 1896. He said Lee, Gililland, and McNew rode into Dog Canyon a few hours after the Fountains went missing and that the three were on fagged horses, were worn out, looked nervous, and slept outside in the brush as if on lookout. Maxwell had been located with some difficulty but proved to be a worthless witness who further diluted his already weak story by saying he had "forgotten" a good many of the details.

Another prosecution witness was Thomas Branigan, an old Indian campaigner and scout, who said on the stand that he had measured a boot track near the place where the Fountain assailants had made a campfire and found an identical track on the roof of Oliver Lee's adobe house at Wildy Well. The track, he said, matched Bill McNew's boot. But McNew was not being prosecuted, and when he was asked for copies of the bootprints, Branigan said he had lost them.

The territory also called a Dr. Francis Crosson, said to be from "somewhere back East," who testified that the blood found at the scene was human blood. This intrinsically useless fact was battered down when Fall cross-examined and forced Crosson to admit that he couldn't be positive that it wasn't horse, coyote, or rabbit blood, he just *thought* the blood was human in origin. (The *Albuquerque Daily Citizen* also revealed that the physician wasn't from "back East" at all, but from Albuquerque.)

Much was expected of Pat Garrett's testimony, but it, too, fell flat, too heavily tinged by his hatred of Fall, Lee, and the others. At one point on cross-examination, Fall asked about Garrett's advent as a hired detective on the Fountain case.

FALL: What was the condition of affairs when you went to Las Cruces?

GARRETT: Oh, you fellows had been shooting at one another and cutting up.

FALL: What fellows?

GARRETT: You, Lee, and others.

FALL: Why did you wait two years to procure a warrant for the arrest of Lee and Gililland?

GARRETT: You had too much control of the courts. It was wise to wait.

When the prosecution rested, Fall and the other defense lawyers asked for a verdict of not guilty on the ground that in the absence of a corpse, no murder could be proved. After Judge Parker denied the motion, the defense opened its case by stating that if necessary they could prove that Colonel Fountain was living after the date of his alleged murder—a naked lie stated for the jury's benefit—and would prove that the defendants were at least sixty miles away from the scene of the alleged murders when they were alleged to have occurred. Fall and company then proceeded to call a string of witnesses, nine men and Lee's sunbonneted mother, all of whom testified that Oliver was at home on the fateful Saturday when Colonel Fountain and his son were alleged to have met foul play. Lee himself took the stand and told his story, that he was working in his ranch when the crimes were said to have taken place, that he did not know of them for several days, and that when he learned of them and found out that he was suspected of complicity in them, he rode to Las Cruces and offered to surrender. Later, he said, he feared mob violence in Fountain's Dona Aña County and refused to give himself up.

The territory's closing arguments failed to bolster their case. District Attorney Barnes spoke too long and too flowery, "quoted from the *Pickwick Papers,* and whipped up soaring metaphors," as historian C. L. Sonnichsen put it. Barnes referred to Mrs. Lee's testimony as a mother's gift to her son: "She laid a wreath of maternal duty on the altar of maternal love." Such words, and quoting Dickens, were not endearing to the bushy-bearded and horny-handed miners who made up the jury.

The defense, on the other hand, conducted a brilliant closing. Fergusson graciously ended his remarks by saying, "Colonel Fountain, who was the soul of honor, would not have lent himself to such methods as have been used to make a case against these two young men." Albert Fall was not so amiable, stating that the case was a political vendetta against his clients and himself. He spoke of "this plot for the persecution of Oliver Lee . . . a conspiracy to send an innocent man to the gallows."

He demanded a verdict of first-degree murder or acquittal, addressing the jury in his low, vibrant, and persuasive oratorical style: "I ask for no mantle of charity for these men, I desire no vindication. I ask simply stern justice. If the evidence in this case convinces you that these men murdered little Henry Fountain, you must convict. If you are not convinced, turn them loose. There is no alternative."

Judge Parker, however, gave the jury the choices of first-, second-, or third-degree murder, or not guilty.

At 11:30 p.m. on June 12, after eighteen days of testimony, the case was handed to the jury. *Eight minutes later* the jury returned with its verdict: "Not guilty" for both Lee and Gililland.

Judge Parker ordered the defendants to be held over for the September term of court to stand trial for the killing of Deputy Kearney at Wildly Well on July 12, 1898, but the indictment was later dismissed.

Lee and Gililland were free men.

The Fountains were certainly dead, beyond question murdered, more than likely at dusk on February 1, 1896, close to the Chalk Hill landmark at the southern end of the White Sands on what is today the Army's White Sands Missile Range.

Searches have gone on periodically for 107 years. There was

even speculation that Pat Garrett bought a ranch in the San Andrés Mountains, only twenty miles from Chalk Hill, so he could continue searching for the bodies and collect the twenty thousand dollars in reward money.

But no remains of the Fountains, father or son, have ever been found.

Who killed them?

George Curry, the Otero County sheriff at the time of the Hillsboro trial, said in his autobiography that he suspected a small-time rancher and cowboy named José Chávez y Chávez, who had expressed his hatred of Fountain after the colonel prosecuted him as a rustler. Chávez was acquitted but told Curry, "I will get that scoundrel Fountain if I have to hang for it." Aside from a report that the night before the murders Chávez had been spotted at Luna's Well, where Fountain watered and fed his buckboard team, he was not questioned, and Curry never saw him again.

Train robber "Black Jack" Ketchum was named as the Fountains' killer in a 1949 report in the *Albuquerque Tribune*. The story that Ketchum cold-bloodedly murdered the colonel and his son was told third-hand to a *Tribune* reporter and, while sensational for moment, quickly expired.

There were other culprits named, but eventually the matter circled back to Oliver Lee, Jim Gililland, and less often, to Bill McNew, with Albert Fall as a sort of aloof but deeply involved puppet-master.

Fall's career continued upward after the Hillsboro Trial. He bought a fine, established ranch at Three Rivers in Lincoln County and, while keeping his New Mexico residency, built a splendid redbrick house on a hilltop north of downtown El Paso and opened a law office. There he welcomed the many distinguished and monied clients who made him wealthy.

His ambition ruled him, and even the vastness of New Mexico, where he ruled as a political king and kingmaker, could not contain him. He quit the Democratic party in 1902 (his friend Oliver Lee joined him), sensing that the Republicans were on the rise and might send him to Washington. He waited, serving as territorial attorney general and, in 1912, one of the first United States Senators representing the new state of New Mexico. He served nine years in the Senate, until 1921, when President Warren Harding selected him as Secretary of the Interior.

After two years, Fall resigned the office, citing failing health and finances as his reasons for returning to private life. He returned to Washington under subpoena when a congressional investigation revealed that he had leased government oil lands at Teapot Dome, Wyoming, and Elk Hills, California, to two business associates and that he had accepted a hundred-thousand-dollar payoff from one of them.

At his trial for bribery in Washington, Fall sat at the defense table in a wheelchair, wrapped in blankets, frail and trapped but denying he had taken money for the oil leases.

He was found guilty and was permitted to serve his sentence in the Santa Fé penitentiary. He spent six months behind bars, most of it in the prison hospital, and was released in May 1932. He lost his beloved Three Rivers ranch to creditors and spent the rest of his life as an invalid, moving from one hospital to another. He was reading Blackstone's *Commentaries* when he died in an El Paso hospital in November 1944, at the age of eighty-three.

George Curry, friendly with Oliver Lee, was convinced that Lee took no part in the murders. This view was also expressed by Albuquerque attorney and New Mexico historian William Keleher, who talked to Lee forty years after the Fountain case and summed up his impressions by writing, "Fate gave Oliver Lee a part to play in southeastern New Mexico, and he played it with a zest for life, with dignity, courage and capability." The part he played, Keleher made clear, did not include murdering the Fountains.

Lee eventually owned and ran a considerable ranching empire and was elected to the New Mexico State Senate in 1922 and again in 1924. He died in Alamogordo in 1941.

Keleher also interviewed Jim Gililland in 1946 and wrote,

"Polite, courteous and responsive up to a certain point, Gililland skirted and evaded all efforts on the author's part to get him to talk about pivotal points in the case. Jim's secret knowledge passed away with him."

In 1903, Gililland and his wife Adelia built a successful cattle ranch in the San Andrés Mountains and operated it for thirty-seven years before retiring to Hot Springs, where he died in August 1946.

William Henry "Bill" McNew died after a stroke in June 1937. He was a minor player in the Fountain case, although, as Pat Garrett's biographer Leon Metz wrote, McNew was reportedly "the meanest and most vicious of the three."

None of the three spoke, publicly at least, about the Fountain case. In his *Tularosa,* C. L. Sonnichsen wrote,

> He [Lee] never discussed the troubles of the nineties. Neither did his friends. For fifty years and more their united front was never broken. Even after McNew, Gililland, and Lee were dead, it was not broken. One by one they died with their lips firmly closed. That was the way of the old-time cattlemen.

At the Masonic Cemetery in Las Cruces, in Section A, Block 12, Lot 18–19, there is a cenotaph thus inscribed:

IN MEMORY OF
ALBERT J.
FOUNTAIN
AND
SON, HENRY,
WHO DISAPPEARED
FEB. 1, 1896

The real graves, of course, are somewhere under the White Sands.

WHO KILLED THE MAN WHO KILLED THE KID?

You will get killed trying to find out who killed Garrett. I would advise you to let it alone.

—EMERSON HOUGH TO
JAMES H. HERVEY, 1909

Some hours after Pat Garrett was killed while urinating beside his buckboard on a lonely New Mexico road, his corpse was taken to Las Cruces in a spring wagon and delivered to a funeral parlor. There, the undertaker unfolded the body and discovered he didn't have a coffin big enough to hold a six-foot-four-inch deceased. So, while waiting for a suitable box to be sent up from El Paso, he filled and fixed the hole in the lawman's head, laid him across five chairs in the viewing room, and opened the doors to the public.

In death, as in life, Patrick Floyd Jarvis Garrett was hard to handle.

For nearly half his life, Pat Garrett was defined by a split-second. That instant passed in the flash and bang of his Colt revolver in the midnight dark of July 14, 1881, when his .44-caliber bullet killed Henry McCarty, also known as William Bonney, best known as Billy the Kid. That deadly moment inside Pete Maxwell's house at Fort Summer, New Mexico, "hung around his neck like a millstone," says Lincoln County War historian Frederick Nolan.

Garrett was only thirty-one years old at the time of the deed, and for a while enjoyed his sudden celebrity status as the Slayer of the Kid. He even published a book in 1882, *The Authentic Life of Billy, the Kid, the Noted Desperado of the Southwest, Whose Deeds of Daring and Blood Have Made His Name a Terror in New Mexico, Arizona and Northern Mexico, by Pat Garrett, Sheriff of Lincoln County, N. Mex, by Whom He Was*

Finally Hunted Down and Captured by Killing Him. The text was little better than the bloated title. Garrett's ghostwriter, a rolling-stone newspaperman named M. A. "Ash" Upon, took the lawman's laconic, straightforward story and served it up in dime-novel prose as a hash of hyperbole, misinformation, exaggeration, and outright fiction. The book not only failed financially, but it elevated the nonentity Henry McCarty to Western legendry, cast a shadow on Garrett's single moment in the sun, and put an end to any celebration of him as a heroic lawman. For a quarter-century thereafter, his life spiraled down until it hit bottom in a quarrel over goats.

After he killed the Kid, Garrett decided not to stand for reelection as sheriff of Lincoln County, ran instead for the territorial legislature, and was soundly defeated. He herded cattle on a New Mexico ranch, and after that briefly supervised a group of hired guns called the L. S. Pat Garrett Rangers, who were assigned to stop cattle rustling in the Texas Panhandle. In 1887, he moved with his wife Apolinaria Gutiérrez Garrett (mother of their eventual nine children) to the Pecos Valley near Roswell, where he involved himself in an irrigation scheme using water from the Hondo River. Upon being voted out of the partnership, he ran for the office of sheriff of Chaves County but was defeated by his former deputy John Poe. Following these and other disappointments, Garrett drifted southeast to Uvalde County, Texas, where he played cards and raised quarterhorses with the encouragement of Uvalde's preeminent citizen, the future Vice President of the United States, John Nance Garner.

In July 1890, he returned to New Mexico and, in Albuquerque, borrowed one thousand dollars from the newly opened Bank of Commerce, the six-month note cosigned by his friends George Curry (the future governor of the territory) and one John F. Eubank. The loan may have furthered Pat's horse-breeding business in Uvalde or paid gambling debts, or both. Whatever the case, he never repaid it. That would not be the last occasion in which he proved to be a deadbeat.

In March 1896, New Mexico Gov. William T. Thornton called Garrett out of "retirement" to return to the territory and investigate the disappearances of attorney Albert J. Fountain and his young son Henry. In the course of his lackluster "investigation," Garrett trained his eye on the ranchman Oliver Lee and two of Lee's cowboys, James Gililland and William McNew, and followed no other leads. When not working on the Fountain case, he gambled in Las Cruces, raced horses, speculated in mining, real estate, and stock-selling. He lost money in them all.

In 1898, while awaiting the trial of Lee and Gililland for the Fountain murders, the beleaguered new sheriff of Doña Ana County somehow acquired a 160-acre homestead in the San Andrés Mountains, thirty miles north of Las Cruces. A year later, he scraped together two hundred dollars for the title to the adjacent Bear Canyon property, consisting of a three-room, board-floored stone house and a corral close to a water source called Sinking Spring.

The ranch made Garrett a neighbor of William Webb (known as W.W.) Cox, a forty-four-year-old Texan, tall and lean with deep-set eyes and a bushy mustache, a profane, quick-tempered, tough-as-a-rope cowman with a violent history. His father, a state policemen, had been killed in a bloody Texas feud, and young W.W. vowed vengeance, ending up with several murder warrants against him and spending some time in jail before drifting to New Mexico Territory in 1886. He started with a modest cow outfit in the San Andrés range that, by 1893, after he bought the historic San Augustín Ranch, evolved into a cattle kingdom of 105,000 acres.

In the period of building up his holdings, Cox became a brother-in-law of the old Garrett adversary, the gun-handy cattleman Oliver Lee.

Soon after the Fountain trial ended in Hillsboro, Garrett's term as Doña Ana County sheriff expired, and after suing the county to recoup expenses incurred during the case investigation, he moved his family fifty miles south to El Paso. He managed to retain his New Mexico ranch properties but angled for new opportunities to feed his family and as well his own gambling and moneymaking hungers.

Toward the end of 1901, with the inauguration of President Theodore Roosevelt, the position of Collector of Customs at El Paso opened, and the one-time Western ranchman Roosevelt, always partial to lawmen (he had several in his Rough Rider regiment in 1898, including George Curry), landed on a candidate: He picked the former sheriff of Lincoln and Doña Ana counties, the man who killed the Kid.

News of Garrett's impending nomination quickly made its way west, and Roosevelt learned that not all were as thrilled with the choice as he and Garrett were. Some influential citizens supported the nomination, these including former New Mexico Governor and *Ben Hur* author Lew Wallace; the soon-to-be congressman John Nance Garner of Uvalde, Texas; and, inexplicably, Garrett's sworn enemy in the Fountain case, the formidable attorney, territorial legislator, and judge, Albert Bacon Fall. But other telegrams and letters arrived from New Mexico, many of them using vague language about Garrett's "unfitness for public office," some more direct, objecting to the appointment of a man whose reputation was that of a killer, a gambler, a debtor, and a chronic barfly.

With the president seeming to be hesitant to put his name forward, Garrett traveled to Washington to plead his case. A persistent story is that after the customary cordialities, Roosevelt handed the lawman a paper and asked him to read it aloud and sign it. The document stated, the story goes, "I, the undersigned Patrick F. Garrett hereby give my word of honor that if I am appointed Collector of Customs at El Paso, Texas, I will totally abstain from the use of intoxicating liquors during my term of office." Garrett is said to have read the letter, said "Mr. Roosevelt, that suits me fine," and signed it.

It was enough for Roosevelt. He officially nominated Garrett for the collectorship on December 16, 1901, and sent Pat's name forward for confirmation. Soon after, with Garrett called for questioning by the Senate Finance Committee, one senator asked the nominee about rumors that he was a gambler. Garrett lied that he didn't know the difference between a straight flush and four-of-a-kind. (A short time later, when he was guest of honor at a luncheon in El Paso, the master of ceremonies told the audience, "Here is the man that President Roosevelt worried about because he had the reputation of being a poker player. Everybody in El Paso knows that Pat Garrett isn't a poker player. He only *thinks* he is a poker player.")

The Senate confirmed the appointment on December 20, and Pat returned to El Paso to begin work.

Within three months he was in a jam.

For one thing, he thought he could save money by doing his own cattle appraising rather than hiring a professional to do it. This idea might have ingratiated him to his customs service superiors except that he made repeated mistakes in evaluating calves as full-grown beeves, forcing cattlemen to file objections with a Board of Appraisers, where Garrett's decisions were invariably reversed.

Finally, he gave in and employed an appraiser, an experienced man named Charles Gaither. The hiring should have solved the problems except that a month after Gaither started work, Pat fired him for incompetence. Gaither was not pleased and soon after met the collector in front of an El Paso butcher shop where the two called each other "a Goddamned liar," squared off, and began throwing schoolboy punches. The El Paso police chief and a group of townspeople waded in and split them up, the chief fined each combatant five dollars for disturbing the peace, and the *El Paso Evening News* described the fisticuffs as "bordering on the comic opera style."

Most of Garrett's five-year tenure as customs collector remained controversial. He became a stickler for rules, and instead of enforcing them with diplomacy and handshakes, used sarcasm and insult, earning him a reputation for rancor in his public dealings, as well as an assortment of unnecessary enemies. He also broke his pact with the president by hanging out at El Paso's watering holes, drinking and gambling, oblivious of the obvious: his conduct would eventually be bruited about in the territory, eventually in Washington, and might cost him his job.

What did cost him the collectorship was his friendship with Tom Powers, the burly, one-eyed owner of Pat's favorite hangout, an El Paso dive called the Coney Island Saloon. Powers became such a confidant that Garrett lent him the .44 Colt that killed the Kid so that Powers could put the gun on display behind the Coney Island bar.

In April 1905, Theodore Roosevelt invited Garrett to San Antonio, where the president would be presiding over a convention of his old regiment, the First United States Volunteer Cavalry, the Rough Riders of Spanish-American War fame. Pat, who had not served in the war but had received a special honor in being invited to sit with some of its heroes, responded by taking Tom Powers with him and introducing the barkeep to Roosevelt as a "West Texas cattleman." This fabrication probably would have gone unnoticed except that photographs of the Rough Rider convention were taken and published, among them one snapshot showing Garrett and Powers sitting at a banquet table with the president. Garrett's enemies back home lost no time in notifying Roosevelt of the real identity of the "West Texas cattleman."

By the end of the year, with his collector's term soon to expire, Garrett learned that he might be replaced and made arrangements to travel to Washington to appeal to the president for reappointment. But, despite warnings from friends, Pat, displaying a pathological unconsciousness, again took Tom Powers along.

Roosevelt, not pleased, allowed the collector a brief, frigid few minutes on December 11 and then, two days later, as the *El Paso Herald* announced, "emphatically declined to reappoint Pat Garrett Collector of Customs at El Paso." The *Houston Chronicle* reported that "the Powers incident at San Antonio is what finished [Garrett]." Roosevelt himself, in a letter to novelist Emerson Hough, referred to the Powers matter as "annoying" and "not a happy incident" but said it had nothing to do with denying the reappointment. He said his secretary of the treasury had reported to him that Garrett "was away a large part of the time from his office; that he was in debt and that his habits were bad."

With his El Paso opportunities lost, Garrett returned to his San Andrés, New Mexico, ranch, a few miles east of the mining settlement of Organ. Speculation had it that he intended to continue the Fountain investigation with the hope of collecting the twenty thousand dollars in reward money offered back in 1896, but Garrett biographer Leon Metz finds no evidence of this. "The two primary suspects had already been acquitted and could not be retried," Metz says. "Furthermore the reward money had dried up. Garrett moved to his ranch because he had nowhere else to go."

Actually, the San Andrés ranch was no longer his. In April 1902, he had mortgaged the 160 acres of land, all fixtures, thirty head of cattle, and 150 horses to Martin Lohman, a Las Cruces businessman and future mayor of the town, and signed a note in the amount of $3,567.50 to be repaid to Lohman within a year. After three years and no payment from Garrett, Lohman sold the note to W. W. Cox for two thousand dollars. Cox had no better luck in collecting on it but rather than foreclose on the property—which he didn't need or want—he extended the due date and let the note gather dust.

Meantime, Garrett spent the Lohman and Cox money, bought horses, dabbled in mining, studied law, spent time in El Paso with a woman reputed to be a prostitute, hung out with his saloon cronies, drinking and gambling and sinking farther into debt. He wrote to his author friend Emerson Hough in March 1906, "I am suffering great distress of mind and soul."

Two months later, the Albuquerque Bank of Commerce, which had not forgotten the thousand dollars it had lent Garrett six years past, filed suit to collect it plus legal costs and interest, which nearly doubled the original amount. When Pat failed to appear to pay the note, the court dispatched the Dona Aña sheriff to take possession of Garrett's ranch—a failed mission, since W. W. Cox held the lien on the property.

Now, too, the chronic debtor was sued by the county for six years of back taxes, nearly one thousand dollars overdue. Once again, Cox stepped in and moved Garrett's cattle to his own ranch to prevent the county from auctioning them. Cox now owned all the lawman's land, buildings, and stock and could take possession at any time he chose.

In 1905, desperately in debt, Garrett began working with the Chicago novelist Hough on a new version of the Lincoln County War and the pursuit and killing of its now legendary central figure. The Slayer of the Kid perhaps dreamed that this return to the event that had defined his life would pay off at last. He hoped to share in the profits from Hough's book and was confident that the two had a verbal, or at least tacit, agreement to this effect. The manuscript, titled *The Story of the Outlaw,* underwent many drafts and revisions as Hough sought a publisher for it and had been completely rewritten by the time Outing Publishers of New York issued it in 1907. When Garrett wrote to inquire about "royalties" for himself, Hough gave his erstwhile collaborator the bad news: the author advance from Outing had been only three hundred dollars: Hough had requested the publisher pay Garrett two hundred dollars, but the contract stipulated that if the book did not recoup Outing's investment, the two hundred dollars would have to be repaid. Hough also stated that his personal investment in the book exceeded a thousand dollars.

When Garrett received copies of *The Story of the Outlaw,* he wrote Hough that he was "well pleased with it as a whole," but said, "there are some parts of it that are not up to what I expected," and offered to discuss these shortcomings with Hough when the two next met.

The author, perhaps nettled by the letter and weary of Garrett's "royalties" expectations and indifference to Hough's investment in the project, closed down the correspondence.

The last sad episode of Pat Garrett's life began in early March 1907, when his son, Dudley Poe Garrett, leased Pat's Bear Canyon property to a thirty-one-year-old cowboy named Jesse Wayne Brazel. A Kansan, Brazel's family moved to New Mexico Territory when Wayne was in his teens and settled near Organ, close by W. W. Cox's ranch in the San Andrés Mountains. At age fifteen, Brazel went to work for Cox and regarded the ranchman as a surrogate father. At the time he leased the Garrett property, the cowhand was a sandy-haired, blue-eyed, six-footer described by friends as quiet, abstemious, and inoffensive.

The five-year lease on the Bear Canyon land was peculiar, if not sinister. The land was Garrett's in name only—the mortgage was held by Brazel's boss, W. W. Cox—and the lease paper was drawn up by Albert B. Fall, defender of the alleged Fountain killers and also Cox's lawyer. Moreover, two months after signing the lease, Brazel borrowed $574 from Cox, put a sizable herd of goats on the land, and had as his silent partner, A. P. "Print" Rhode, Cox's brother-in-law.

Garrett seems not to have known of the lease his son had arranged until that summer when he saw the first goat herd passing the front door of his ranch house headed to the Bear Canyon pasturage. He flew into a rage, made worse when he learned the details of the lease and that W. W. Cox had financed Wayne Brazel's goat operation. The wealthy ranchman had saved Garrett from destitution by buying the mortgage on the lawman's property and not foreclosing on it, and had saved Garrett's livestock from confiscation for delinquent taxes, but Pat hated him. Cox had a stranglehold on virtually all Garrett's assets and had even refused to return Pat's small cattle herd until the two-thousand-dollar mortgage was paid off.

After a futile attempt to break the Brazel lease in a court session in Organ (during which Print Rhode, his dander up, challenged Garrett to a fistfight), the local justice of the peace put the matter off until spring. By then, he hoped, tempers would cool and some reasonable solution to the case could be reached.

Unforeseen by the JP was the eventuality that by the spring the whole matter would be moot since Pat Garrett would be dead.

The goat issue lay dormant until January 1908, when James B. Miller came to El Paso, claiming to have a thousand head of Mexican cattle south of the Rio Grande waiting for shipment to Oklahoma. Miller, known as Deacon Jim, was a mild-mannered Arkansas native and former Texas Ranger who shunned alcohol, tobacco, and foul language, and was faithful to his wife. His main source of income, however, was denoted by his other nickname, not used to his face, Killin' Jim. A hired assassin, he was said to charge from fifty to two thousand dollars for a killing, depending upon what the employer could afford. He was suspected of at least twenty murders, perhaps twice that number, had often been charged, indicted, and tried for his handiwork, but never convicted. Across the Southwest, he was recognized as an excellent hand with a firearm, particularly with a shotgun.

In El Paso and Las Cruces, Miller let the word spread that he and his brother-in-law, Carl Adamson, needed a place to fatten their Mexican cattle before shipping them to the Oklahoma market. After an inquiry or two, Deacon Jim made his way to Pat Garrett's place.

Although neither man wrote or spoke of it—neither lived long enough to memorialize the event—the meeting between Miller and Garrett must have been a trifle tense. Each knew the other's reputation, but they tiptoed around their past histories and did business. After taking a tour of the Bear Canyon ranch, Miller offered three thousand dollars for it and as a bonus proposed to hire Pat to drive the cattle up from Mexico and onto the ranch pasturage.

This was the opportunity Garrett had hoped would fall out of the sky. As the ostensible "owner" of the San Andrés ranches, he could sell the relatively useless Bear Canyon land and its stone building and spring. The sale would enable him to pay off W. W. Cox, get his stock returned, retain his other ranch, settle some other debts, and have money left over after running Miller's cattle up from Mexico.

There remained one obstacle to this dream opportunity: Wayne Brazel's lease and Wayne's Brazel's goats.

At some point, probably in early February 1908, Garrett, Jim Miller, and Brazel met in an El Paso hotel, and Brazel offered to cancel the lease if Miller would buy the goats, 1,200 of them, at $3.50 a head. Miller must have thought he could at least break even on reselling the animals, since the *El Paso Herald* reported that the three men signed a contract. Miller, the *Herald* said, agreed to purchase the Bear Canyon ranch for three thousand dollars and pay another one thousand dollars for Patrick F. Garrett to drive a cattle herd up from Mexico to put on it.

Then, on about February 20, while Garrett and Miller were working out details of the arrangement, Wayne Brazel threw a handful of grit into the machinery by announcing he had miscounted his goats. He had 1,800 of them instead of 1,200, and unless Miller bought the additional animals, there would be no deal. Miller, not interested in goats to begin with, said he doubted he could raise the money for the added six hundred. Garrett could barely restrain his rage but agreed on another meeting, this time in Las Cruces, on February 29, where the three would attempt to resolve the problems and proceed with the sale.

Garrett, in the period between the meetings, wrote to George Curry, now territorial governor: "I am in a hell of a fix. I have been trying to sell my ranch but no luck. For God's sake send me fifty dollars." Curry sent the check, and Pat stuck it in his pocket, intending to cash it when he reached Las Cruces on the twenty-ninth.

Carl Adamson, Jim Miller's ne'er-do-well brother-in-law, spent the night of the February 28 at the Garrett ranch and next morning climbed into Pat's buckboard. The former lawman snapped the reins, and the two sorrel mares trotted down the dirt trail and up toward San Augustín Pass. They bumped along at an easy pace past Chalk Hill, a place haunted by the Fountain ghosts, through the dilapidated mining town of Organ, and down the mail road that cut a swath through the colorless winter desert to Las Cruces.

Less than a mile past Organ, they caught up with Wayne Brazel—or he caught up with them; the record is not clear. Some say Brazel was riding alongside the buckboard; others claim that the cowboy was talking with his goat operation partner Print Rhode when he spotted Garrett and Adamson approaching and that Rhode spurred his horse and departed as the buckboard reached them.

Whatever the case, with the day now warming, Brazel rode beside the buckboard as it bounced down the road toward Las Cruces and the meeting with Jim Miller. Adamson later said Garrett was angry and cussing at Brazel over the goat situation.

About five miles past Organ, at a desert crossroad called Alameda Arroyo, Garrett pulled the wagon to the side of the road, and he and Adamson climbed out while Brazel remained in his saddle. Adamson walked toward the buckboard mares and Pat to the rear, apparently taking his Burgess folding shotgun with him. While he was urinating, there was a flat bang of a gunshot, a split-second echo. Garrett was knocked to the ground as if poleaxed as a .45 slug blew through the back of his head. A second bang followed, the bullet hitting him in the back.

After covering the body with a carriage robe, Brazel and Adamson raced the buckboard into Las Cruces where Brazel burst into Sheriff José Lucero's office and yelled, "Lock me up. I just killed Garrett!" He pointed to Adamson. "He saw the whole thing and knows I shot in self-defense."

Lucero put the cowboy in a cell, called for his deputies, and raced to Alameda Arroyo. They found Garrett in a sand drift off the side of the road, his shotgun about four feet from the side of his body, his trousers unbuttoned, a glove on his right (gun) hand. The head shot had driven his long hair into the brain along with pieces of bone and scalp and had exited through the right eyebrow. Dr. William C. Field later extracted the other .45 bullet from shoulder muscles and said the first shot appeared to have been fired from horseback, the second from ground level.

The sheriff and his men took the body on to Las Cruces in a wagon, and the next day, Pat's wife, Apolinaria, and their daughter Pauline arrived and saw his corpse laid out across five chairs in Strong's Undertaking Parlor.

Wayne Brazel was to be tried for murder in Las Cruces with Albert B. Fall, who had defended Oliver Lee and Jim Gililland in the Fountain case, as his attorney. Carl Adamson testified at a preliminary hearing (before a non-English-speaking magistrate) on March 3 and corroborated Brazel's story, although he said he had also stepped down from the buckboard to urinate and was "looking the other way" when the shots were fired.

The indictment against Brazel charged, in typically florid frontier legal jargon, that he "did on the 29th Day of February, 1908, in Dona Aña County, Territory of New Mexico, with force and arms in and upon one Patrick F. Garrett, there and then with a certain pistol, loaded with gunpowder and various leaden bullets, did kill and murder the said Patrick F. Garrett."

The accused was released on a ten-thousand-dollar bond with W. W. Cox among the bail signees.

Thirteen months passed before a fifteen-minute verdict was reached by a jury of Wayne Brazel's peers.

The farcical trial began on April 19, 1909, with Judge Frank W. Parker (he of the Hillsboro trial ten years past) presiding. Fall quickly called his client to the stand, where Brazel related how he and Garrett had argued about the goats, how Garrett was enraged and threatening, with a "killer look" in his eyes, saying "Brazel, I want you to get them damned goats off that range; if you don't, I'll make you take them off." The defendant, as expected, claimed that Garrett had threatened him with a shotgun and that he killed in self-defense.

Brazel was not asked by the prosecutor Mark Thompson (a friend and ally of Albert Fall's) how he could see that "killer look" with Garrett's back to him, or why a second shot was necessary, or how a man in the act of urinating would have posed a threat.

Beyond comprehension, even in the rough-and-tumble arena of Old West justice, Carl Adamson, the only witness to the killing, was not called to testify, nor was Capt. Fred Fornoff of the New Mexico Territorial Mounted Police, who had visited the site of Garrett's killing. Fornoff, a conscientious lawman, had compiled interviews, chased down rumors, conducted the only genuine investigation into the killing, and made a report to the New Mexico attorney general, James H. Hervey. Nor was Fornoff's report introduced into evidence at the trial. This important document, in fact, was subsequently "lost," although Fornoff's findings were eventually made public. He claimed to have found a Winchester cartridge case, some cigarette butts, and horse tracks on a sandhill overlooking the killing site, told others he believed a conspiracy lay behind Garrett's death, and that Wayne Brazel was not the killer.

An interesting sidelight on Fornoff's report came to light many years later. Attorney General Hervey seems to have read the report when he wrote a letter to the author Emerson Hough, some months after Garrett's death. In the letter, Hervey asked Hough if he would help finance an investigation into the case, presumably a kind of private inquiry. The novelist, who had picked Garrett's brain for months in the course of writing the ill-fated *Story of the Outlaw,* declined to write a check. Hough said his sometime friend had died owing him "considerable money," but a more likely reason for not assisting in an investigation lay in his admonition to Hervey. Hough said, "You will get killed trying to find out who killed Garrett. I would advise you to let it alone."

Hervey took the advice, writing later, "I decided not to be so active."

As for the man whose offer to buy the Bear Canyon spread had seemingly precipitated Garrett's death, Jim Miller took no part in the Brazel trial and for good reason: on April 19, the day the trial opened in Las Cruces, Deacon Jim was busy getting lynched in an Ada, Oklahoma, barn. He had been arrested in March 1909, near Hicks, Texas, a few miles west of Fort Worth, accused with three other men of killing a prominent farmer and former U.S. deputy marshal. All were extradited to Oklahoma, where the murder had occurred, and just before dawn on April 19, a mob overpowered the jailers at the Ada lockup, dragged Miller and the other three culprits out, took them to an old barn, and hanged them from the rafters.

The Brazel jury got the case at 5:30 p.m. on May 4, 1909, and returned at 5:45 with a verdict of "Not guilty of murder," having apparently divined that shooting a man in the head and back, a man who was urinating with his back turned to his assailant, was "self defense."

That night the verdict was celebrated at a big barbecue at W. W. Cox's San Augustín ranch.

There were, and still are, differing theories about how Pat Garrett met his death. Most of the speculations, while ingenious, are dismissable because they involve top-heavy intrigues that defy the cardinal rule that one out of every two people involved in a conspiracy will talk and blow the whole plot wide open.

For example, it is impossible to believe, as some contemporaries did, that W. W. Cox wanted Garrett's land and hired Jim Miller, or maybe Print Rhode, or Carl Adamson, or all of them, to lure Pat into the desert and kill him. This overly complex script has Wayne Brazel selected as patsy, taking the blame for the murder with the assurance that the cunning defense tactics of Albert Fall would keep his head out of the noose. There were even reports that Cox brought all the plotters together (adding Oliver Lee, a Garrett enemy and defendant in the Fountain disappearances in 1896) in an El Paso hotel to hammer out the details.

Of this cabal, Garrett's biographer Leon Metz states, "How all these 'authorities' document their allegations is in itself something of a secret, since many of them cite dead men who meant to talk for the record but never quite made it." This ludicrously elaborate scheme, Metz says, has "enough romance and mystery for a saddlebag full of paperback thrillers. It seems a shame that none of it is true."

The biographer points out that W. W. Cox already owned the land adjacent to Garrett's, held the lien on Pat's land, could have foreclosed on it at any time but gave Garrett ample time to pay the two thousand dollars due to keep possession of it. Cox, Metz says, clearly did not want Garrett's "poverty-stricken land." If he *had* wanted it, he had the perfect device to take it—the unpaid, overdue mortgage. And, even without the paper, Cox, a savvy, tough customer, would have found a way to acquire it without financing Brazel's goat operation, involving such a notorious character as Jim Miller, or lending his name and influence to a plot involving as key figures the likes of drifter Carl Adamson and the simple bronc-buster Wayne Brazel.

Metz, whose research into Garrett's life continues long after his prize-winning book on the lawman was published, says, "I am convinced that Brazel did it, and he did it because he feared and hated Garrett. The motive was that simple." He points out that Brazel confessed and so far as is known, never recanted the confession. Moreover, the cowboy's plea of "self-defense," Metz says, while not consistent with the facts, does not signify innocence or point to another gunman; it "simply means he [Brazel] was lying about *how* he did it." The El Paso author adds that "Brazel feared the old manhunter. . . . The two men had argued bitterly, and when Garrett turned his back, Brazel took the safe way out and shot him.

"There were no conspiracies, no large amounts of money changing hands, no top guns taking positions in the sandhills. It was simply a case of hate and fear erupting into murder along a lonely New Mexico back road."*

Jesse Wayne Brazel, a few months after his acquittal, acquired land near Lordsburg, New Mexico, and homesteaded on it. He married and fathered a son, but after his wife's untimely death from pneumonia in 1911, Brazel sold his ranch and moved to Arizona Territory, where he lived for a time and then vanished from the historical record. There were stories that he died from a fall from a windmill or was killed after being pitched off a horse. In 1935, an El Paso attorney, hired by the cowboy's son, investigated Brazel's disappearance and reached the colorfully tentative conclusion that Brazel ended up in South America during World War I and was probably killed in Bolivia by one of Butch Cassidy's former Wild Bunch crew.

*In an interview with Leon Metz in April 2003, nearly thirty years after publication of his *Pat Garrett: The Story of a Western Lawman,* the author told me, "I've read all the theories—and, believe it or not, there are new ones still occasionally coming out—and I haven't changed my mind. In fact, I am more than ever convinced that Wayne Brazel, acting on the spur of the moment, shot and killed Pat Garrett."

Later in the same year as the Garrett murder, Carl Adamson, the other man present at the killing, was indicted in Alamogordo for "unlawfully, feloniously, knowingly, wickedly, falsely, and corruptly" conspiring to bring "certain Chinese persons" into the United States from Mexico. He served eighteen months in prison and died in Roswell of typhoid fever in 1919.

W. W. Cox died in December 1923.

Pat Garrett was buried in the Odd Fellow Cemetery in Las Cruces on March 5, 1908. He was an affirmed agnostic and wanted no religious rites at his funeral. He loved the work of Robert G. Ingersoll, the great Illinois orator and religious skeptic, especially a passage from an elegy Ingersoll wrote to his dead brother. Garrett asked in his will that his friend George Curry, now governor of the territory, read the passage, but Curry, politically sensitive to Ingersoll's reputation as a heretic, declined to read the oration. Saloon man Tom Powers, Pat's steadfast friend, did read it:

> Life is a narrow vale between the cold and barren peaks of two eternities. We strive in vain to look beyond the heights. We cry aloud and the only answer is the echo of our wailing cry. From the voiceless lips of the unreplying dead there comes no word; but in the night of death hope sees a star and listening love can hear the rustling of a wing.

THE
CALAMITY
PAPERS

><+>—<+>—<○>—<+>—<+><

*Blue, why don't the sons of
bitches leave me alone and let me
go to hell by my own route?*

—MARTHA CANARY, ABOUT 1901

I

MARTHA CANARY

There is a famous photograph of Calamity Jane standing in the weeds at Wild Bill Hickok's grave at the Mount Moriah Cemetery in Deadwood, Dakota Territory. The picture was taken in 1900 by a master of the camera, and it captures Calamity daintily holding a daisy in her left hand, the right pressed to the crown of her flat-brimmed hat, perhaps against a gust of wind. She is wearing a voluminously ruffled, dark-colored day dress, the white collar of her shirtwaist wrapped around her throat like a neckerchief. Her face is suntanned and leathery, the features—except for her wide-awake eyes looking off the shoulder of the photographer—seem sculpted harshly by alcohol and hard living: the downturned mouth, the nose that seems to have met a fist in a brawl or two. She is a homely but not ugly woman who clearly has always taken care of herself, needs no instruction, and requires no assistance.

She seems to be familiar with the grave, too. She has visited Wild Bill there before, and in three years will return there permanently.

The picture is a perfect publicity still. For one who had a walk-on role on the stage of the Old West, Calamity Jane played it so well the reviews are still coming in.

She was a creative, chronic prevaricator made worse by all the tale-telling help she had while she was living and in the hundred years since she died. The lies she told about herself, and most of those told about her, suited her just fine. Without them, we'd never know about Calamity Jane, and to her that would have been the greatest calamity of all.

At one time or another she claimed to be an army scout, an Indian fighter, a pony express rider, a bullwhacker and mule team driver, a stagecoach jehu, a frontier Florence Nightingale, and (maybe) Mrs. James Butler "Wild Bill" Hickok. In the Beadle & Adams "Deadwood Dick" dime novels of the 1880s and '90s, she was *The Beautiful White Devil of the Yellowstone,* the *Queen of the Plains,* and *The Heroine of Whoop-Up,* also the "West's Joan of Arc" and its "Hellcat in Leather Britches." A typical passage about her is to be found in the yellowback titled *Deadwood Dick's Doom, or, Calamity Jane's Last Adventure*:

> That day a horseman, or rather a girl dressed in male attire drew rein before the Poker House, and slipping from the saddle, she strode into the bar-room, and took a glance over the crowd therein. The woman was the notorious free-and-easy reckless waif of the rocky Western Country, Calamity Jane. . . . Few there were in Death Notch who had not heard of the notorious girl. . . . Calamity had changed but little since the time when this pen last introduced her: she was the same graceful, pretty girl-in-breeches that she had always been, but if there was any change it was in the sterner expression of her sad eyes.
>
> A murmur of "Calamity Jane" ran through the bar-room as she entered, proving that she was recognized by more than one. "Yes, Calamity Jane!" she retorted. "I see I am not un-

known even in this strange place. Better perhaps, it is so, for you'll have a clearer idea of whom you have to deal with . . ."

She is credited with inspiring the character "Cherokee Sal" in Bret Harte's immortal yarn "The Luck of Roaring Camp"* and has been depicted in film as the endearing sharpshooting tomboy played by Jean Arthur to Gary Cooper's Hickok in Cecil B. DeMille's *The Plainsman* (1936); by the voluptuous Jane Russell in the Bob Hope film *Paleface* (1948); the almost-as-voluptuous Yvonne DeCarlo in *Calamity Jane and Sam Bass* (1949); by Doris Day, driving the Deadwood stage through the hostiles and singing "Secret Love" in the 1953 musical show *Calamity Jane*; by Jane Alexander in the television show *Calamity Jane* (1984); Anjelica Huston in Larry McMurtry's novel-to-miniseries, *Buffalo Girls* (1995) with Sam Elliott as Hickok; and by Ellen Barkin to Jeff Bridges's Hickok in *Wild Bill* (1995).

She was also depicted in her own day as a camp follower and drunken prostitute; by James D. Horan in his *Desperate Women* (1952) as "a grotesque creature, dressed in a ragged black dress, battered flowered hat, worn boots, a drunken grin framing two yellow teeth"; as "a widely traveled, coarse, slovenly, frontier whore" in Harry Sinclair Drago's *Notorious Ladies of the Frontier* (1969); and as a vile slut in Pete Dexter's novel *Deadwood* (1986)—which also portrays Hickok as syphilitic and going blind.

Her first biographer, El Paso newspaperman Duncan Aikman, had a kinder assessment, calling Calamity "an amusingly rakish camp follower and kind-hearted demi-mondaine with an exceptional passion for plains life and male abundance," and Hickok biographer William E. Connolley urges us to scratch "the coy charmer, the buckskin-clad belle of the plains" to find

---

*Which seems unlikely, since Harte's story appeared in 1868, four years before Calamity was called Calamity and too early in her career to have earned enough notoriety to reach Harte's attention in San Francisco.

the "fascinating woman, and a most interesting personality" beneath.

The venerable *Encyclopedia Britannica* surrendered after trying to portray her, ending the entry on her with a limp truth: "The facts of her life are confused by her own inventions and by the successive stories and legends that accumulated in later years."

For 130 years, legends and lies have defined Calamity Jane. Just to take her word for it that "My maiden name was Marthy Cannary" and "I was born in Princeton, Missourri, May 1st, 1852," presents problems in taking her word for anything. Marthy? Did her people call her that in backwoods Missouri or was she *really* Marthy and not Martha? Modern researchers dispute the spelling of her last name, as well, finding *Canary* more provable. The year of her birth is debatable, too. Her original tombstone in Deadwood, Dakota Territory, said she died in 1903, "Aged 53 years," which would put her birth year at 1850; an 1860 census of the township of Princeton listed her parents and their three children and appeared to give Martha's birthdate as 1856.

These confusions, and a hundred others, spring from an eight-page "autobiography" titled *Life and Adventures of Calamity Jane by Herself* which she wrote, or had written, in 1896 to sell to customers when she was performing on stage with the Kohl & Middleton Dime Museum shows in Minneapolis and points east. If she wrote the booklet, the misspellings of Martha and Missouri are understandable—she had, after all, no schooling, at least none on record. But except for a highly suspect "diary" (of which more later), nothing she ever wrote, not even her signature, has survived, giving rise to the suspicion that she was probably illiterate and the booklet ghostwritten by someone who added the misspellings for "local color."

As to the "Jane" commonly attached to her birth name, it is not mentioned in her *Life and Adventures* and cropped up, according to her own testimony, in 1872, when she was called "Calamity Jane" for the first time during what she called the "Nursey Pursey" (Nez Percé) campaign. As to why she was not called "Calamity Martha" (or "Marthy"), several researchers have pointed out that on the Western frontier in her time, a "jane" was a prostitute—her customer, a "john," the latter usage surviving today.

That she was born on her grandfather's farm in Princeton in north-central Missouri is not in dispute, nor the fact that Robert, her father, was a farmer. There is speculation that Martha's mother, Charlotte, may have been working in an Ohio brothel when she met and married the feckless Robert Canary.

There were at least three Canary kids, Martha the roughest of them, learning to ride the woods and Missouri byways and by age nine acquiring an extensive vocabulary of cuss words learned from the boys she fought with for a place at the swimming hole.

In 1863, Robert Canary sold his farm and took the family, a two-horse wagon, two cows, and a couple of dogs, to Virginia City, Montana, after hearing of a gold strike in the vicinity. Martha, already described as "wild as a lynx's kitten," said in her 1896 pamphlet that they joined an emigrant train on the trail out of Independence, moved on to Colorado, through Cheyenne and Laramie, Wyoming, into Utah and across Idaho into the Montana gold diggings. "While on the way the greater portion of my time was spent in hunting along with the men and hunters of the party," she wrote. "In fact I was at all times with the men when there was excitement and adventures to be had. By the time we reached Virginia City I was considered a remarkable good shot and a fearless rider for a girl of my age." During the five-month journey, she learned to use the thirty-foot teamster's bullwhip and the blistering oaths that went with it, and developed at age eleven a taste for the firewater the teamsters doted on—a thirst that went unslaked for the rest of her life.

There are various stories about where the Canarys roosted. They were in the Virginia City diggings for a while, among an estimated ten thousand miners scattered in a six-mile stretch of meadows and flats. This was an exciting place to Martha, drawn to its riotous boomtown saloons, gambling and dance halls, and the drunken fights and wrestling matches in its muddy streets. Some sources say Martha and the other Canary children were abandoned in Virginia City and were taken in by a good citizen while other townsfolk appealed to the newspapers to "do something about the Canarys," calling the father a low-down gambler, the mother a prostitute. On these matters Martha was mute, skipping the years between 1864 and 1866, saying only that "Mother died at Black Foot, Montana, 1866, where we buried her. I left Montana in Spring of 1866, for Utah, arriving at Salt Lake City during the summer. Remained in Utah until 1867, where my father died . . ."

Charlotte's death was reported to be from "wash-tub pneumonia," signifying that she was probably working as a laundress in the mining camps. Robert had apparently taken up farming on forty acres of land near Salt Lake City when he died. The fate of the other Canary children is unknown, but they were believed to have been adopted into Mormon families.

Martha, now about twelve or eighteen, probably somewhere between, struck out on her own, showing up at Fort Bridger, Wyoming Territory, in May 1868, then on to the town of Piedmont, where she claimed to have worked on Union Pacific track-laying gangs, and to Laramie and Cheyenne and God knew where else. One thing is certain: she told a demonstrable windy when she wrote, "Joined General Custer as a scout at Fort Russell, Wyoming in 1870, and started for Arizona for the Indian Campaign."

It made no difference to her that somebody in the future would discover that Custer was never at Fort D. A. Russell, Wyoming, and never went on an Indian campaign in Arizona. She also said, "Up to this time I had always worn the costume of my sex. When I joined Custer I donned the uniform of a soldier. It was a bit awkward at first but I soon got to be perfectly at home in men's clothes," and there was some truth in this. She wore men's clothes, probably including cast-off soldier's trousers, shirt, and boots, since her wanderings took her to cow towns, miner and railroader camps, and army posts. In these places, she worked as a laundress but also learned the teamster's trade, becoming a proficient muleskinner (driver of a mule train), bullwhacker (driver of an ox train), and packer—men's work requiring men's dress.

She seems to have passed muster as a man with only occasional difficulty. By now she was a tall, big-boned, and muscular red-haired roughneck, somewhat attractive with a good figure. By the early 1870s, she was said to have married at least three times—two soldiers and a brakeman in Rawlings, Wyoming— but these unions were not blessed by clergy or law. Her habit was to move in with a man, stay until he wore out his welcome, or she hers, then move out and move on.

In about 1870, she landed for a time in the raw cow town of Hays City, Kansas, and was spotted there by a boy named Miguel Otero, the son of a storekeeper.* Otero vividly recalled spotting the new Hays marshal, James Butler Hickok, recently hired by the town's Vigilance Committee, and remembered Wild Bill as "cool, polite, well-mannered, and handsome." The boy also recalled the woman subsequently called Calamity Jane, thought that she was about twenty years old, said she was "extremely good-looking" but "was regarded in the community as a camp-follower."

Martha said she acquired the "Calamity Jane" nickname in 1872, while serving as a scout at Goose Creek (later the town of Sheridan, Wyoming), during the "Nursey Pursey outbreak." She claimed to have rescued her commanding officer, Capt. Patrick Egan, who had been wounded and fell from his horse. "I turned my horse and galloped back with all haste to his side

*The same Miguel Otero who, twenty-six years later, then governor of New Mexico Territory, became involved in the disappearances of Judge Albert Jennings Fountain and his son, as told in the "Under the White Sands" chapter in this book.

and got there in time to catch him as he was falling," she said. "I lifted him onto my horse in front of me and succeeded in getting him safely to the Fort. Capt. Egan on recovering, laughingly said: 'I name you Calamity Jane, the heroine of the plains.'"

The quote, and Martha's entire story, were patently pulp-paper, "reckless waif of the rocky Western country" stuff. There is no record of the "numerous skirmishes" with Indians at Goose Creek and, in fact, Egan himself had no recollection of the rescue incident but did recall Martha Canary worked from time to time as a laundress among his troops.

Another, and more likely, story has the name given her by Bill Nye, editor of the *Laramie Boomerang,* who took note of her presence at such calamities as saloon shootouts and brawls.

Duncan Aikman said that whatever its origin, the name was appropriate "because of her notoriously down-at-the-heels appearance when returning from her trail expeditions or when liquored up," looking like she had been involved in some calamity or other.

Calamity's own incessant self-mythologizing has submerged her real accomplishments as a frontierswoman.

While in Fort Laramie in the spring of 1875, she managed to join Gen. George Crook's Black Hills expedition against the Sioux, working as a teamster, a courier, and later as a scout under William Frederick "Buffalo Bill" Cody. This employment is on record: her name appears in the muster rolls of Frank Grouard, Crook's chief of scouts, and Cody acknowledged her service by saying, "Her courage and good fellowship made her popular with every man in the command."

Now perhaps twenty-five years old and strong as the mules she handled, she was enjoying the labor and the company—soldiers were among her favorites—until she was "discovered" as a woman. Col. Anson Mills, one of Crook's officers, who had met and observed Calamity on the trail, knew her reputation as a camp follower and remembered her being removed as civilian teamster and scout. Mills particularly recalled his embarrassment the day she was placed under guard and he passed the stockade. She saw him and sprang up, Mills said, and shouted, "There is Colonel Mills, he knows me." After which, he said, "everybody began to laugh, much to my astonishment and chagrin, being married." Even so, he said she "was a woman of no mean ability and force even from the standard of men."

In his 1893 memoir, *With Crook on the Border*, Lt. John G. Bourke, aide-de-camp to General Crook, also recalled Calamity's service as one of the command teamsters. "She was eccentric and wayward rather than bad," he wrote,

> and had adopted male attire more to aid in getting a living than for any improper purpose. "Jane" was as rough and burly as any of her messmates, and it is doubtful if her sex would ever have been discovered had not the wagonmaster noted that she didn't cuss her mules with the enthusiasm to be expected from a graduate of Patrick and Saulsbury's Black Hill Stage Line, as she had represented herself to be.

According to Calamity's autobiographical pipe dream, she escaped death at the Little Big Horn when she contracted pneumonia as a result of swimming the flooded Platte River in a desperate effort to reach Custer's column with important messages. She was "laid up," she said, in the Fort Fetterman infirmary for two weeks, then, "When I was able to ride I started for Fort Laramie where I met Wm. Hickok, better known as Wild Bill, and we started for Deadwood, where we arrived in June."

That Calamity didn't remember that Hickok's name was James and not William is probably a simple slip of the pen—hers or her ghostwriter's—but it serves as a starting point for the greatest of Calamity Jane controversies, her relationship, if any, with the man she called "my friend Wild Bill."

James Butler Hickok, born in Homer, Illinois, in 1837, came from a farm family as Martha Canary had, only one more prosperous and less footloose. The Hickoks, originally from Vermont, were abolitionists, participated in the underground railroad, and became strong Unionists in the Civil War. James, after a farm-boy's rudimentary education, had his first taste of law work in 1858, when he served as a constable in Monticello, Kansas, after which he drove freight wagons on the Santa Fé Trail.

In July 1861, at Rock Creek Station in Nebraska Territory, he killed a man named David McCanles, a bully and horse thief, and wounded two other men. A lurid account of the gun battle was published as "Wild Bill" in *Harper's New Monthly Magazine* in February 1867 and gave Hickok his first national exposure.

(A popular version of the "Wild Bill" name has its origin in the 1860s, when Hickok and his brother Lorenzo were wagoning supplies out of the towns of Rolla and Springfield, Missouri. In Rolla, the story goes, a young man was in jail and being threatened by a mob because he was a Union sympathizer. The Hickok brothers broke up the mob, and somebody, perhaps a newspaper reporter, dubbed James "Wild Bill." (The "Bill" appears to have been informally adopted by Hickok, for reasons unknown, after his father, William, died in 1852.)

After the McCanles fight, Hickok enlisted as a Union Army civilian scout at Fort Leavenworth and fought in the battles at Wilson's Creek in Missouri and Pea Ridge in Arkansas. By 1864, while working for the army's provost marshal's office, he had begun the transformation into the Wild Bill character dime novelists doted on: the tall, grim-faced, long-nosed, oddly handsome, flamboyantly dressed, pistol-bedecked frontiersman with the drooping blond mustaches and wavy hair falling from his flat-brimmed hat to below his shoulders.

Following the Civil War, in which he had served as scout, wagonmaster, sharpshooter, and spy, Hickok gambled for a time in Springfield, Missouri, and there killed a man, allegedly over a woman, in the kind of "walk-down" street duel that became a standard movie cliché. In 1867, he enlisted for a six-month stint (at one hundred dollars a month) as scout for Lt. Col. George A. Custer's Seventh Cavalry, served as deputy United States marshal in the Kansas towns Fort Riley and Hays City, and in 1871 as city marshal of Abilene. In the latter town, he had trouble with one gambling-whorehouse establishment owned by English-born gunman Ben Thompson and a roughneck named Phil Coe. In October 1871, Coe took a shot at Hickok and missed; Wild Bill didn't. He shot Coe twice in the belly and accidentally killed a good friend named Mike Williams in the bargain. After the incident, he went on a rampage, shutting down saloons, backing down drunks and running them out of town, and for his zeal was discharged at the end of the year.

He traveled with Buffalo Bill Cody's stage troupe in 1873, appearing in a production called *The Scouts of the Plains*—a popular but miserable melodrama written by dime novelist E. Z. C. Judson ("Ned Buntline"). Hickok could not abide the discipline required to memorize such lines as "Fear not, fair maid; by heavens, you are safe at last with Wild Bill, who is ever ready to risk life and die if need be in the defense of weak and helpless womanhood," probably because they were unlike anything ever uttered by a human being. When he left town before the season ended, he left word with Cody's stage manager. "Tell that long-haired son-of-a-bitch I have no more use for him and his damned show business." (The message was playful badinage: the two remained friends, "the best of friends," Cody later said.)

During his Abilene, Kansas, days, Hickok fell in love with Agnes Thatcher Lake, a horsewoman, dancer, actress, and lion tamer with a traveling circus. The two corresponded after the show left town, reunited and married in Cheyenne on March 5, 1876. Soon after, with his wife heading east, Wild Bill departed for the boomtown of Deadwood, where he hoped to make a strike, mostly at gambling, and eventually to bring Agnes out to join him.

The town, originally Deadwood Gulch and named for the litter of splintered timber downed by lightning storms, was the biggest of several mining camps that erupted in 1875 and '76 after gold was discovered in the Black Hills. Within six months, ten thousand miners were swarming the Dakota settlements, squatting in kindling-wood shacks and tents up and down the ravines and hillsides. The Cheyenne and Deadwood Stage meantime brought more drifters and would-be miners to Deadwood from Fort Laramie and points beyond and took a half-million dollars in gold back to Cheyenne after the first few weeks.

By July 1876, a month after news of the Custer massacre reached the town and about the time Hickok arrived there, Deadwood had a Main Street, several stores, a theater, and many gambling dens, among the latter the popular Lewis & Mann's Number 10 Saloon. There Wild Bill, now thirty-nine years old, his eyesight failing—perhaps from untreated gonorrhea—became a familiar figure, drinking and playing poker with his back to a wall, facing the bar and door.

Since bald-faced invention, pulp-novel tale spinning, and tangled testimony are the foundation stones of Calamity Jane's life and career, there can be little surprise that nobody knows with certainty when she met Hickok or precisely what they had in the manner of an acquaintanceship.

She was in her early to mid-twenties, and, Duncan Aikman says, her "charms were still in a state in which they were presentable when they got a good scrubbing," at the time she came to Deadwood in the summer of 1876 and met Wild Bill en route, or so she claimed in her *Life and Adventures*. In the pamphlet she states that after being hospitalized at Fort Fetterman during the time of the Custer march to the Little Big Horn, she "started for Fort Laramie where I met Wm. Hickok, better known as Wild Bill."

One of Hickok's friends, Joseph "White Eye" Anderson, later confirmed that the two indeed met for the first time in June 1876, on the trail to the Black Hills. Anderson said Hickok had "deserted" Agnes Lake for the lure of gold and was accompanying thirty wagons, including "a load of whores" from Fort Laramie to Deadwood. White Eye said Wild Bill turned over wagon train duties to two other gambler friends, Colorado Charlie and Steve (no known nickname) Utter, and that Calamity, who had been in a Laramie guardhouse after a drunken spree, tagged along. "She was nearly naked," Anderson said, and remembered that the Utters outfitted her in a buckskin shirt and pants and a wide-brimmed hat.

Most Hickok authorities agree that Wild Bill did not desert Agnes Lake, indeed professed his love for her to the last, and that he never had a close association with Calamity. Charley Utter is quoted as saying, "Wild Bill would have died rather than share a bed with Jane," a strange pronouncement given Hickok's familiarity with frontier brothels and the likelihood that he had contracted some variety of venereal disease in them. It is also passing strange given the testimony of others who said that Steve (or maybe Charlie, or maybe both) slept with Calamity en route to Deadwood and continued to do so after their arrival.

A better source, perhaps the best source, Joseph G. Rosa, the British authority on Hickok, wrote, "Of all the women associated in any way with Wild Bill, she had the least to do with him." As early as 1927, Calamity's biographer Duncan Aikman was writing, "Mr. Hickok was the real thing in western derring-do and Calamity was merely a western spectacle. . . . It was good to be Calamity Jane on your own account, but it was better still to be the recognized, even if condescendingly recognized, as walking companion of Wild Bill." Hickok's attitude, Aikman said, was one of "genial tolerance."

One feature of their association is certain: its duration was brief.

On the afternoon of August 2, 1876, twenty days after he arrived in Deadwood, Hickok was playing stud poker with three friends at Lewis & Mann's Number Ten Saloon on Main Street. He customarily sat with his back to the wall but found that seat taken and rather than disrupt the game, sat facing the wall with his back to the bar and door. At a little past four in the afternoon, as he sat holding a hand of aces and eights with a jack of diamonds kicker, a cross-eyed, twenty-six-year-old Kentucky-born drifter named John "Jack" McCall ("one of the sorriest specimens of humanity to be found in the Hills," said the *Black Hills Pioneer*) entered the saloon and walked up to the bar. He turned, drew a navy revolver, took two steps to where Hickok sat, placed the muzzle two inches from Wild Bill's head, and fired a single shot which, as the *Black Hills Daily Times* reported clinically, "entered the base of the brain, passed through the head and upper and lower jaw bones, breaking off several teeth and carrying away a large piece of the cerebellum through the wound." The ball passed through Hickok's head and struck the player across the table, Capt. William R. Massie, a one-time Missouri riverboat pilot, in the left arm.*

A choice example of Calamity's tendency to create a yellow-back story and believe in it was her claim to have rushed to the scene of the shooting where she "found my friend had been killed by McCall":

> I at once started to look for the assassin and found him at Shurdy's butcher shop and grabbed a meat cleaver and made him throw up his hands; through the excitement of hearing of Bill's death, having left my weapons on the post of my bed. He was then taken to a log cabin and locked up, well secured as

---

*Joseph Rosa wrote that the bullet was never removed from Captain Massie's arm and that he often invited people to shake the hand on the end of the arm that carried the bullet that killed Wild Bill Hickok.

every one thought, but got away and was afterwards caught at Fagan's ranch on Horse Creek, on the old Cheyenne road and was then taken to Yankton, Dak., where he was tried, sentenced and hung.

In fact, she was not involved in the aftermath of the Hickok murder and probably was not present in Deadwood at the time of it.

McCall surrendered outside the saloon, did not escape or attempt to escape, and was tried by a miner's court in Deadwood the day after the shooting. Several witnesses attested to McCall's sterling character and Hickok's reputation as a "terror in every place he has ever lived in." McCall told the jury, "Men, I have but a few words to say. Wild Bill killed my brother and I killed him. Wild Bill threatened to kill me if I ever crossed his path. I am not sorry for what I have done. I would do the same thing over again."

Even if McCall had a brother, no evidence was presented (nor is there any today) that a McCall was among the estimated ten men Hickok killed in his career, yet the jury believed the story and after ninety minutes of deliberation delivered a "not guilty" verdict. The *Black Hills Daily Times* reported sourly, "The prisoner McCall was at once liberated, and several of the model jurymen who had played their part in the burlesque upon justice, and who had turned their bloodthirsty tiger loose upon the community, indulged in a sickening cheer. . . ."

There were overnight rumors that the twelve-man jury had been bribed by a thrown-together confederation of gamblers who feared that Hickok might be elected city marshal in Deadwood and launch a town-taming campaign as he had attempted in Kansas. This, of course, was a patently unlikely prospect for a man depending upon gambling for income.

McCall's taste of freedom lasted only a few months. Toward the end of 1876, while working as a freighter in Wyoming, he was arrested after bragging in a saloon of lying to a jury and getting away with murdering Wild Bill Hickok. A United States marshal escorted him to Yankton, capital of Dakota Territory, for trial in the federal district court there. He changed his story of the killing, claiming he was hired by a gambler who had a grudge against Hickok, but the jury determined the story to be ludicrous and found him guilty of murder. He was hanged in Yankton on March 1, 1877.

Hickok's funeral was held at Colorado Charlie's camp, with burial at Deadwood's Ingleside graveyard. Three years later, his remains were moved to the new Mount Moriah Cemetery above the town, the plot and headstone paid for by the ever-faithful Charlie Utter.

Calamity told friends she was too distraught to attend Wild Bill's last rites, but she returned to Deadwood after his death, delivered government mail (which she elevated to "acted as a pony express rider") in the Black Hills, and on occasion, she said, drove an overland mail stagecoach.

She lived up to her nickname in the late 1870s in times of "mountain fever" (typhoid) and cholera epidemics, and during a "black diphtheria" outbreak on the Green River in Wyoming. In mining camps and homesteader lands, despite the danger of contagion, she performed valiant volunteer services where it was said she "dropped all her vices and spent day and night nursing."

In the Deadwood smallpox calamity in 1877–78 she nursed eight stricken men in a log cabin in Spruce Gulch, claiming to be immune from the disease because she had contracted it as a child. She said she aimed to live at the pesthouse until the epidemic passed, raised hell to get fresh water delivered, ransacked the general store and drew her six-shooter when anybody complained about the grocery bill, and treated her wards with Epsom salts, tartar emetic, and whatever pills and poultices she could confiscate. When a man died she wrapped him in a blanket and had the "boys" dig a hole and carry the body to the grave, where she recited the only prayer she knew: "Now I lay me down to sleep . . ." Her tireless efforts were attested to by the town's only physician, Dr. L. F. Babcock, and the men she saved.

Among her friends in these post-Hickok days was the cowboy E. C. "Teddy Blue" Abbott, later author of *We Pointed Them North,* one of the classic books on the cattle drive in pre-fencing days of the West. He saw her in Deadwood in 1878: "I didn't meet her then," he recalled,

> but I got a good look at her, when she was at the height of her fame and looks. I remember she was dressed in purple velvet, with diamonds on her and everything. As I recall it, she was some sort of madam at that time, running a great big gambling hall in Deadwood.

Teddy Blue appears to have confused Calamity with a Deadwood bordello madam on that first glimpse, but he came to know and appreciate her in Miles City, Dakota Territory, in the early 1880s. He wrote of encountering her at a hotel where he and his cowhand friends were staying, of offering her drinks and enlisting her help in a memorable prank. Abbott explained that his trail boss was an old, dour, puritanical slave driver, despised by all who worked for him, and that this man was presently in the saloon evil-eyeing his punchers, intent on keeping them sober. Abbott took Calamity aside and said, "I'll give you two dollars and a half if you'll go sit on his lap and kiss him." She was game, he said, and described how she walked up to the old man with everybody watching, plopped in his lap, threw her arms around him, pinned his arms to his side and began kissing his face and yelling, "Why don't you ever come see me anymore, honey? You know I love you!"

Abbott saw her toward the end of her life, too, and asked her how she liked the idea of going back East to perform on stage. He wrote,

Her eyes filled with tears. She said, "Blue, why don't the sons of bitches leave me alone and let me go to hell my own route? All I want is to be allowed to live out the rest of my life with you boys who speak my language. And I hope they lay me beside Bill Hickok when I die."

In the early 1880s, she had once again returned to Deadwood and was remembered there by the actor Charles E. Chapin who was appearing with the Lord Players in a production of *East Lynne* at the town's Opera House. Chapin wrote of Calamity strutting into the theater chewing tobacco "as industriously as any miner present," with another local character called Arkansas Tom, said to be an infamous gunslinger. During the second act, when the female lead appeared on stage in a pink evening gown, the crowd booed—in the play she deceived her husband— whereupon, Chapin said, Calamity swaggered up to the stage apron and, to the loud approval of the miner audience, spat a stream of juice that landed on the hem of the actress's dress. After the curtain fell and the lady's real-life husband stormed onto the stage in a fury, Calamity "threw some gold pieces across the stage to pay for the gown she had so ruthlessly desecrated."

Despite countless drunken sprees, she was prosecuted only once, for rolling a drunk for thirty dollars. She told the judge, "I had to take it [the money], judge, before somebody else took it. The damn fool was drunk under the table." She was acquitted after testifying that she used the money to pay a sick girl's hospital bill.

In her scrambled *Life and Adventures,* Calamity recounted her travels and exploits, some few of which might have actually occurred. She wrote of driving ox-teams in Dakota, taking up a ranch on the Yellowstone, where she raised cattle and horses and "kept a wayside inn, where the weary traveler could be accommodated with food, drink, or trouble if he looked for it." She said she left the ranch in 1883 and traveled, for unstated reasons, to San Francisco, ventured into the Southwest in 1884, where she visited Fort Yuma, Arizona Territory, "the hottest spot in the United States," while en route to Texas.

In 1885, she told of meeting a man named Clinton (later called "Charley") Burk (or Burke) and marrying him in El Paso in that summer, "as I thought I had traveled through life long enough alone and thought it was time to take a partner for the rest of my days." Martha and Burke, a one-legged Civil War veteran who earned a living as a hack driver, remained in Texas "leading a quiet home life" for four years, she said, adding that "On October 28th, 1887, I became the mother of a baby girl, the very image of its father, at least that is what he said, but who has the temper of its mother."

Although Calamity claimed that she, Burke, and their daughter left Texas in 1889 and "kept a hotel" in Boulder, Colorado, until 1893, at least part of the story was a sad fantasy, a dressed-up dream of respectability. Researchers have found no record of their marriage or a birth certificate on the child; moreover, Calamity probably was not in Texas in 1885 or '86 since there are newspaper records of her being elsewhere, including one Rapid City, Dakota Territory, write-up about her drunken stunt of riding a bull through downtown streets.

Burke may have been a common-law husband—Calamity had several of these—and the child is believed to have been Burke's from an earlier marriage. That he deserted her, probably about the time she said they quit the hotel business in Boulder, and that there *was* a child in the story, seems clear since Calamity, accompanied by a little girl, showed up in Deadwood in 1895. Estelline Bennett, in her 1928 memoir *Old Deadwood Days,* wrote that funds were raised in the town's saloons for the child's education, that at the Green Front gambling hall enough money was collected to pay "for the convent" (Saint Mary's convent in Sturgis, South Dakota) and that Calamity got roaring drunk thanking her benefactors.

In the years during and following the Burke episode, her notoriety spread afar, her name linked with Hickok's in such dime

novels as *Calamity Jane, Queen of the Plains,* which featured
tender love scenes between the two; in *The Beautiful White Devil of the Yellowstone,* the *Queen of the Plains,* and *The Heroine of Whoop-Up.* She was even featured in an ostensibly serious
book portentously titled *The Coming of Empire,* published in
1878. The author, one Horatio N. Maguire, included an engraving of her, as "Miss Martha Canary, the Female Scout," in which
she stares from horseback across a sun-dappled prairie, as if on
lookout for hostiles.

She was featured in stories so preposterous, even Calamity, a
fabulist of the first order, must have choked on some of them:
she personally killed Crazy Horse, was the only scout to escape
from the Custer massacre, had a belt with forty Sioux scalps on
it, helped build the Union Pacific Railroad, assisted Wild Bill
Hickok in "cleaning up" Abilene. Duncan Aikman wrote that
her reaction to such yarns was "a grin of mildly alcoholic candor" followed by advice to pay no attention to "the damn lies of
them joshers," ending the discussion by asking who was going to
buy her a drink.

In 1893, she told friends that she toured in the East with Buffalo Bill's Wild West and went to Europe with him, but unfortunately, there is no record of this, since Cody and his Wild West
extravaganza spent most of 1893 in Chicago performing at the
Columbian Exposition and World's Fair. Significantly, she did
not mention Buffalo Bill in her *Life and Adventures* autobiography.

While visiting her favorite haunts in Deadwood in 1895,
Calamity said she met

> several gentlemen from eastern cities who advised me to allow
> myself to be placed before the public in such a manner as to
> give the people of the eastern cities an opportunity of seeing
> the Woman Scout who was made so famous through her daring career in the West and Black Hill countries.

Among these agents, one represented Kohl & Middleton, a company that signed up celebrities and produced stage lectures and "exhibitions" in dime museums for them. This agent booked Calamity and paid her train and hotel expenses, first to Minneapolis, where she appeared at the Palace Museum in January 1896, then to Chicago, Saint Louis, and Kansas City. Playbills advertised her as

.

The Famous Woman Scout of the Wild West!

.

Heroine of a thousand thrilling adventures!

.

THE TERROR OF EVIL-DOERS IN THE BLACK HILLS!

.

The Comrade of Buffalo Bill and Wild Bill!

.

Her act consisted of striding onto the stage in buckskins and six-shooters, mugging the audience, and describing her Western exploits in colorful but clean language. She drew good crowds, earning the fifty dollars a week she was paid. According to Duncan Aikman,

> Mornings off, she lounged about the swanky hotel lobbies of the mauve decade to the admiration of young drummers, with airs of appropriately aloof ferocity. She learned to carry liquor on her hip and no longer to punish Palmer House bartenders for not extending to her weaker sex the courtesies of Deadwood.

But she was no Annie Oakley, had nothing to show off but a recitation of her "hair-raising adventures"—which metastasized with each telling—and inevitably her drinking and profanity cut the engagement short. She was sent back to Deadwood in the summer.

For nearly five years following the Kohl & Middleton engagement, Calamity lived hand-to-mouth in the mining camps in
and around Livingston, Montana, shacking with the miners,
cadging drinks, and working as laundress. Toward the end of
1900, she was found near Livingston, sick, drunk, and sleeping
in a bordello, by an agent who sobered her up and signed her to
perform in the Pan-American Exposition in Buffalo, New York,
the following year. Part of the agreement seems to have been that
Calamity would quit drink, foul language, and roistering for the
duration of her stint in New York, stipulations she agreed to
readily and broke quickly. Aikman describes her "triumphal entry" into Buffalo brandishing the reins of a four-horse team
hitched to an old-fashioned buckboard, her nose suspiciously
red, and with whiskey bottles in her back pockets.

Even so, in an exposition later ruined by the assassination of
President William McKinley on September 6, 1901, some remembered Calamity as a hit, dressed in her familiar buckskins
and leather gauntlets, a big sombrero on her head, galloping her
horse around an outdoor arena, waving her pistols and shouting
at the crowd. Once again, however, drink did her in, and she was
fired. She had apparently blown all her salary money (she claimed
to have been earning five hundred dollars a week but, as Aikman
says, a tenth of that is more likely), buying drinks for the house.
Bill Cody found her stranded and destitute and paid her rail
ticket back to Montana.

The New York show was to be Calamity's last hoo-raw. She
spent her declining days, her eyesight failing, around Livingston,
selling her skimpy autobiography to tourists visiting nearby Yellowstone Park. Harry Sinclair Drago, one of her least admiring
chroniclers, believes she was also suffering from some form of
venereal disease.

In the spring of 1903, she returned to the Black Hills for the
last time, sick and nearly blind, carrying her belongings in a battered suitcase, and found refuge in Belle Fourche, cooking and
laundering at Dora Dufran's brothel. Dufran recalled her as loud

and boisterous when drunk and that she "even had a band of coyotes beat for howling."

In July she went on a bender, rode an ore train to Terry, a little mining town near Deadwood, and fell violently ill. A benevolent bartender got her a room at the Calloway Hotel and sent for a doctor. On Saturday, August 1, 1903, she died of "inflammation of the bowels and pneumonia," and the Society of Black Hills Pioneers paid for her funeral, one of the biggest Deadwood ever witnessed, at the First Methodist Church. Both the undertaker who donated the pine coffin and the caretaker of Mount Moriah Cemetery had been boys when Calamity nursed them through the smallpox epidemic of 1878.

She was buried at Mount Moriah in a plot next to Wild Bill Hickok's.

For all its sordid episodes, there is more triumph than sadness in Martha "Calamity Jane" Canary's story, more to admire than to pity. As a child, barely into her teens and penniless, she was thrust into the man's world of the old, still very wild, western frontier, forced to learn to survive and make her way alone. That she did so, and lived forty of the fifty-odd years of her life by some discovered wit and strength, is little short of miraculous.

At least as unaccountable is that she is virtually all mystery, that aside from a handful of usable facts, we know almost nothing about her, yet she is among the most readily identifiable of Old West characters, the precise definition of "Western legend." While it is true that the legendary Calamity Jane was the product of her own invention, aided by dime novelists and eager newspaper writers, there is more to it.

Buffalo Bill Cody said of her, "Only the old days could have produced her. She belongs to a time and a class that are fast disappearing. Calamity had all the rough virtues of the Old West as well as many of the vices."

John Wallace "Captain Jack" Crawford, the Irish-born

scout and poet, wrote, "Calamity Jane was a good-hearted woman. . . . She grew up in a wild unnatural manner which we wonder did not quench out every spark of womanhood in her, and it is to her credit that she did retain a kind and generous heart. . . ."

And her great friend Teddy Blue Abbott said, "I've been in the plains for fifty-eight years, and I've never heard of an old-timer that knew her but what spoke well of her."

Compared to many Western figures whose legendry is inexplicable—Billy, Jesse, Wyatt, Doc, Wild Bill, and similar bloodletters—Calamity's place among them is above them.

II

THE ALBUM

In her 1896 *Life and Adventures,* Calamity Jane claimed Wild Bill Hickok only as "my friend." Thirty-eight years after her death, some other claims came to light.

On May 6, 1941, a tiny sixty-eight-year-old woman who identified herself as Jean Hickok McCormick appeared on the CBS radio program *We the People,* hosted by the popular newscaster Gabriel Heatter. Mrs. McCormick had a newsworthy announcement to make: She said she was the daughter of Martha "Calamity Jane" Canary and James Butler "Wild Bill" Hickok, and that she had "indisputable proof" of her claim. She had with her an old bound album consisting of letters written to her, she said, by her mother, Martha Canary, between 1877 and 1903, a handwritten marriage certificate in a Bible, dated September 1, 1870, and miscellaneous other papers.

The album and its diary-like letters and documents had a complex history. McCormick explained that as a baby she was "given away" by her mother to a British Cunard Steamship captain named James O'Neil and his wife, Helen, who were traveling in the American West. The O'Neils, she said, had befriended Martha Canary, then alone, ill, and destitute, and offered to raise her child in England and provide her a good education. Martha turned her baby over to the O'Neils in Omaha, and the child was taken by train to their home in Richmond, Virginia, and subsequently to Liverpool, England.

The daughter's birth name apparently was Jane, which the O'Neils changed, for reasons unknown, to Jean Irene. Jane grew up as Jean, believing the O'Neils were her parents.

After she gave up her daughter, Martha returned to her wanderings in Montana, Wyoming, and Dakota territories and elsewhere. McCormick said her mother always carried with her the "album," a sort of scrapbook, in which she wrote a diary-like series of letters to Janey—her nickname for the daughter now known as Jean. The letters were never mailed to Jean or the O'Neils, but the album was discovered among Martha's belongings after she died, and in 1903 had been sent to Captain O'Neil. Then, when O'Neil died in 1912, the album was given to Jean, who discovered her "real" parentage for the first time.

In her foreword to a selection of the Calamity-Janey letters published in 1951, Jean McCormick (who died that year) wrote that her mother had been living many years on money sent to her from England by Captain O'Neil, "the sea-captain who had adopted Calamity Jane's one and only daughter." The letters, she said, were written "by lonely campfires in the Yellowstone Valley where savages lurked," that the Indians called Calamity the "crazy woman," which enabled her to move about among them unmolested, and that she "nursed among the Indians." McCormick added, "Almost every page shows Calamity Jane's hatred for the sordid life she was forced to live, as well as the devotion she had for her daughter." She signed the foreword "Jean Hickok McCormick, Calamity Jane's daughter and foster daughter of James O'Neil."

The diary-letters, although with substantial time gaps between them, are filled with details on Calamity's whereabouts, activities, and innermost feelings. They are a record of a Calamity Jane nobody ever suspected lurked inside the "Hellcat in Leather Britches" of dime novel fame or the boozy, profane, camp follower depicted by such writers as James D. Horan and Harry Sinclair Drago.

The opening entry in the diary, dated "Sept. 25, 1877, Deadwood, Dakota Terr.", was preceded by a note: "Jim O'Neil— Please give this album to my daughter, Janey Hickok, after my death," and is signed "Jane Hickok." The letter, Calamity said, was written in her shack on Janey's fourth birthday, that "I visited your father's grave this morning at Ingleside," and that "They are talking about moving his coffin to Mt. Moriah cemetery in Deadwood."

Three days later she wrote of her mail route through Sioux lands ("I guess I am the only human being they are afraid of"), and that she carries the "diary" tied to her saddle. She also mentioned O'Neil sending her a bottle of ink and a pen so she could write to him—a strange matter, since pen and ink would have been available in Deadwood for a few pennies.

In a July 1879 entry, noting that Janey is now almost six and that Helen O'Neil has died, Calamity wrote of taking care of a boy named Jackie, about eleven years old, whose parents were killed by Indians. She said she found the boy on the "day your father [Hickok] was killed." She also wrote of visiting the Custer battlefield, where she saw disemboweled horses and human corpses with cut legs and arms and with "their eyes poked out."

The September 1880 letter, written from Deadwood, was the most important—at least to Janey—in the album:

Your picture [a photo sent to her by O'Neil] brought back all the years I lived with your father and recalled how jealous I was of him. I feel like writing about him tonight so I will tell you somethings you should know. I met James Butler Hickok Wild Bill in 1870 near Abilene Kansas—I heard a bunch of outlaws planning to kill him. I couldn't get to where my horse

was so I crawled on my hands and knees through the brush
past the outlaws for over a mile and reached the old shack
where he was staying that night. I told him and he hid me back
of the door while he shot it out with them. . . . Bill killed them
all. Ill never forget what he looked like with blood running
down his face while he used two guns he never aimed and I
guess he never known to miss anyone he aimed at.

After this concoction she offhandedly added the great revelation:

Then he was quite sick I nursed him several days and then
while on a trip to Abilene we met Rev Sipes and Rev Warren
and we were married there will be lots of folks doubt that we
were ever married but I will leave you plenty of proof that we
were. You were not a woods colt Janey don't let any of these
pusgutted blatherskites every get by with that lie.

Of the marriage "certificate," she said it was "fixed up by
the two revs far from civilization."

In this key letter, Calamity confessed that jealousy over Wild
Bill's other women drove him from her:

I lost everything I ever loved except you I gave him a divorce so
he could marry Agnes Lake. I was trying to make amends for
the jealous times and my spells of meanness. If she had loved
him she would have come out here with him but she didn't and
I was glad to have him again even if he was married. . . . A
man can love two women at one time he loved her and he still
loved me.

She said that Hickok was fifteen years older than she when
they met, that she had been born May 1, 1852, in Princeton,
Missouri, and that "your father was born in 1837 in Troy Grove,
Ill." (The town was actually called Homer when Hickok was
born there.)

In the letters Calamity revealed that she and Janey actually met on two occasions, on neither of which was their relationship revealed. The first meeting occurred in Richmond, presumably in 1890. There, Calamity claimed to have given ten thousand dollars to O'Neil for her daughter's education, money she said she won in a poker game with some Northern Pacific railroad barons. She wrote in her diary in October 1890:

I cherish my visit to you and your Daddy Jim [O'Neil]. . . . I am driving a stagecoach these days. . . . Rev. Sipes and Teddy Blue Abbott got me the job—they seemed to think it was better than being a saloon hostess. You see your mother works for a living. One day I have chicken to eat and the next day the feathers.

On September 25, 1891: "I did a most crazy thing sometime ago. I married Charley Burke. He got me in a weak moment."

On May 10, 1893, she wrote Janey, then twenty years old, about taking up a homestead west of Billings, Montana, and that her horse Satan had died. In July she was driving a stagecoach in a hailstorm and had been invited by Buffalo Bill to join his Wild West show and said she would ride bareback for Cody, "standing up shoot my old Stetson hat twice after throwing it in the air before it falls back on my head." She told Janey that she had bought acreage west of Billings and had a log cabin, then gave her daughter a "receipt" for "Twenty Year Cake" ("start with 25 eggs") which she said was "unexcelled and will keep to the last crumb twenty years." She also wrote plaintively that "They are telling awful things about me None of it is true every man I speak to I'm accused of being an immoral slut," and mentioned the outlaw Belle Starr—"She's bad but she's becoming famous."

In an entry marked "New York City 1893," Calamity said she was with the Wild West, heading for Richmond and then to Europe: "Buffalo Bill is so good to me. He and your father [Hickok] were great friends." A week later, from Richmond, she wrote, more diary-like than as a letter, "Saw Janey there [while I was] performing on bareback and rode close to her and O'Neil." With Janey and O'Neil returning to England, Calamity said she would be traveling with them on the *Madagascar,* presumably a Cunard steamer conveying Cody and his Wild West troupe to Europe for a tour. She added, "Your old mother is going down hill."

Following a long gap in the diary, she wrote a "Last Will" from Billings, Montana, in April 1898, bequeathing "to my only heiress my daughter Janey Hickok O'Neil all my possessions." These she enumerated as a ranch at Canyon Creek, a log cabin, saddle, trunk of possessions, the diary, a brooch of gold, and two pearls. She signed the entry "Jane Hickok Burke" and had it witnessed by men named John Tinkler and Joe Stager.

In May, from Stringtown, Montana, she wrote a letter to O'Neil:

> I may never write to you again Jim so I must tell you I have always loved you not the way I loved Bill Hickok but more idolatrous like you were something divine above me. . . . I haven't long to live Jim. The Dr. says I am going blind, My arms and legs are so numb at times I am afraid of paralysis. . . . I am not afraid to die but I don't want to die alone.

(O'Neil's response, dated Liverpool, August 25, 1898, was included in the diary: "You are just as good as I am. . . . I am old and lonely too." He also said that Janey was planning to "marry again," adding in Calamity-styled humor, "If she burns her behind she will have to sit on the blisters.")

From Deadwood, dated July 1898, Calamity made an apparently much belated entry on her experiences with Cody's Wild West in 1893: "Lord! how I did hate England—with its snobs . . . human parasites . . ." Now, she said, "My eyes are bothering me a lot. . . . The Spanish American War is on. If I wasn't so old I would go to nurse the boys who are sick and dying in that awful country."

In April 1903, some three months before her death, she wrote from Deadwood of finishing the diary: "Oh how I wish I had my life to live over." Then, in June she wrote that she couldn't see to write anymore: "Forgive me Janey, if they fail to bury me beside your father you will see that it is done should you ever get this." Then, on June 3: "I Jane Hickok Burke better known as Calamity Jane of my own free will and being of sound mind do this day June 3, 1903 make this confession. I have lied about my past life." This peculiar admission was accompanied by an even odder claim, that the outlaw Belle Starr was her sister, that Calamity had raised Starr's daughter and passed her off as her own child, and that Starr had married William Hickok, a cousin of Wild Bill's.

She ended her diary with the defiant line, "I was legally married to Hickok and Burke. I dare anyone to deny these facts," and signed the entry "Jane Hickok Burke."

Inserted in the album was a page from a Bible on which was written something resembling a marriage license:

En route to Abilene, Kansas, Sept. 1, 1870. I, W.F. Warren, Pastor, not having available a proper marriage certificate find it necessary to use as a substitute this page from the Holy Bible and united in Holy Matrimony Jane Cannary, age 18, and J.B. Hickok—31.

The crude certificate was witnessed by Carl Cosgrove, Abilene, Kansas; Rev. W.K. Sipes, Sarasville, Ohio; and Tom P. Connel, Hays City, Kansas.

Naturally, there were disputes over Jean Hickok McCormick's "indisputable proof" of her parentage. While the severest of the charges against her and the album—that both were frauds—came after her death in 1951, there were doubters at the outset.

The *Rapid City Journal* on September 12, 1941, four months after her appearance on the *Meet the People* program, carried an admiring story of McCormick's visit to Deadwood, where she "tenderly placed flowers on the Wild Bill and Calamity Jane graves," but others were pondering the matter of the album of letters and documents—the Calamity Papers. How could a woman whose formal education ended at about age ten, who was widely believed to be illiterate, who had never written anything, whose skimpy pamphlet of her *Life and Adventures* was clearly ghostwritten, have composed such letters? Why had she not boasted of her marriage to Hickok, or at least confided it, to others while she lived and after his death? Why had nobody ever noticed her toting an album around and scribbling in it? Why could no single example of Calamity's handwriting—not even a signature—be found?

And what of Jean Hickok McCormick? Who *was* she, anyway?

She claimed to have been born in Benson's Landing (later Livingston), Montana Territory, in September 1873, and that as a baby had been taken by Capt. James O'Neil and his wife to Richmond, Virginia, and to Liverpool, England, where she was raised and educated. She did not learn the identity of her "true parents" until her adoptive father died in 1912. She told the *Billings Gazette* in June 1941, that she "eventually returned to the United States," traveled in Montana, and from 1898 to 1902 taught penmanship in the Butte area.

She married at least twice, first to a "Virginia state senator" named Robert Burkhart* whom she said divorced her after learn-

---

*There was a Robert C. Burkhart who served in the *West* Virginia State Senate 1899–1901 (and who died in 1929), but no Robert Burkhart is to be found in the Virginia senate archives.

ing of her parentage and fearing that a scandal might ensue that would interfere with his political aspirations. In 1918, she said she married Ed McCormick, a pilot in World War I who died of wounds soon after their wedding. She had met McCormick, she told the *Gazette* reporter, while serving as a volunteer nurse in France.

After the World War, she returned to Montana and apparently, for twenty-odd years, worked as teacher, cook, and nurse, until, at some unspecified time, she revealed to her coworkers her parents' identity. Eventually, some of those who knew her secret contacted *We the People* and in 1941 she was invited to bring her documents to New York and to appear on the program and reveal publicly that she was the daughter of two of the most familiar names in Old West history. The producers of *We the People* were apparently convinced of the truth of her story after a cursory examination of her papers. One document that seemed particularly convincing was a letter from a daughter of W. F. Warren, the minister who "married" Jane Cannary and James B. Hickok on the trail out of Abilene on September 1, 1870. The letter attested that the marriage document was authentic.

Calamity Jane authority James D. McLaird, history professor at Dakota Wesleyan University in South Dakota, investigated McCormick's claims and her shadowy life and in a 1995 magazine article recounted some of the many problems with her credibility. She gave varying stories on how she came to be unofficially adopted by Captain O'Neil, one of her tales worthy of a Deadwood Dick novel.

She told a newspaper writer that O'Neil was in Montana in 1873, looking for the grave of a brother who had been killed by a Sioux chief named Howling Wolf when he stumbled upon Calamity Jane's cabin in the wilderness. McCormick's inclination toward variations on pulp melodrama cropped up again when she told of her mother taking her infant daughter from Montana to Omaha to meet the O'Neils in 1873. Calamity, Mc-

Cormick said, rode through "ferocious Sioux lands" and through their villages "doing a handstand on the saddle" which convinced the Indians that she was crazy and, since they revered the insane, permitted her to proceed unmolested.

Elsewhere she spoke of her son, fathered by Senator Burkhart, being killed in an accident on Chesapeake Bay involving the senator's yacht and, in a monumentally freakish coincidence, another yacht belonging to her future husband Ed McCormick—the man whom she said elsewhere she met in France during World War I. She also mentioned a daughter born of the Burkhart marriage who had been kidnapped as an infant and never recovered.

Beyond such lamentable examples of an old woman's overcooked ruminations, McLaird found no trace of her residence or history in either Montana or Virginia—not so much as a name in a census report or city directory. He also found it remarkable that there were over forty *loose* letter pages inserted in the bound album, allowing the suspicion that they had been written later as McCormick came across new information on Calamity and added it to the collection.

In the ten years she lived following the public disclosure of her parentage, Jean Hickok McCormick enjoyed her moment in the sun of the Big Sky Country and elsewhere. A librarian interviewed her toward writing her biography; she appeared in rodeos and frontier celebrations, visited Deadwood several times to place flowers on the graves of Calamity and Wild Bill, and even attended a Hickok family reunion in LaCrosse, Wisconsin, where she was greeted warmly by Wild Bill's distant cousins. There, a local newspaper reporter took a picture of her togged out in fringed buckskin skirt, red silk shirt, yellow neckerchief, cowboy boots, and a wide-brimmed Hickok-like sombrero. The photograph, in which she is flanked by two grinning Hickok cousins, reveals a tall, thin, sad-faced woman who appears to be trying, with mixed success, to be the daughter of Calamity Jane.

Jean McCormick died of heart failure in Billings, Montana,

on February 21, 1951, age seventy-seven (according to her stated birthdate). The Billings *Gazette* reported that she had lived in the city since 1922 and that she left "no known survivors."

McCormick's revelations were treated as semi-sensational feature-story fodder during her lifetime. Many who read of her claims were dubious of them but nobody knew much about Calamity Jane and, perhaps in deference to a kindly lady's harmless claims, most readers greeted her story with a grin and a ho-hum shrug and moved on to the important news of the new World War.

Probably the greatest initial blow to McCormick's revelations came from a Beloit, Wisconsin, librarian, Clarence S. Paine, who had sought out McCormick, soon after her *Meet the People* appearance, with the idea of writing her life story. He interviewed her, and the two corresponded for years as he painstakingly researched Calamity's life and attempted to mesh his findings with McCormick's album of Calamity letters. He was honest and meticulous, and despite his subject's impatience—the two grew distant as time passed—insisted on thorough research before writing the book.

Paine found certain particulars of the Calamity letters and documents disturbing. For example, there was the matter of the handwritten marriage certificate, dated September 1, 1870, and signed by Reverend W. F. Warren, "En Route to Abilene, Kansas." This page-in-a-Bible had been accompanied by a letter from Rev. Warren's daughter attesting to its authenticity, but Paine believed that the daughter was mistaken and the certificate bogus. Reverend Warren had indeed conducted a marriage ceremony for Hickok, but it was in Cheyenne, Wyoming, on March 5, 1876, when Wild Bill married the circus woman Agnes Lake. To Paine it seemed unlikely that the same minister would have conducted two Hickok marriages, one in Cheyenne and the other on the trail out of Abilene, Kansas, within five and a half years.

The librarian also investigated Calamity's claim to have participated in Buffalo Bill's Wild West in Richmond, Virginia, in 1893. During this episode Calamity allegedly said she had met her daughter Janey in Richmond (without Janey knowing her parentage) and subsequently traveled with her and Captain O'Neil to England on the Cunarder *Madagascar*. Paine found no record of Cody's Wild West performing in Richmond in 1893.

Paine never wrote the McCormick biography, but he did publish some random articles about her and the Calamity album. He did not ascribe to the putative daughter any attempt to defraud, rather seemed to believe McCormick was honest in her beliefs. But he determined that any claim that Calamity and Hickok were married had been "spun from the whole cloth" and wrote that the Bible-page "marriage certificate" was a crude forgery.

Subsequent researchers were not so forgiving.

In his *Desperate Women*, published a year after McCormick's death, James D. Horan, a popular historian of the West, revealed that Cunard Lines had no record of a captain named O'Neil or a vessel named *Madagascar*.

Hickok authority and biographer Joseph G. Rosa found that a photograph of O'Neil in McCormick's possession was actually that of a Capt. A. C. Grieg, a Cunard captain in the years 1906–1945. Rosa, in his several exhaustively researched books on Hickok (see under "Sources") gives no credence to any serious relationship between Calamity Jane and Hickok, and gives none whatever to the Calamity letters and documents McCormick revealed in 1941.

In her 1958 book *Calamity Jane: A Study in Historical Criticism,* Roberta Beed Sollid expressed the belief that the Calamity–Wild Bill "marriage" was either a fantasy of Martha Canary's or a tall tale fomented by others, and expressed the belief that the McCormick story was a hoax.

Harry Sinclair Drago, another popularizer of Old West historical figures, wrote in 1969 that the Calamity–Wild Bill marriage was a laughable invention, that at the time it was supposed to have occurred, Calamity was employed in a low brothel five miles west of Fort Laramie. Drago described her as "a widely traveled, coarse, slovenly, frontier whore . . . with her looks gone" and "reduced to finding employment in the various 'hog ranches,' the cheapest houses of frontier prostitution."

In 1941, when McCormick unveiled the album, the available factual data on Calamity Jane was so meager that the claims of her putative daughter were scarcely challenged even though many of the Calamity stories were clearly absurd. There was the bizarre business of being Belle Starr's sister, of rescuing Wild Bill from outlaws in 1870 after crawling a mile through the brush on her hands and knees, of performing in Buffalo Bill's Wild West "standing up [on horseback to] shoot my old Stetson hat twice after throwing it in the air before it falls back on my head," of winning ten thousand dollars in a poker game with Northern Pacific railroad barons, and the like. These were dismissed as typical Calamity Jane inventions, the kind of wholesale fabrication on which she had built her dime-novel reputation. And as for McCormick herself, since nothing substantial was known of her history, newspapers tended to believe what little she told them, even when the information grew contradictory in her embellished retellings. In this, at least, she resembled Calamity Jane.

With the passage of sixty years from disclosure and fifty years from McCormick's death, tenacious Western historians have not only challenged the papers, but also pronounced them counterfeit—and many of the experts are convinced that Jean Hickok McCormick was their author.

History professor John D. McLaird, without formally indicting McCormick as the source, called the Calamity album and its contents "clumsy forgeries" and titled his 1995 article in *Montana: The Magazine of Western History,* "Calamity Jane's Diary and Letters: Story of a Fraud." McLaird found McCormick on a par with Calamity in credibility and a woman with just as shadowy a past: she seemed to appear out of nowhere, with no imprint left on the places she claimed to have lived, made her startling announcement of May 6, 1941, and died a decade later leaving behind a cloud of mystery.

McLaird, in posing the great question on the Calamity Papers—"Who wrote them and why?"—states that virtually all the material appearing in the "Dear Janey" letters was in print before 1941, when the diary-album was first revealed. Calamity's whereabouts, friends, and exploits had appeared in stories in Montana and other Northern Plains newspapers and were readily available to any diligent researcher. Moreover, McLaird found that "documentable" places where Calamity was known to sojourn but which were not mentioned in newspaper coverage were not mentioned in the diary, and the same held true of known acquaintances of Calamity's—if they did not appear in newspaper reports, they did not appear in the letters. Further, the major historical events of which Calamity wrote in her *Life and Adventures* pamphlet—her claims of scouting for General Crook, of helping capture Hickok's murderer, and the like—are conspicuously missing from her letters. The implication here is that whoever fabricated the diary eliminated many of Calamity's wildest tales, those commonly laughed at, to add credibility to her Janey letters.

McLaird even solved one particularly troublesome mystery within the Calamity Papers raised by Elizabeth Stevenson in her 1994 book, *Figures in a Western Landscape.* This issue involved a man named William Lull, a tenderfoot from New York who, after trying his hand at gold mining, became the assistant to the owner of Porter's Hotel in Deadwood, where Calamity often stayed. In letters Lull wrote to his family in New York of his adventures in the Wild West, he spoke of his admiration for Hickok. He even claimed to have ridden in a posse with Wild Bill to rescue some miners under attack by Indians, and said he was a witness to Hickok's murder on August 2, 1876. Lull also wrote that he knew and had befriended Calamity Jane. He called her a "lone wolf," said she was honest and generous, a marvelously skilled horsewoman, bullwhacker, and teamster, and that he treated her like a lady at the hotel, in response to which she would say "Go to Hell, Baby Face." Once, he wrote, he found a doctor for her when she fell ill of a fever at the Porter, and not only helped nurse her back to health but corralled some of the "girls"—prostitutes—into taking care of her "woman's needs."

He said Calamity was not as calloused as people thought and in his letters and in a memoir of his Deadwood days written later seems to have taken it for granted that she and Hickok were at least friends. He said she was a "frequent companion [of Wild Bill's] in the search for adventure."

In the purported letters Calamity wrote to Janey, one dated July 1880, from Coulson (later Billings), Montana, is evidence of her acquaintanceship with Lull:

> I met a man here today from Deadwood who knew my best friend there, Mister Will Lull. I was sick with a fever of some sort while rooming at his hotel. The Hotel Baby Face took over from New Orleans man, Porter, and Lull was so good to me. He knows his business. I like him very much, he always treats me with "Howdy Jane, little girl. Keep a stiff upper lip, remember you're a good girl."

Calamity even gave Lull a tintype of herself and told him, "If you show it to some nice young girl, don't tell her it was your sweetheart or she might give you the bounce!"

Eventually William Lull returned East and never saw Calamity again, although he would occasionally see her name in the papers, as when she appeared at the Pan-American Exposition in Buffalo, New York. Following his death, his letters and memoir were placed in the family archives. They were never published.

This last fact struck Elizabeth Stevenson as significant enough to give new credibility to McCormick's claims and perhaps to the authenticity of the Calamity Papers. In her *Figures in a Western Landscape,* Stevenson wrote that McCormick may have read the Calamity Jane passages in Teddy Blue Abbott's *We Pointed Them North* since it was published in 1939, but how could she have known of Lull's friendship with Calamity when his letters and memoir had never been published?

McLaird, in his "Calamity Jane's Diary and Letters: Story of a Fraud," provides the answer to this significant question. "In fact," he wrote, "the resourceful McCormick utilized Lull's memoirs and those of many others in the production of her forged diary and letters."

The loose pages in the bound album provided a clue that McCormick added material to the album after her initial disclosure on *We the People* and that among these additions were the William Lull passages. McLaird discovered the proof of this: After her parentage claim went public in May 1941, McCormick received letters from people who claimed to have know Calamity personally and among these informants was William Lull himself, writing to her in 1941 from his home in Yonkers, New York. He told McCormick of his meeting Calamity and Wild Bill in Deadwood in gold rush days, of his working for the owner of the Porter Hotel, and of the time Calamity fell ill and he found a doctor for her—all the ingredients for the July 1880 passage in the "Dear Janey" letter.

If Jean McCormick assembled the album, forged its letters and documents, invented not only her Calamity–Hickok parentage but also her "adopted" parents, the O'Neils, what was her motive for so intricate a deception, and what did she gain from it?

McLaird believes she sought notoriety, some form of "self-identity," and money for personal appearances and for the story of her life. That money was a factor seems indisputable: four months after her *We the People* appearance, she was able to convince Yellowstone County welfare officials in Billings that she was eligible for old-age benefits. Her claim was based upon her birthdate of September 25, 1873, as stated in the first letter of the diary in which Calamity writes from Deadwood on September 25, 1877, Janey's "fourth birthday."

There remain questions about the timing and the massive elaborateness of the hoax. McCormick was sixty-four years old when she told her story publicly. She supposedly knew of her parentage for at least twenty-nine years (since 1912 when James O'Neil was said to have died) before revealing it. Why had she delayed until her advanced age letting the world know she was the daughter of Calamity Jane and Wild Bill Hickok?

The album of letters and documents required a staggering amount of research—months, probably years, spent winnowing through old newspapers in an era not only before computer-assisted searches but also before microfilm. McCormick not only reconstructed Calamity's exploits and whereabouts and learned of her friends, but also planted certain clever clues that would add authenticity to the "Janey" letters. Since she must have known that Calamity was believed illiterate, "Janey" even had to emulate her mother's "voice," how Calamity would write if she *could* write, down to the missing punctuation and occasional misspellings. In her scheme, if that is what it was, Mc-Cormick often displayed flashes of brilliance, as when Calamity tells Janey in September 1880 that she is the legitimate child of Martha and James Butler Hickok: "You were not a woods colt Janey don't let any of these pusgutted blatherskites every get by with that lie." And in such a passage as that of October 1890: "I am driving a stagecoach these days. . . . You see your mother works for a living. One day I have chicken to eat and the next day the feathers."

These passages sound precisely like Calamity Jane would talk and, if she could, write.

While piecing together Calamity's chronology, whereabouts, exploits, friends, voice, and character, McCormick also had to construct her own biography, and it is in itself a rather marvelous work. She had to invent James and Helen O'Neil, her adoptive parents, and O'Neil's Cunard history, his Richmond and Liverpool homes, his venture into the American West and meeting with Calamity in Montana, Nebraska, and Virginia. She had to invent O'Neil's voice, as well, as when he writes in August 1898, to assure Calamity, "You are just as good as I am. . . . I am old and lonely too," and with special astuteness, even plant in O'Neil's and Calamity's letters clues to "Janey's" early and failed marriage.

All this clever, painstaking, years-consuming work—to what end? To gain a few rodeo appearances and a welfare pittance from Montana authorities?

While it is common currency to denounce the McCormick Calamity papers as a fraud and a hoax, and the weight of the evidence supports the censure, there *must* be more to the story.

But until we know more about Jean Hickok McCormick, the case is cold.

THE
JACK LONDON
CASES

I am sick, very sick. . . .
Something has gone out of me.
I have always been unafraid of
life, but I never dreamed of
being sated with life.

—JACK LONDON
Martin Eden, *1909*

I

WOLF HOUSE BURNING

The trail begins at an elegant fieldstone house, headquarters of the Jack London State Historic Park, fifty miles north of San Francisco and just a mile or two west of the village of Glen Ellen. The hike from this "House of Happy Walls," once the home of London's widow Charmian Kittredge, is a deceptive half-mile downhill that seems twice as long climbing back up. In August, a hinges-of-hell month in this place early-day Indians called the Valley of the Moon, there is scarcely a breeze. Nearby, the celebrated Sonoma County vineyards thrive. On either side of the dirt roadway, where golden specks of pollen hang in the still air, are old oaks, California buckeyes, Douglas firs, redwoods, and madrones, their peeling bark like shaved chocolate. Behind the trees, ferns, and manzanita shrubs, in the leaf-covered, mulchy soil, are some bright spots of buttercup and poppy, Indian warrior, and hound's tongue.

This is an eerie, primitive place, dead quiet except for birdsongs, the buzz of bees, and the rustling of small forest creatures scurrying through the leaves.

About three quarters of the way downtrail is a turnoff path to the east that opens into a small clearing at the center of which is a weathered picket fence surrounding an immense native rock, burgundy-colored and greened with moss. Under it, in a copper urn, are Jack London's ashes.

The trail ends in a bigger clearing, one with picnic benches, where the visitor can rest before starting back. Dominating this shady place are the tumbled, fire-blackened native stone walls, chimneys, and cobblestone rubble of Wolf House, so called by London's closest friend, the poet George Sterling.

The grave and the ruins lie in close, some say symbolic, proximity. Wolf House burned in 1913, London died in 1916, and each of the two events has its mysteries.

In 1913, the year Wolf House burned, Jack London, at age thirty-seven, had already finished what every boy of his era dreamed of doing and what every man wished he had done. He had risen in genuine Horatio Alger style, by strength of character, daring, a wondrous work ethic, and a consuming ambition, to become America's favorite author, the creator of *The Call of the Wild, White Fang, The Sea-Wolf, Martin Eden,* and all those stories of exotic places, from the wolf-haunted white silence of the Yukon to the sultry islands of the South Seas. Everybody knew his name, knew he had been to the places he wrote about, knew at least some of his adventuresome, at times contentious, history.

He was born John Griffith Chaney in San Francisco on January 12, 1876, the American centennial year in which Alexander Graham Bell introduced the telephone in Philadelphia and George Armstrong Custer and two hundred of his cavalrymen were massacred by Indians above an obscure river in Montana. *Griffith* derived from a nephew of the baby's mother, Flora Wellman of Massillon, Ohio, an unstable woman who made a marginal living as a spiritualist, conducting séances and astrological readings. Age thirty-three when her son was born, Flora had lived the year prior to the birth with "Professor" William H. Chaney of Maine, a wandering astrologer in his fifties at the time he met Flora. Chaney deserted his common-law wife about six months before his son was born.

In September 1876, Flora married a Pennsylvanian, John London, a widower and impecunious Civil War veteran in chronic ill health who earned a subsistence living as farmer, grocer, store-keeper, and sewing-machine salesman. He was a gentle, kindly man with children of his own and was much loved by Flora's son, to whom he gave his name.

Young Jack described his youth as that of a "work beast" and wrote of "becoming a man very early in life" in such auto-biographical works as *Martin Eden, John Barleycorn,* and "The Apostate." In the latter story, published in 1906, a boy works dawn to dusk in a jute mill, "toiling centuries long in a single night at tying an endless succession of weaver's knots," breath-ing lung-clogging lint amid the deafening roar and crash of the looms, and prays,

> *Now I wake me up to work;*
> *I pray the Lord I may not shirk.*
> *If I should die before the night,*
> *I pray the Lord my work's all right.*
> AMEN.

Jack had been a bobbin boy in a jute mill, also a cannery worker, and a coal-heaver in a power plant, in grammar school days. In his teens, he learned to sail a boat and raided oyster beds on San Francisco Bay, then put his sailor skills to work as an able seaman on a sealing schooner in the Bering Sea. As "Skysail Jack" and "the Kid," he hoboed with other vagabonds in the

---

*A collection of unemployed men, led by Ohioan Jacob S. Coxey, which marched to Washington in 1894. London put his experiences riding the rails and hoboing across the country into *The Road,* published in 1907.

western detachment of Coxey's Army,* was arrested for va-grancy in Buffalo, New York, and spent a month in the Erie County Penitentiary.

Before his twentieth birthday, London joined the American Socialist Labor Party; at age twenty-one, he followed the Klondike gold rush into Canada's Yukon Territory; at twenty-three, he saw his first professional story published; and in 1900, the year his first book was published, he stood on the brink of the fame he dreamed of and hungered for from his childhood.

Jack London had sixteen years to live and lived them as furi-ously as he had the previous twenty-four.

He lived six weeks as a "denizen" of the East End ghetto of London, England, in the summer of 1902 and wrote a stinging book-length exposé, *The People of the Abyss,* on the poverty and hopelessness he observed there at the time of the sumptuous coronation of King Edward VII.

In 1903, the year he separated from his wife and left behind two baby daughters, *The Call of the Wild,* his most enduring book, was published, selling ten thousand copies on the day of its release.*

In the first half of 1904, London served as a war correspon-dent for the Hearst newspapers in Manchuria during the Russo-Japanese War, managing to report from the battle front while the other correspondents, including the venerated Richard Harding Davis, luxuriated in a Tokyo hotel. *The Sea-Wolf,* among his finest novels, appeared during his absence.

In 1905 and the year following, he lectured on socialism in New York's Carnegie Hall, at Yale, and at the University of

---

*By 1964, it had sold six million copies. In 2003, a century after it first ap-peared, the novella remained in print, in thirty or more editions in America alone and in an estimated forty languages. London received two thousand dollars from the *Sat-urday Evening Post* for the magazine serialization, and Macmillan offered another two thousand dollars for all book rights. London, always money-desperate, took the deal and earned no royalties from the single book that alone would have earned him a comfortable fortune.

Chicago; began building a ranch in the Valley of the Moon; and for *Collier's* wrote one of the finest of all eyewitness accounts of the San Francisco earthquake and fire.

In April 1907, with his second wife, Charmian Kittredge, and a small crew, he sailed from the Oakland wharf in his own ketch-rigged yacht, the *Snark,* to Hawaii, the Marquesas Islands, Tahiti, the Solomons, Samoa, Fiji, the New Hebrides, and Australia. During the two-year voyage, London contracted malaria, pellagra, and painful skin abscesses that introduced him to morphine, a drug he would depend upon in years to come. But even in the midst of the miseries of the voyage, he kept up his daily work "stint" of a thousand words a day and wrote such books as *The Road,* on his days as a cross-country tramp, and *The Iron Heel,* a fiery novel of socialist revolution. The voyage also produced the unforgettable "To Build a Fire," his most popular and anthologized story, a tale of a man freezing to death in the Canadian wilderness, written in Hawaii while the *Snark* was undergoing repairs.

There were other adventures, as well: the Londons made a horse-drawn wagon trip to Oregon and back in 1911, voyaged from Baltimore to Seattle via Cape Horn on the four-masted barque *Dirigo* in 1912, and sailed his sloop *Roamer* on San Francisco Bay and up the Sacramento River.

His adventures, misadventures, his occasionally scandalous behavior and personal life attracted national press coverage, giving him the uncomfortable distinction of being the first American writer-as-celebrity, a star in a time of a single news medium.

He also became the richest socialist in the country, the first American author to earn a million dollars from his work.

The Jack London credo, written in about 1902, before he could look back with confidence that he had lived up to it, ends,

The proper function of man is to live, not to exist.
I shall not waste my days in trying to prolong them.
I shall use my time.

No man of his time, and few of any other time, did more with the years allotted to him.

To Jack London, home was literally wherever he hung his hat. One researcher has identified thirty-three places he lived as a youth—in San Francisco, Oakland, Livermore, Alameda, and San Mateo County—as he followed the fading fortunes of his stepfather, John London. The young wanderer also found a home on any seagoing craft, skiff to schooner, with sails; in a tramp's boxcar and tent, and around his campfire; in a log cabin outside Dawson City; in a correspondents' camp in frozen Korea or arid Mexico; a jail cell in Buffalo, New York; a workhouse in an East End ghetto in London; a hotel in Tokyo, Hobart, or Panama City; a grass hut in Fiji; a bungalow in Honolulu.

In 1909, he had to abandon the *Snark* voyage to recuperate in a Sydney, Australia, hospital from the tropical ailments he had contracted. He and Charmian made a roundabout return voyage home on the Scotch collier *Tymeric,* touching at Pitcairn's Island, Ecuador, and New Orleans, then traveling overland by train to California. He reached Glen Ellen in July, and by the time *Martin Eden* was published in September, began concentrating his energy and funds into expanding and building up his property in the Valley of the Moon. Important in this planning was the idea of a great mansion, his first real, permanent, home.

Back in July 1905, London bought a 130-acre ranch in Sonoma County, fifty miles north of San Francisco, "the most beautiful, primitive land to be found in California," he said of the one-time Tokay vineyard and winery. He fell in love with the place, its fertile soil, its ancient redwoods, firs, tanbark oaks, maples, madrones, and manzanitas, its canyons, silvery streams and springs, and its isolation. The new Mrs. London, Charmian Kittredge, loved it, as well. She had been raised in Oakland, attended Mills College, worked as a secretary and reviewed books for *The Overland Monthly,* the magazine founded by Bret Harte which in 1899 gave London his first national exposure as a writer. Charmian, a breezy, pretty, athletic horsewoman who disdained the sidesaddle and rode like a man, shared her husband's adventures in the South Seas, and wherever he roamed, shared his agrarian dream and the planning of what the two called their "Beauty Ranch."

By buying six adjacent properties over the next eight years, the Londons increased their land holdings to 1,400 acres and operated an innovative farming and livestock operation. London often consulted his neighboring rancher Luther Burbank, the celebrated horticulturist, studied and learned soil conservation to renew worked-out lands, employing terracing techniques he had observed in his travels as war correspondent in Manchuria, Japan, and Korea in 1904. He raised Shire horses, chickens, fruits, vegetables, and grains; built the first concrete silo in the state and a "pig palace" to feed, water, and raise his Jersey Duroc hogs, sows, and broods; brought in huge hay crops said to be the finest in northern California; and planted eucalyptus trees as a future lumber source.

The year 1911, a signal year for his ranch, also became the most productive of London's literary career: Twenty-four of his stories appeared in the best-read and highest-paying periodicals in the country and, under the Macmillan imprint appeared one novel, one nonfiction book, and two story collections, much of the work the beginning harvest of his South Seas voyage. He was earning seventy thousand dollars a year, a rich man's earnings in pre–World War I dollars, and spending one hundred thousand dollars, pouring his royalties and book contract advances into his land and the great stone and redwood house that would be his home and headquarters.

In fact, he was publishing too much, writing furiously to keep ahead of his bills, and, worse, borrowing on work to come.

In May 1911, he wrote to George Brett, the Macmillan president: "Having now a beautiful dream-ranch, I am doing on this dream-ranch two things: I am planting eucalyptus trees by the hundreds of thousands, and I am also building my dream-house." He proceeded to ask Brett for a thousand-dollar advance each month for five months to complete a new novel, *The Valley of the Moon.* Brett, nearly always amenable to his star author's appeals, advanced some money but warned Jack to slow down, that he was clogging the market with his work.

This was not welcome news and in 1912, after twenty-six books in ten years with Macmillan, London switched publishers. Doubleday, Page, brought out a collection of his South Sea stories, *A Son of the Sun,* and in 1912–1913, the Century Company published four London books. Only one of these, *John Barleycorn,* was remarkable. He called it, somewhat extravagantly, a "bare, bald, absolute fact, a recital of my own experiences in the realm of alcohol."

In July 1912, the *Santa Rosa Press Democrat* reported that "Jack London is building a charming home on his country estate at Glen Ellen," and said, "When London is not grinding out fiction for the *Saturday Evening Post,* or some other periodical, at the rate of ten cents a word, he is directing the pouring of concrete or the placing of beams and rafters in his new residence."

That December he wrote Frank H. Scott, president of the Century Company, for an advance of three thousand dollars against the nearly completed *John Barleycorn:* "In order that you don't think me a wastrel," Jack wrote, "I enclose herewith a very inaccurate article upon the home I am building." He said the tile roof alone cost $2,500, and that he had stonemasons, plumbers, and carpenters to pay.

London had, in fact, fifty-three employed workers on the ranch, including a thirty-five-man construction crew building Wolf House, and was supporting an extended family: mother, Flora; a nephew; his stepsister Eliza Shepard and her son; his ex-wife, Bess Maddern London; his daughters from that marriage, Joan and Bess; and "Aunt Jennie" Prentiss, a black woman who had been his wet nurse as a child and to whom Jack was devoted.

Century published *The Abysmal Brute,* a prize-fight novella and his thirty-fourth book, in May 1913, and while awaiting publication of *John Barleycorn,* London negotiated with George Brett to return to Macmillan. Brett agreed to take him back but advised him to slow down production. Jack agreed but wrote a friend, "If I should die at this precise moment I would die owing $100,000."

Meantime, *Cosmopolitan* paid him one thousand dollars for the serialization of *The Valley of the Moon* and contracted him for another novel and a dozen stories. He also made some pocket money from a photo and endorsement that ran in the magazine, a testimonial to his status as a national celebrity: "I am tremendously pleased with the antiseptic qualities of your Formamint tablets. Formamint is a real cleanser of mouth germs."

That spring and early summer of 1913 he juggled checks and bills and worker schedules, wrote his voluminous correspondence (experimenting with a new Dictaphone), bought farm equipment, ordered lumber, and worked on a big sea novel, *The Mutiny of the Elsinore.* One of his greatest triumphs in his role as gentleman farmer was buying an imported Shire stallion for the horse-breeding enterprise on the ranch. The horse cost $2,500.

Except for playing pinochle with guests at the cottage he and Charmian occupied while awaiting construction of their new residence, the ranch and "castle" absorbed what time he could spare from his writing. Eventually, he would even mortgage the cottage to continue construction of Wolf House.

⬡

They had planned the house as the centerpiece of the Beauty Ranch even before they were married in 1905, and the plot of

land for it—on a bank of Asbury Creek at the extreme north-
western border of the ranch—was landscaped before they departed on *Snark* voyage in 1907. Jack was a wanderer, Charmian
London later wrote, and needed a big place for his treasures.

> It [Wolf House] should be thought of . . . in relation to Jack,
> not as a mansion, but as a big cabin, a lofty lodge, a hospitable
> teepee, where he—simple and generous despite all baffling
> intricacy—could stretch himself and beam upon you and me
> and all the world that gathered by his log fires. Why the very
> form of the rough rock hacienda was an invitation, with its
> embracing wings, its sunny pool between the wide, arched cor-
> ridors and grape-gnarled pergola.

The *Overland Monthly* described it as "essentially a home
for the two people building it—a workshop for Mr. London, a
home for Mrs. London, and a place where they can gather and
entertain friends."

Even so, Wolf House was never to be a simple domicile; in
fact, from the beginning plans, it was to be a "castle," as London
himself referred to it repeatedly, or at least a château: a four-story,
eighty-by-eighty-two-foot, twenty-six-room hospitable teepee of
fifteen thousand square feet of space designed by the eminent San
Francisco architect Albert Farr.

In 1911, the lofty lodge began taking shape as huge volcanic
boulders were hauled by draft horses from a quarry three miles
distant to the landscaped site. These maroon-colored lava rocks,
uncut and unmodified, were cemented in place and blended with
unpeeled redwood logs to form the house walls. These walls, re-
inforced against seismic shocks by steel straps, were attached to
an enormous earthquake-proof slab, strong enough, it was reported, to support a forty-story building. The roof was fashioned of dark red Spanish-style tiles.

Two of the giant redwood trunks, bark and branches in

place, also formed the supports for the massive porte-cochère leading to a courtyard and breezeway that extended through the house. A patio, reflecting pool (to be stocked with mountain bass), redwood-paneled guest rooms, and the library opened on the left of the breezeway; a gun room, stairs, servants' quarters, utility rooms, and banquet hall seating fifty guests, all were situated on the right side.

The ground floor also held the eighteen-by-fifty-eight-foot living room—two stories high with rough redwood balconies extending around three quarters of it, one side occupied by an huge fireplace of blue slate, red rock-and-cobbles, biggest of the nine fireplaces in the house and extending up through the ceiling rafters. A large alcove nearby held Charmian's Steinway grand piano.

London's nineteen-by-forty-foot workroom on the third floor was isolated from the rest of the castle with a same-size library for his eighteen thousand books beneath it on the second floor, connected by a spiral staircase. His bedroom on the fourth floor lay just above Charmian's personal apartment.

Wolf House had its own heating, electric lighting, and refrigerating plants; a laundry, wine cellar, and, also in the basement, a fireproof vault for London's manuscripts and other valuables.

"I have a wage list of $3,000 this month, which I must pay," Jack wrote to his editor at *Cosmopolitan* on August 19. He appealed for $2,500 and got the money. The magazine had been a steady source of income since 1911, when it published the series of twelve "Smoke Bellew" Klondike tales at $750 each. At the time of London's August appeal, *Cosmopolitan* was serializing *The Valley of the Moon* and paying advance money for the novel-in-progress, *The Mutiny of the Elsinore*.

On August 21, 1913, on the eve of occupying the place, and with but three hundred dollars cash in the bank, London negotiated with a Santa Rosa bank for a five-thousand-dollar final mortgage on the Beauty Ranch to complete Wolf House. The insurance on the mansion amounted to only six thousand dollars, since everyone agreed, as a newspaper article put it, that "rock and concrete, massive beams and redwood logs with the bark on, were practically fireproof unless ignited in a dozen places, owing to the quadrangular construction and cement partitions."

By that sweltering summer of 1913, London had spent at least seventy-five thousand dollars (in modern dollars, probably a million) on his home and was ready to move in. He and Charmian had all their scattered belongings brought north from San Francisco and other storage places to fill the barns and cottages of the Beauty Ranch: furniture and furnishings, iron bedsteads, wall hangings, animal skin rugs and throws, trunks of clothing, Jack's manuscripts and books, file cabinets, scrapbooks, photographs, the Steinway piano, curios and native crafts collected in the South Seas, and such priceless items as the dinner china once belonging to Robert Louis Stevenson that Charmian had purchased in Samoa.

On August 22, 1913, the day of final cleanup, the day before the move, the temperature in the Valley of the Moon, always cloying in the summer, rose to one hundred degrees Fahrenheit.

At two o'clock on the morning of August 23, Charmian London woke up to the sound of a voice and found Eliza Shepard, Jack's stepsister and manager of the ranch, at the cottage window pointing toward Wolf House, a half mile south. The night sky was glowing orange and billowing with smoke as Jack was awakened and dressed frantically.

They reached the house just as the roof collapsed, the tiles clattering down between the fire-blackened rock partitions. Only the walls, three stories high, a rubble of smaller stones, and the six fireplace chimneys were left standing. All the redwood timber had been consumed and lay in piles of glowing embers.

The Londons, the wakened building crew and neighbors, remained at the ruins until dawn. The fire continued to burn for several days while the surrounding redwoods were soaked by a bucket brigade to prevent further destruction.

The *Santa Rosa Press Democrat* carried the story on August 24:

> The spirit of Jack London is not depressed by fire, even if the flames do devastate the interior of a majestic castle he has been building on the hillside on his big ranch near Glen Ellen, occupying the most romantic spot in all the country round.

The paper stated that London "decreed Saturday that the work of reconstruction of the castle shall commence immediately after the insurance adjuster has inspected the premises. . . . As to the origin of the fire, it may have been the work of a discharged employee and it may not."*

A day after the fire, Charmian wrote in her diary: "Feel terribly shaken—heart seems to be jumping out of my body and tears are very close to the surface. Our dear dreamed of home." Of her husband: "Dear mate—he is so brave and cheerful. I don't believe a soul knows his secret heartsorrow." Years afterward she said, "The razing of his house killed something in Jack, and he never ceased to feel the tragic sense of loss."

"It isn't the money," he told her. "The main hurt comes from the wanton despoiling of so much beauty."

A few days later, he returned to his desk, writing to pay the bills and payrolls. He took another two-thousand-dollar advance from *Cosmopolitan* and added a workroom to the cottage, giving him a small but efficient space with windows all around.

---

*Exactly a month later the paper reported that Glen Ellen had been saved from destruction when a great fire jumped Sonoma Creek and threatened the town and that London "arrived upon the scene with a small army of his ranch employees . . . at once took command of the situation . . . [and] was acclaimed the hero of the day."

As pieced together from neighbors, workers, and investigators, the fire began near midnight and destroyed Wolf House in about three hours. Constructed in a hollow, the fire could not be seen until the roof began caving in and the flames and smoke leaped out. By then, with no water available, it was too late to do anything but watch it burn.

But the suddenness of it seemed suspicious, and newspapers in San Francisco, Oakland, and Santa Rosa were the first—after the Londons themselves—to speculate that an arsonist, or gang of them, might have been responsible. In November, Charmian wrote in a letter, "the deepest hurt lies in the indisputable fact that it was set afire by some enemy . . . Who it could be we have no idea."

Among the possible malefactors was Eliza London Shepard's elderly husband, James, a former sea captain, from whom she was estranged. Three months before the fire, James Shepard had returned to the ranch, where he had been invited to dinner with Eliza, Jack and Charmian, and Jack Byrne, married to Eliza's sister. During an argument with Eliza, Shepard drew a pistol and threatened to shoot her, was wrestled to the floor by the men and disarmed. London threw Shepard off the ranch, and the next day he found himself and Jack Byrne under arrest for "assault." The case was thrown out of court, but for a time Shepard remained a suspect.

Disgruntled workmen were also mentioned as potential arsonists. London had fired one man for laziness and insolence only a few days before the fire, but the other workers said they had been paid and treated well and this possibility was eventually rejected.

The idea of "agents"—Socialist Party minions or perhaps a cell of the IWW (Industrial Workers of the World, the "Wobblies," as they were popularly known) cropped up early in the arson speculation. London's advocacy of socialist beliefs had never been wholly convincing; he seemed to embrace party ideas and in his time became the most eloquent spokesman for the "working

class" and against the "monied captains of industry." But his es-
pousals in fiction, essay, and speech were romantic and sentimen-
tal, outgrowths of a stormy youth in ten-cent-an-hour sweatshops
and on the boxcar road with Coxey's army of unemployed. What
he embraced was also the product of his self-education wherein
he read deeply and eclectically but without direction.

He wrote "Dear Comrade" and "Yours for the Revolution"
on many of his letters, gladly debated socialism in comfortable
surroundings, before a podium at Yale or among friends at the
Beauty Ranch, but he never walked a picket line or stood at the
barricades against the scabs hired to break a strike. He believed
in socialism, as biographer Richard O'Connor wrote, "as an actor believes in the lines he is declaiming," and London seemed to
admit this in a letter he wrote in 1913: "I have never taken any
part in the policy of the [Socialist] party. I have never spoken out
in a meeting. I've just been a propagandist."

At the time Wolf House burned to embers, what fire remained in him for the socialist movement was also dying out,
and since, to many of London's one-time comrades, Wolf House
was an ugly monument to capitalism, its ruins now stood as a
grim reminder of the price of betrayal of the militant socialism
he once espoused.

However, these speculations, entertained by Jack and Charmian and many among their circle of friends, remained dead ends.

Natale Forni, the general contractor for the Wolf House project, had a more workable and believable theory on the disaster.
He was devastated over the fire, knew the house to be Jack's great
dream, the focus of his energy and funds since the day the great
earthquake-proof slab had been poured and work had begun on
the walls. The day before the fire, Forni said, electricians finished
their work and the cleanup crew used turpentine and linseed oil
to clean and rub down the redwood paneling and other wooden
fixtures in preparation for the move-in the next day. These workers dumped their rags in a corner when they ended the day, and
the contractor believed that the combination of turpentine, oil,

and the 100-degree heat created a spontaneous combustion that spread to all the chemical residue on the exposed wood. Forni even took some of the blame. He personally inspected the house at the end of each workday and had often removed the flammable rags left behind. But this time, he said, he had been distracted and forgot the inspection.

Whether the Londons accepted this theory of the fire is not known, but eighty-two years after the event, Forni's ideas were tested.

In May 1995, a ten-member forensics team was assembled by Robert Anderson, a retired San Jose State University engineering professor and member of the American Academy of Forensic Science, to bring modern investigative techniques to the study of the Wolf House fire. Among the experts were a state criminologist, a specialist in hydrocarbon and chemical fires, an electrical engineer, an arson authority, and another expert on fire burn patterns.

For four days the team examined the evidence: the design and construction plans and documents, witness statements, historical records, weather reports for August 1913 (lightning was ruled out based on these reports and from testimony of Glen Ellen residents), a computer reconstruction of Wolf House, and the remains of the mansion itself, seemingly unlikely to give up any secrets after eight decades.

The team found that the house had been wired for electricity, as evidenced by junction boxes, conduit embedded in the walls, copper wire, and porcelain-knob-and-tube insulators found in the ruins, but the system had not been connected to a generator at the time of the fire.

Important evidence was uncovered in the moss-invaded stone walls and chimneys. Pieces of charred wood were discovered in notched masonry pockets where the redwood beams connected to the stone walls. These were important in determining the most likely progression of the fire. In the dining area, on the ground floor under London's library and study, ceiling beams were canted and showed signs that they had failed first, caving in by the force of the tile roof dropping down on them. These beams and timbers were found to be burnt more severely than in other rooms, indicating that the dining hall was the most likely locus of the fire, the point of origin. The hall also had the largest fireplace in the house and the only one with a redwood facing—all the others were finished in stone and loose cobbles. The significance seemed to be that the day before the fire, workmen had applied linseed oil to the redwood paneling around the fireplace and threw their rags in the corner of the room when they finished the day's work.

Although the forensic team could not completely rule it out, arson was considered a "low probability": the tall-ceilinged dining area would not have been a natural choice for an arsonist nor would an arsonist have been content with a single place to start a fire in so huge a structure. Also, the site was so remote that traveling in the dark would have required a lantern, and a moving light might have come to somebody's attention.

The investigators adopted the Forti theory. There were no furnishings in the house, but the cabinetry had been finished the day before the fire. (The *Santa Rosa Press Democrat* described the walnut and oak "interiors" and redwood paneling and said all were "magnificent.") The finishes applied to the woodwork were surmised to be linseed-oil-based stains and varnishes, "industry standards" of the day for fine woods.

The self-heating process of linseed oil on cotton, the investigators said, releases large quantities of a choking, white, lachrymatory (tear-making) smoke. A loosely piled handful of cotton rags dampened with boiled linseed oil was shown by forensic experiments to be capable of self-heating to flaming ignition in a few hours. The fire created by even a modest pile of such rags can be sustained, the experts wrote in their report, "as a very energetic fire for more than an hour. This was enough heat and time to insure the ignition of any wooden shelves or cabinetry in close proximity."

The final key, they reported, was the temperature: the higher the ambient temperature, the faster the spontaneous combustion of the flammable rags would have occurred, and the night temperature at Wolf House on August 23, 1913, was at least 100 degrees Fahrenheit.

"I've been down there at midnight on August 23," the late Russ Kingman wrote in May 1980, referring to the Wolf House ruins, "and I can testify that Forti had it right." A Jack London biographer and authority on the writer's life, Kingman was also a former navy firefighter who, after moving to Glen Ellen, made a study of the 1913 disaster. "Spontaneous combustion is a dull finding," he wrote, "not as interesting as arson by some Molotov cocktail–throwing socialist, but dull or not, that's what happened."

I I
WOLF DYING

His entire life had been an uphill scramble, a tale of veritable
Darwinian survival and one he proudly told and retold in his
fiction: outlasting frustration, persevering, turning disappointment into triumph. The destruction of Wolf House devastated
him but momentarily. He went back to work, the Jack London
anodyne, and in many ways the three years and three months
separating the fire and his death were the happiest and most productive of his life.

John Barleycorn, that "bare, bald, recital of my own experiences in the realm of alcohol," appeared in August, the month
Wolf House burned, and earned a rhapsodic endorsement from
the Women's Christian Temperance Union of California. (Later,
the National Prohibition Party also adopted it and, to his amusement, suggested Jack might run for president on its ticket.) The
book was a lighthearted but devastating first-person insight into
alcoholism from his first drunk, at age five as he carried a pail of
beer to his father plowing in the fields and drank from the
bucket. He told of bouts with whiskey that almost cost him his

life, and of his self-imposed rule not to drink aboard the *Snark* or at home during his daily thousand word "stint." He had mixed success with hard liquor to the end of his life.

The Abysmal Brute, an exposé of the prizefight game, and *The Valley of the Moon,* a pastoral novel set in London's own adopted paradise of Sonoma County, were also published in 1913, and before the year ended, he began writing another Sonoma novel, a love-triangle melodrama, *The Little Lady of the Big House.*

He wrote his daily thousand words and answered a flood of correspondence on the Dictaphone in a new workroom attached to the cottage—still dreaming of rebuilding Wolf House—and ran his ranch, now 1,439 acres in size. He oversaw the building of a dam and the terracing of the grain and produce acreage, adding to his Jersey cattle herd and starting another of Angora goats. He relaxed with Charmian, watching Charlie Chaplin movies in San Francisco, dined with friends at the Saddle Rock Restaurant in Oakland, and cruised on the bay on his yawl *Roamer.*

Outwardly, his riotous life seemed to have taken a tranquil turn: the sailor had been becalmed, enjoying a homebody's routine of work and play, friends and family.

The looming threat to his happiness was the state of his health, which had declined steadily from about 1910, following his return from the South Seas, the decline exacerbated by a life too suddenly sedentary and excessive in drink and diet. After an appendectomy two months before the Wolf House fire, London's physician, William S. Porter, told him his kidneys were infected, that uremia was taking its toll, and that he must switch instantly to a bland diet with no alcohol and strengthen his body by a rigorous exercise regimen.

Jack respected Dr. Porter but ignored the medical advice and proceeded to embark on a strenuous assignment offered him by *Collier's* in the spring of 1914. The magazine wanted him to serve as its correspondent in Mexico to cover an explosive international incident. Some American sailors had been arrested in Tampico, and while they were released soon after, the Woodrow Wilson administration had made certain demands of the Mexican government, which were denied. Wilson authorized the navy to seize the harbor at Vera Cruz, a strategy that resulted in a two-day fight in which nineteen American sailors and marines and 126 Mexican troops were killed.

Collier's offered London the unprecedented salary of $1,100 a week plus expenses to report from Vera Cruz on the fight and its aftermath. Perpetually in debt and forever neglectful of his health, he accepted the assignment. He arranged for Charmian to travel with him, and the two rode the Sunset Limited from Los Angeles to El Paso in mid-April, then on to Galveston and to Vera Cruz on a transport ship. In the Mexican port city, he reunited with Richard Harding Davis and other correspondents from the Russo-Japanese War a decade past and spent a month interviewing soldiers in the field, sailors on warships in the harbor, and soaking up information. He saw no fighting—it had ended before he reached Vera Cruz—but wrote several long and colorful dispatches, which put *Collier's* readers in the midst of the tense military and political atmosphere of a country still in the throes of a bloody revolution. The articles also served to further alienate him from the American Socialist Party, which accused him of reversing his opinions on the justice of the revolution, and of being co-opted by American oilmen in the country.

In late May, he took to his hotel bed with dysentery, ran a high fever, complained of pain in his colon and bloody diarrhea, and returned home, shaken and weak from the brief Mexican venture.

The year ended with publication of his rousing sea story, *The Mutiny of the Elsinore,* and good news from two of his mainstay magazines: the *Saturday Evening Post* offered him $750 for all the stories he could supply, and *Cosmopolitan* agreed to pay two-thousand-dollar advances to serialize *The Little Lady of the Big House* and a novel he was planning, a dog story set in the South Seas.

But the decline continued: the uremic infection, recurring dysentery, vomiting, and "gripes"—stomach and colon pains. He and Charmian shipped to Honolulu in January 1915, hoping the sun and sea breezes might invigorate him. He rested and worked, wore a loose kimono, and sat at his desk on the lanai of a guest bungalow facing the sea. There he wrote *Jerry of the Islands,* his dog story set in the New Hebrides, and dreamed of books he longed to write. ("Lord, Lord, man," he wrote to Roland Phillips, his editor at *Cosmopolitan,* "I haven't begun to write yet.")

They sailed home in July. Jack's last great novel, *The Star Rover,* appeared in October. The book was based upon the experiences of a San Quentin inmate named Ed Morell who wrote of tortures in prison, including being straitjacketed for days at a time. The ex-convict told of learning to escape the jacket by "astral projection," in which his spirit left his body and roamed through time and space. London heard of Morrell's claims and invited him to the ranch to tell his story. The resulting novel, said Joan London,* the author's daughter, "was Jack's last attempt at a serious work. Into this extraordinary and little-known book he flung with a prodigal hand riches which he had hoarded for years, and compressed into brilliant episodes notes originally intended for full-length books."

The Londons returned to Honolulu in December 1915, and on New Year's Eve attended a reception for Queen Liliuokalani in the throne room of her palace. The seven months they spent in Jack's beloved islands provided few clues to his wide circle of

---

*Joan London Miller (1901–1971) and Bess "Becky" London Fleming (1902–1991) were London's only children, both from his first marriage, to Bessie Maddern.

friends there of the dire state of his health, his advancing uremia, his morphine-induced sleep to escape the agony of kidney stones. The Londons entertained friends at their Waikiki cottage, held card parties where everybody talked about the Great War in Europe and the chances of American involvement, attended banquets, minstrel shows, movies, charity balls, luaus, polo games, and picnics. He managed to write *Michael, Brother of Jerry,* a sequel to his island dog novel, and a few Hawaiian stories before returning home in August.

Outwardly at least, his routine seemed little changed. He wrote his stories, answered correspondence, rode the ranch, greeted and entertained guests—a good many of them complete strangers, old hoboes, sailors, down-and-out pugs from the boxing ring, seeking a handshake, a handout, and a meal from the notorious soft touch, Jack London.

Few of the visitors saw beneath the generosity and joviality the pale, irritable, despondent, dying man suffering from the agonies of advanced kidney disease, finding peace only in morphine-induced sleep.

One of the joys of these last days was London's discovery of Carl Jung's newly published *Psychology of the Unconscious.* In Jung, he said, he saw a whole new world opening up for his fiction and experimented with a long fever-dream sequence in a final Klondike story, "Like Argus of the Ancient Times," later published in *Hearst's Magazine.*

On November 20, he rode up to the top of Sonoma Mountain to look at some land he hoped to buy. That night he barely slept and spent the twenty-first listless, fatigued, unable to hold his breakfast. He wrote his stint on a Hawaiian novel, *Cherry,* he had begun and wrote a letter to his daughter Joan, the last letter he would write. In it he asked that she and her sister Bess join him for lunch at the Saddle Rock in Oakland. He suggested taking in a matinee movie and a sail on Lake Merritt and wrote of leaving in a few days for New York.

In the evening, London talked with Eliza about the chores he wanted done on the ranch while he was away, talked with Charmian for an hour, then, at eight, went to his room to read. His last words to her were cryptic: "Thank God you're not afraid of anything."

She took a walk, returned at nine, and saw a light in his room—her bedroom only a few feet from his with a porch between. He had fallen asleep, feet propped up, chin on his chest, green eyeshade on his head, while reading *Around Cape Horn, Maine to California in 1852,* by James W. Paige.

At 7:45 on Wednesday morning, November 22, 1916, Sekine, London's Japanese houseboy, brought Jack's accustomed cup of coffee and tried to awaken the author, who lay in a fetal position on a couch in his workroom. When he failed to get a response, Sekine roused Eliza Shepard at her nearby house, and the two awakened Charmian. After holding Jack upright and trying to pour black coffee into his mouth, Charmian dispatched Jack Byrne, London's secretary, to Santa Rosa to fetch Dr. Allen M. Thompson, nearest of the family's physicians. The doctor arrived quickly and later said he found Jack doubled up in bed, propped on a pillow, head thrown forward, his face a ghastly bluish black.

Thompson, who immediately diagnosed a narcotic overdose, summoned a colleague, Dr. W. B. Hayes of Sonoma, and asked him to bring a stomach pump and an antidote for morphine poisoning. Soon, the two physicians were attempting to revive their patient with artificial respiration, a stomach lavage of potassium permanganate in solution, vigorous massage of arms and legs, and attempts to walk London around while Charmian and others shouted "Wake up! Wake up!" in his ear. He was also given an injection of atropine sulphate, a central-nervous-system stimulant.

By midday, Dr. William S. Porter, Jack's personal physician, arrived from Oakland, together with another medical doctor, a

London friend from San Francisco, J. Wilson Shields. Now four doctors were trying to revive the comatose patient, continuing to walk the rag-doll-limp author around the room, inventing crises—"The dam has burst!"—to shout at him, massaging his limbs and checking his respirations, pupils of his eyes, and reflexes. Once or twice London seemed to respond languidly but only for seconds.

At 7:45 p.m., twelve hours after Sekine found him unconscious, Jack London died at the age of forty years, ten months and six days.*

Dr. Porter did not agree with Thompson's diagnosis that the coma had been induced by an overdose of morphine. Porter had been treating Jack for three years for uremia and kidney disease, and he said it was possible that Jack had taken extra morphine in the throes of renal colic—the agony, the most excruciating pain known to inflict a human, of passing renal calculi, kidney stones. But, Porter said, the coma was the product of retention of bodily poisons London's diseased kidneys could no longer release and not the result of morphine poisoning.

Dr. Thompson was persuaded, if only temporarily, by the argument and signed the joint press release with the other physicians:

> At 6:30 p.m., November 21, 1916, Jack London partook of his dinner. He was taken during the night with what was supposed to be an acute attack of indigestion. This, however, proved to be a gastro-intestinal type of uremia. He lapsed into coma and died at 7:45 p.m., November 22.

On the death certificate, Porter wrote that death occurred from "Uremia following renal colic," and a kidney specialist

---

*In his seventeen-year professional writing career (1900–1916), he produced fifty books, forty-three published in his lifetime, seven posthumously. Of the fifty titles were twenty-four novels, seven nonfiction books, three plays, and sixteen collections containing most of his two hundred short stories.

writing in the *San Francisco Examiner* on December 14, 1916, agreed with the diagnosis. A Dr. William Brady, writing of "The Mysterious Disease that Killed Jack London" gave as common warning signals of uremia as headaches that can persist for days or weeks without relief, unusual daytime drowsiness but night insomnia, shortness of breath on moderate exertion, nausea and vomiting, the sudden onset of watery diarrhea, a peculiar odor resembling ammonia on the breath and skin. Brady said uremia was often mistaken as dyspepsia, asthma, and even drunkenness.

Virtually all the symptoms were recognizable in London's decline and death.

For twenty years the idea that Jack London may have killed himself remained speculative among a handful of the author's friends. The poet George Sterling, chief proponent of the idea, had for more than a decade been London's closest friend and confidant, and the virtues of suicide had been among their philosophical musings. Sterling was convinced his friend knew precisely what he was doing in taking an overdose of morphine, but the poet's views were tainted by his own self-destructive inclinations. For years he carried a vial of cyanide in his pocket, and in 1926, at the Bohemian Club in San Francisco, the man who called Jack London "Wolf" (and gave Wolf House its name), swallowed the poison and died.

Within five years of Jack's death, two biographies appeared. *Life and Jack London* by Rose Wilder Lane (daughter of Laura Ingalls Wilder, author of the Little House of the Prairie books), was serialized in *Sunset: The Pacific Monthly* in 1917–1918, and in 1921, The Century Company published Charmian Kittredge London's *The Book of Jack London*. Lane's book was highly fictionalized, and Charmian's two-volume memoir, while valuable, seemed an overly worshipful work by a widow who saw no faults in her hero. Neither book added details to the circumstances of London's death.

The London-as-suicide theory arrived full force in 1938 with publication of *Sailor on Horseback* by Irving Stone, a thirty-four-year-old former political science professor whose 1934 novel about Vincent Van Gogh, *Lust for Life,* launched his literary career. He subtitled his book *The Biography of Jack London,* not "*A* Biography" but "*The* Biography," and he seemed to know all the Jack London secrets.

Sailor on Horseback was a massively flawed book, a light-year from the publisher's claim that it was "The definitive biography." The author depended too much on London's fiction, in particular the half-factual novel *John Barleycorn* and such "work-beast" stories as "The Apostate," to recreate the author's life. And, while Stone the novelist could not escape novelizing *Sailor on Horseback* (later editions were more factually subtitled "A Biographical Novel"), *Sailor* was nonetheless a pioneering work, presenting original research on the circumstances of both London's birth and his death.

Stone's research identified for the first time the vagabond astrologer William Henry Chaney as the author's father and printed the 1897 exchange of letters between the two in which Chaney admitted living with Jack's mother, Flora Wellman, at the time of conception but denied paternity: "I was impotent at that time," he said, "the result of hardship, privation, and too much brain work. Therefore I cannot be your father, nor am I sure who your father is." Every London biographer since 1938 (including the author's daughter Joan, who researched Chaney's life) has followed Stone's lead, and despite his denial, Chaney has been named by all as Jack's "putative father."*

The second of the revelations in *Sailor on Horseback* was the story that London had calculated a lethal dose of morphine and killed himself with it some time during the night of November 21-22, 1916.

---

*Chaney died in 1903, the year his son's great novella, *The Call of the Wild,* was published.

Irving Stone's sole source behind this stunning finding was the first physician to reach London's bedside on the morning of November 22. In 1936, the author discovered Allen M. Thompson still residing in Santa Rosa, twenty years after he rode down to the Beauty Ranch the fateful morning. The doctor had a clear recollection of what he saw and what he diagnosed. He told Stone that when he arrived at the London cottage he found the author doubled up in bed, unconscious, breathing stertorously, his face bluish black. Thompson said that a morphine sulphate vial and another of atropine sulphate was found on the floor near London's bed and that on the nightstand lay a pad with some figures on it representing a calculation of a lethal dose of twelve and a half grains of morphine.

"If he had taken 12½ grains early in the evening, he would have been dead," the doctor stated somewhat obscurely. "If he had been accustomed to morphine, had a tolerance for it, he might have lasted; but if he had not been taking it, he wouldn't have lasted more than four hours."

Moreover, Thompson said that later in the day as he and the others continued their efforts to revive London, Charmian told him "it was important that the now probable death of Jack London should not be ascribed to anything but uremic poisoning." Thompson said he told her that "it would be difficult to ascribe it [London's death] to that alone, as any of the telephone conversations overhead that morning, or any information supplied by the druggist who prepared the antidote, would tend to ascribe his death to morphine poisoning." Thompson went on to say that the two physicians who superseded him (William S. Porter and J. Wilson Shiels) concocted the cause of death to avoid an inquest and autopsy. He continued to maintain that a *calculated* overdose of morphine and atropine had allowed deadly toxins to build in Jack's system, resulting in coma and death.

But there were grave problems with Thompson's story that Irving Stone either did not explore or chose not to report.

Neither Eliza Shepard, who was at Jack's bedside the entire

day of his death, nor the houseboy Sekine, nor the other doctors in attendance, nor anybody else, ever saw the empty vials or the notepad Thompson cited as evidence of a purposeful drug overdose. Further, the suicide skeptics point out, how could anybody assert that London "calculated a lethal dose" of the drugs without knowing how much morphine and atropine sulphates were in those elusive vials at the moment he reached for them? He was a veteran morphine user and may have taken the drugs several times after they were purchased. Moreover, as a seasoned morphine user, Jack had built up some tolerance for the drug, and even his regular doctor, Porter, would have had difficulty making such a calculation.

As London biographer Andrew Sinclair put it, "All in all, if Dr. Thompson saw some arithmetic on the night table, it was more likely to refer to 12½ percent royalties than grains of morphine for a fatal dose."

(After *Sailor on Horseback* appeared in 1938, Dr. Porter insisted adamantly to Joan London that uremic poisoning was the cause of her father's death, complicated by whatever morphine he ingested, and not vice versa. Joan London remained suspicious, however, and seemed to side with the Thompson thesis, but without using the word *suicide*, in her own book, *Jack London and His Times*, published in 1939.)

"More than likely," wrote London authority Alfred Shivers, a former pharmacist, "London had injected one or more doses of the drugs during a sharp seizure of pain from his kidney stone, and did not give sufficient heed to possible toxicity." Shivers, for his 1969 study of London's death, consulted three medical authorities who agreed there was no mathematically precise method for calculating a lethal dose of morphine.

The cause of Jack London's death has never been in serious question: He died of kidney failure complicated by a toxic dose or doses of morphine, most likely taken in the throes of pain resulting from kidney stones. The question has always been whether he premeditated his death—*knowingly* killed himself.

The suicide idea, first advanced in print in Irving Stone's *Sailor on Horseback*, has been tenacious, as if suicide were more romantic, a more fitting death for a man of action than the sordid business of kidney failure. London, after all, wrote often of suicide. In a symposium on euthanasia published in the *Medical Review of Reviews* and quoted by Joan London, he stated, "Man possesses but one freedom, namely, the anticipation of the day of his death. . . . I believe in the individual's right to cease to live."

Those searching for suicide clues in London's work point out that in *The Little Lady of the Big House,* the last novel published in his lifetime (written in 1913, the year Wolf House burned), the wife of a scientific rancher with a northern California domain of a quarter-million acres is torn between her love for her husband and another man. She shoots herself, is revived by stimulants, then is given a large dose of morphine and slides into death.

Even in his earliest fiction, there were suicidal themes, and he loved the lines from Longfellow and often quoted them:

> The sea is still and deep;
> All things within its bosom sleep;
> A single step and all is o'er;
> A plunge, a bubble and no more.
>
> A plunge, a bubble and no more.

The lines were particularly poignant in *Martin Eden,* London's most ambitious and important novel. Written during the *Snark* voyage and published in 1909, *Eden* is a novel of disillusionment, of the struggles of a common, self-educated sailor to become a successful writer and how Martin's rise is also his fall, especially from his real world into an artificial "civilized" life he cannot abide.

In a shocking (for 1909) ending, Martin commits suicide.

The book is autobiographical; it is also fiction.

On the eve of his death, London made plans to meet his daughters for lunch in Oakland, a movie, and a sail on Lake Merritt. He had purchased rail tickets and made hotel reservations on November 21 for the trip to New York. There, he told friends, he hoped to find a correspondent assignment in Europe, where the Great War was raging. He talked to his daughter Joan about his hope to visit Scandinavia and perhaps return to Japan to study their agricultural methods, and he gave his half sister and Beauty Ranch manager Eliza Shepard instructions to be followed during his absence.

During the night of November 22–23, he was stricken by the unendurable pain of passing a kidney stone and reached for his drugs.

If quick suicide had been on his mind, he need not have waited for the effects of morphine sleep. He had a loaded .45-caliber Colt revolver in a holster suspended near his cot to be used to scare off varmints and trespassers.

On November 23, Jack London's body lay in a gray coffin in his study at the Beauty Ranch. The next day Eliza Shepard accompanied the body to the train station in Glen Ellen, then to Oakland, where his daughters Joan and Bess, his first wife, Bessie Maddern, and scores of friends waited. Jack's mother, Flora, now age seventy-five, had been notified of her son's death but could not attend the funeral or burial.

He was cremated, his ashes placed in a copper urn. The funeral was simple, as he wished, with a short oration, the reading of William Cullen Bryant's "Thanatopsis," one of Jack's favorite poems, and a poem written for the occasion by George Sterling containing the lines:

> Unfearing heart, whose patience was so long!
> Unresting mind, so hungry for the truth!

Now hast thou rest, gentle one and strong,
Dead like a lordly lion in its youth.

On Sunday, November 26, Sterling brought the urn back to the ranch, where Charmian decorated it with ferns and primroses. The burial place had been selected by Jack years before, a knoll about a half-mile downhill from the cottage he and Charmian shared. There were already graves there, marked by plain wooden crosses, of two pioneer children, David Greenlaw, who died in 1876, the year of Jack's birth, and Lillie Greenlaw, who followed her brother in death a year later. London loved the silent place amidst brush and flowers and shaded by tall oaks and redwoods, and told Charmian, "If I should beat you to it, I wouldn't mind if you laid my ashes on the knoll where the Greenlaw children are buried. And roll over me a red boulder from the ruins of Wolf House."

The burial was unceremonial, attended by Charmian, Eliza and her son, a few of the ranch employees and old friends such as George Sterling. The copper urn was placed in the ground, sealed within a cement sarcophagus, and, as Sterling wrote, "Amid the profound silence of the on-lookers, a huge boulder—a great block of red lava long-pitted by time and enriched by the moss of uncounted years—was urged by roller and crowbar above the sepulcher."

Charmian London died in 1955, and her cremated remains were buried under the boulder with her hero. Four years after her death, the Shepard family gift-deeded thirty-nine acres of land, Charmian's House of Happy Walls, the Wolf House ruins, and the gravesite to the state of California.

The Jack London State Park is visited by an estimated seventy-five thousand visitors each year.

AFTERWORD: THE WOLF DISEASE

In 1993, a new theory on Jack London's fatal disease came to light in an article in the *Journal of Rheumatology,* written by Charles W. Denko, M.D., of the Division of Rheumatic Disease, Case Western Reserve University School of Medicine. Based upon his study of London's symptoms, beginning with the self-diagnosis of scurvy in the Klondike in 1897–98, Denko believed the author died of systemic lupus erythematosus. This chronic disease, in which the body's immune system attacks connective tissue causing inflammation, is "systemic" when it attacks such systems as kidneys, joints, and the heart.

Denko asserted that London displayed lupus clues when he reported contracting scurvy—with bleeding, swollen gums, and joint pain—in the Klondike in 1896, while others in his party, eating the same diet, showed no signs of the ailment.

In June 1898, at Anvik, Alaska, London wrote of eating fresh potatoes and a can of tomatoes for his scurvy, which he said "has now almost crippled me from my waist down. Right leg drawing up, can no longer straighten it, even in walking must put my whole weight on toes." London said his condition improved after eating the vegetables, but Denko stated that the scurvy self-diagnosis was unlikely since hundreds of milligrams of vitamin C are required for a cure, many times what could have been contained in the vegetables London consumed.

Denko wrote that the symptoms London described "could be better explained as an attack of acute lupus involving the mouth and joints, two areas commonly attacked by episodic lupus."

London continued to have mouth and gum problems, the rheumatic specialist said, together with severe headaches, facial neuralgia, pulmonary problems, grippe, bronchitis, colds, chest pains, and pleurisy (diagnosed on the transport when London was en route to Mexico in 1914), all common manifestations of lupus.

Denko said that London's skin problems—recurring rashes,

urticaria, itching and painful hands and peeling skin, thickened toenails, the other dermatological disorders he experienced in the South Seas—were flare-ups of lupus rather than the diagnosed psoriasis and pellagra. For the author's repeated attacks of fever, diagnosed as malaria, he received antimalarial drugs such as quinine, which Denko pointed out is a modern treatment for lupus.

Lupus erythematosus, Dr. Denko wrote, was the name used by early observers of the disease to describe the severe lesions on the faces of untreated victims that resembled wolf bites. "London's fame, in part, was due to writing about wolves," he said. "Even his beautiful, ill-fated dream house was given a 'wolf' association. . . . It is ironic that Jack London himself succumbed to an acute flare of lupus, the wolf disease."

ACKNOWLEDGMENTS

I'm especially grateful to the writer-researchers whose published works and personal assistance were invaluable and pointed me toward certain trails I would otherwise never have followed: Leon C. Metz of El Paso, Pat Garrett's biographer, for our many breakfast talks about Garrett's murder; and Richard S. Wheeler of Livingston, Montana, who lent me the research materials he accumulated in writing *The Exile*, his novel about Thomas Francis Meagher.

These distinguished historians read my chapters—Metz on Garrett and the Fountain case, Wheeler on Meagher—and were immensely helpful in their critiques. Neither of these generous gentlemen, of course, are responsible for anything I have written, nor do I expect them to subscribe to all my interpretations.

For pursuing scarce books and scarcer pieces of information I'm grateful to my daughter Dianne L. Walker in Virginia; and to Kate Ryan in Washington, D.C.; Catherine Crawford in New York City; Edith L. MacDonald in Cocoa Beach, Florida; and Sue Wimberly in Pleasant Valley, Arizona.

Many thanks, too, to my other writer friends, Elroy Bode, Win Blevins, and Richard C. House, for their helpful comments on portions of the manuscript.

Winifred Kingman of the Jack London Foundation in Glen Ellen, California, allowed me access to the archives in the London Research Center and answered many questions during the writing of the London chapters; the friendly professional staff of the Montana Historical Society in Helena helped me winnow through the society's extensive archives on Calamity Jane, Jean Hickok McCormick, and Thomas F. Meagher (even showing me Meagher's "Convict Profile" document from Van Diemen's Land). I was also assisted by the Lewis and Clark Trail Heritage Foundation and its magazine *We Proceeded On,* and by George Skanse Jr. of the Book Gallery in El Paso, Texas.

Thanks also to Gregory Lalire, editor of *Wild West* magazine, for publishing in 2001 an early version of the "Yazoo Pilgrim" story, which won a Spur Award from Western Writers of America, Inc.

SOURCES

THE YAZOO PILGRIM

Bancroft, Herbert Howe. *History of the Northwest Coast.* New York: The Bancroft Co., 1884; two volumes.
———. *History of the Pacific States of North America: California.* San Francisco: The History Company, 1886–1890; seven vols.
Brebner, John B. *The Explorers of North America, 1492–1806.* London: A. & C. Black, Ltd., 1933.
DeVoto, Bernard, ed., *The Journals of Lewis and Clark.* Boston: Houghton Mifflin, 1953.
Du Pratz, Antoine LePage. *The History of Louisiana.* London: T. Becket, 1774. (Reprinted in New Orleans by J.S.W. Harmanson, n.d.)
Moulton, Gary, ed., *The Journals of the Lewis and Clark Expedition.* Lincoln: University of Nebraska Press, 1989–2001, 13 vols.

"OH HOW HARD IT IS TO DIE"

See Breben, Moulton, above.
Allen, John L. *Lewis and Clark and the Image of the American Northwest.* London: Contable & Co., Ltd., 1975.
Ambrose, Stephen. *Undaunted Courage: Meriwether Lewis, Thomas Jefferson, and the Opening of the American West.* New York: Simon & Schuster, 1996.

Bakeless, John. *Lewis and Clark: Partners in Discovery*. New York: William Morrow, 1947.

Bowers, Claude. *Jefferson in Power*. Cambridge, Mass.: Houghton Mifflin Co., 1936.

Brodie, Fawn. *Thomas Jefferson: An Intimate History*. New York: W. W. Norton, 1974.

Brown, Dee. "What Really Happened to Meriwether Lewis?" *Columbia: The Magazine of Northwest History*, Winter 1988.

Chandler, David L. *The Jefferson Conspiracies: A President's Role in the Assassination of Meriwether Lewis*. New York: William Morrow, 1994.

Chuinard, Eldon G., "How Did Meriwether Lewis Die? It Was Murder." *We Proceeded On* (August, 1991–January, 1992).

———. *Only One Man Died: The Medical Aspects of The Lewis and Clark Expedition*. Glendale, Arthur H. Clarke, 1979.

Clarke, Charles G. *The Men of the Lewis and Clark Expedition*. Glendale, Calif.: Arthur H. Clarke, 1970.

Colver, Ann. *Theodosia: Daughter of Aaron Burr*. New York: Holt, Rinehart and Winston, 1941.

Côté, Richard N. *Theodosia Burr Alston: Portrait of a Prodigy*. Mount Pleasant, S.C.: Corinthian Books, 2003.

Coues, Elliott, ed., *The History of the Lewis and Clark Expedition*. New York: Dover Books, n.d. (3-volume facsimile reprint of 1893 edition.)

Cutright, Paul R. *A History of the Lewis and Clark Journals*. Norman: University of Oklahoma Press, 1976.

———. "Rest, Rest, Perturbed Spirit," *We Proceeded On*, March, 1986.

Daniels, Jonathan. *The Devil's Backbone: The Story of the Natchez Trace*. New York: McGraw-Hill, 1962.

Danisi, Thomas C., "The 'Ague' Made Him Do It," *We Proceeded On*, February, 2002.

Dillon, Richard, *Meriwether Lewis: a Biography*. New York: Coward-McCann, 1965.

Fisher, Vardis. *Suicide or Murder? The Strange Death of Meriwether Lewis*. Athens, Ohio: Swallow Press, 1962.

Guice, John D. W., "Moonlight and Meriwether Lewis," *We Proceeded On*, February, 2002.

Hays, Wilma P. *The Meriwether Lewis Mystery*. Philadelphia: The Westminster Press, 1971.

Holmberg, James J., ed. *Dear Brother: Letters of William Clark to Jonathan Clark*. New Haven: Yale University Press, 2002.

Hough, Emerson. *The Magnificent Adventure*. New York: D. Appleton Sons, 1916.

Jenkinson, Clay S. *The Character of Meriwether Lewis*. Reno, Nev.: Marmath Press, 2000.

Lavender, David. *The Way to the Western Sea: Lewis & Clark Across the Continent*. New York: Harper & Row, 1988.

Malone, Dumas, ed. *Dictionary of American Biography*. New York: Scribner's, 1929–1933.

Montgomery, M.R. *Jefferson and the Gun-Men: How the West Was Almost Lost*. New York: Crown Publishers, 2000.

Norfleet, Fillmore. *Saint-Memin in Virginia: Portraits and Biographies*. Richmond, Va.: The Dietz Press, 1942.

Parton, James. "Theodosia." *Harper's New Monthly Magazine*, August, 1864.

Pidgin, Charles F. *Theodosia: The First Gentlewoman of Her Time*. Boston: C.M. Clark, 1907.

Ravenholt, Reimert Thorolf, M.D. "Triumph Then Despair: The Tragic Death of Meriwether Lewis." *Epidemiology*, May, 1994.

———. "Trail's End for Meriwether Lewis: The Role of Syphilis. Presented to the Coroner's Inquest into the Mysterious Death of Meriwether Lewis—Revisited," *American Academy of Forensic Sciences*, February 21, 1997.

———. "Self-Destruction on the Natchez Trace." *Columbia: The Magazine of Northwest History*, Summer, 1999.

Seton, Anya. *My Theodosia*. Boston: Houghton Mifflin, 1941.

Van Doren, Mark, ed. *Correspondence of Aaron Burr and Daughter*. New York: Covici-Friede, 1929.

Wilson, Charles Morrow. *Meriwether Lewis of Lewis and Clark*. New York: Thomas Y. Crowell, 1934.

SAM HOUSTON'S DILEMMA

Crook, Elizabeth. "Sam Houston and Eliza Allen: The Marriage and the Mystery." *Southwestern Historical Quarterly*, July, 1990.

Day, Donald, and Hary H. Ullom. *The Autobiography of Sam Houston*. Norman: University of Oklahoma Press, 1954.

Gregory, Jack, and Rennard Strickland. *Sam Houston with the Cherokees, 1829–1833*. Austin: University of Texas Press, 1967.

Haley, James L. *Sam Houston*. Norman: University of Oklahoma Press, 2002.

James, Marquis. *The Raven: A Biography of Sam Houston*. New York: Blue Ribbon Books, 1929.

Lester, Charles E. *Sam Houston and His Republic*. New York: Burgess, Stringer Publishing Co., 1846.

Williams, Amelia, and Eugene C. Barker, eds. *The Writings of Sam Houston, 1813–1863*. Austin, Texas: Pemberton Press, 1970.

Williams, John Hoyt. *Sam Houston: The Life and Times of the Liberator of Texas, an Authentic American Hero*. New York: Simon & Schuster, 1993.

MEAGHER OF THE SWORD

"Accident or Suicide." *Eureka* [Mont.] *Journal*, February 26, 1928.

Athearn, Robert G. *Thomas Francis Meagher: An Irish Revolutionary in America*. Boulder: University Press of Colorado, 1949.

Callaghan, James. "Red on Green: 'Meagher of the Sword and the Irish Brigade at Fredericksburg." *Civil War Times*, December, 1998.

Callaway, Lew L. *Montana's Righteous Hangmen: The Vigilantes in Action*. Norman: University of Oklahoma Press, 1982.

Cavanaugh, Michael. *Memoirs of General Thomas Francis Meagher Comprising the Leading Events of His Career*. Gaithersburg, Md.: Olde Soldier Books, n.d. (Reprint of 1892 edition.)

Clarke, Joseph I. C. "Death of 'Meagher of the Sword' a Mystery of Fifty Years." *The New York Sun*, June 8, 1913.

"The Fighting 69th." *The World of Hibernia*, Summer, 1995.

"General Meagher Executed by Vigilantes, Dave Mack Says." *The Anaconda* [Mont.] *Standard*, June 2, 1913.

Glynn, Gary, "Meagher of the Sword." *America's Civil War*, September, 1995.

Haines, Aubrey. *Yellowstone National Park: Its Exploration and Establishment*. Washington, D.C.: National Park Service, 1974.

Howard, Joseph K. *Montana: High, Wide, and Handsome*. Lincoln: University of Nebraska Press, 1983. (Orig. Published in 1943).

"How Gen. Meagher Met His Death." *The Butte* [Mont.] *Inter Mountain*, March 15, 1902.

Keneally, Thomas. *The Great Shame*. New York: Doubleday, 1999.

Langford, Nathaniel P. *Vigilante Days and Ways*. Helena, Mont.: American and World Geographic Publishing, 1996.

"Late Col. W. F. Sanders Described in Detail the Death of General Meagher." *The Butte* [Mont.] *Miner*, June 10, 1913.

Longergan, Thomas S., "General Thomas Francis Meagher," January 11, 1913. (A paper read at the 15th annual meeting of the Irish Historical Society, New York City, in files of Montana Historical Society, Helena, Mont.)

Lyons, Capt. W. F. *Brigadier General Thomas Francis Meagher: His Political and Military Career with Selections from His Speeches and Writings.* Montreal: D. & J. Sadler & Co., 1886. (Reprint of 1870 edition.)

Malone, Michael P. and Richard B. Roeder. *Montana, A History of Two Centuries.* Seattle: University of Washington Press, 1976.

Mather, R. E. and F. E. Boswell. *Hanging the Sheriff: A Biography of Henry Plummer.* Missoula: Historic Montana Publishing, 1998.

Overholser, Joel. *Fort Benton: World's Innermost Port.* Fort Benton, Mont., privately published, 1987.

Phillips, Paul C., ed. *Forty Years on the Frontier as seen in the Journals and Reminiscences of Granville Stuart.* Cleveland: Arthur H. Clark Company, 1925.

Stevens, Christian D. *Meagher of the Sword.* New York: Dodd, Mead, 1967.

Wheeler, Richard S. *Exile.* New York: Forge Books, 2004.

UNDER THE WHITE SANDS

Bethune, Martha Fall. *Race With the Wind: The Personal Life of Albert B. Fall.* El Paso: Novio Books, 1989.

Casey, Robert. *The Texas Border and Some Borderliners.* Indianapolis: Bobbs-Merrill, 1950.

Condia-Williams, Charlotte. *The Unsolved Murders of Colonel Albert Fountain and His Son Henry.* Hillsboro, N.Mex.: Sunrise Publishing, 1995.

Curry, George. *George Curry, 1861–1947: An Autobiography.* Albuquerque: University of New Mexico Press, 1958.

Gibson, Arrell M. *The Life and Death of Colonel Albert Jennings Fountain.* Norman: University of Oklahoma Press, 1965.

Hutchinson, W. H. *Another Verdict for Oliver Lee.* Clarendon, Tex.: Clarendon Press, 1965.

Kelleher, William A. *The Fabulous Frontier.* Albuquerque: University of New Mexico Press, 1962.

Metz, Leon C. *Pat Garrett: The Story of a Western Lawman.* Norman: University of Oklahoma Press, 1974.

Owen, Gordon. *Las Cruces, New Mexico, 1849–1999: Multicultural Crossroads.* Las Cruces: Red Sky Publishing, 1999.

Simmons, Marc. "Animosity lives on in century-old murder mystery." *El Paso Times*, April 14, 1996.

Sonnichsen, C. L. *Tularosa: Last of the Frontier West.* Old Greenwich, Conn.: Devin-Adair, Co., 1972.

WHO KILLED THE MAN WHO KILLED THE KID?

See Curry, Keleher, Metz, Sonnichsen, above.

DeMattos, Jack. *Garrett and Roosevelt.* College Station, Tex.: Creative Publishing Co., 1988.

Hall, Ruth K. *A Place of Her Own: The Story of Elizabeth Garrett.* Santa Fé, N.Mex.: The Sunstone Press, 1976.

James, Bill. *Jim Miller: The Untold Story of a Texas Badman.* Carrollton, Texas, 1980.

Mullin, Robert N. *The Strange Story of Wayne Brazel.* Canyon, Tex.: Palo Duro Press, 1959.

Nolan, Frederick, ed. *Pat Garrett's The Authentic Life of Billy the Kid.* Norman: University of Oklahoma Press, 2000.

Rickards, Colin. *Sheriff Pat Garrett's Last Days.* Santa Fé, N.Mex.: The Sunstone Press, 1986.

Thrapp, Dan. *Encyclopedia of Frontier Biography.* Glendale, Calif.: Arthur H. Clark Co., 1988. Three vols.

THE CALAMITY PAPERS

Aikman, Duncan. *Calamity Jane and the Lady Wildcats.* Lincoln: University of Nebraska Press, 1987. (Reprint of 1927 edition.)

Bennet, Estelline. *Old Deadwood Days.* New York: J.H. Sears & Co., 1928.

Burke, Marthy Cannary. *Life and Adventures of Calamity Jane by Herself.* Fairfield, Wash.: Ye Galleon Press, 1979. (Reprint of pamphlet [ca. 1893] written by or ghostwritten for, Martha Canary, "Calamity Jane."

Connelley, William E. *Wild Bill and His Era.* New York: Press of the Pioneers, 1933.

Drago, Harry S. *Notorious Ladies of the Frontier.* New York: Dodd, Mead, 1969.

[Foote, Don C. and Stella A.]. *Calamity Jane's Diary and Letters.* Foreword by Jean Hickok McCormick. N.P., 1951.

Holbrook, Stewart. *Little Annie Oakley and Other Rugged People.* New York: Macmillan, 1948.

Horan, James D. *Desperate Women.* New York: G.P. Putnam Sons, 1952.

McLaird, James D. "Calamity Janes's Diary and Letters: Story of a Fraud." *Montana: The Magazine of Western History,* Autumn-Winter, 1995.

Riley, Glenda, and Richard W. Etulain. *By Grit and Grace: Eleven Women Who Shaped the American West*. Golden, Colo.: Fulcrum Publishing, 1997.

Rosa, Joseph G. *They Called Him Wild Bill*. Norman: University of Oklahoma Press, 1964.

———. *The West of Wild Bill Hickok*. Norman: University of Oklahoma Press, 1994.

———. *Wild Bill Hickok, Gunfighter*. Norman: University of Oklahoma Press, 2001.

———. *Wild Bill Hickok: The Man and His Myth*. Lincoln: University of Nebraska Press, 1996.

Sollid, Roberta B. *Calamity Jane: A Study in Historical Criticism*. Helena, Mont.: The Western Press, 1958.

Stevenson, Elizabeth. *Figures in a Western Landscape*. Baltimore: Johns Hopkins Press, 1994.

THE JACK LONDON CASES

McKee, Martha L. *Jack London in California*. Ketchum, Idaho: The Computer Lab, 1995.

Haughey, Homer L. And Connie K. Johnson. *Jack London Homes Album*. Stockton, Calif.: Heritage Publishing Co., 1995, 1987.

———. *Jack London Ranch Album*. Stockton, Calif.: Heritage Publishing Co., 1995.

Bamford, Georgia Loring. *The Mystery of Jack London*. Oakland, Calif.: privately printed, 1931.

Denko, Charles W., M.D. "Jack London: A Modern Analysis of His Mysterious Disease." *The Journal of Rheumatology*, 1993.

Kingman, Russ. *A Pictorial Life of Jack London*. New York: Crown Publishers, 1979.

Labor, Earle. *Jack London*. New York: Twayne, 1974.

———. *The Letters of Jack London*. Earle Labor, Robert C. Leitz III, and I. Milo Shepard, eds. Stanford, Calif.: Stanford University Press, 1988, three vols.

London, Charmian Kittredge. *The Book of Jack London*. New York: The Century Co., 1921; 2 volumes.

Noel, Joseph. *Footloose in Arcadia*. New York: Carrick & Evans, 1940.

O'Connor, Richard. *Jack London: A Biography*. Boston: Little, Brown, 1964.

Sherman, Joan. *Jack London: A Reference Guide*. Boston: G.K. Hall & Co., 1977.

Shivers, Alfred. "Jack London: Not a Suicide." *The Dalhousie Review*, Spring, 1969.

Stone, Irving. *Sailor on Horseback: A Biography*. Boston: Houghton Mifflin, 1938.

Walker, Dale L., and James E. Sisson III. *The Fiction of Jack London*. El Paso: Texas Western Press, 1972.

Walker, Franklin. *The Seacoast of Bohemia*. San Francisco: The Book Club of California, 1966.